C000129905

LD 4644896 9

OVER
THE
OCEAN

ERICA FISCHER

For my parents

*Translated
by Andrew Brown*

nova

Published by Hesperus Nova

Hesperus Press Limited

28 Mortimer Street, London W1W 7RD

www.hesperuspress.com

Originally published under the title

Königskinder by Erica Fischer

The translation of this work was supported by a

grant from the Goethe-Institut which is funded by the

German Ministry of Foreign Affairs.

English translation © Andrew Brown, 2014

This edition first published by Hesperus Press Limited, 2014

Typeset by Madeline Meckiffe

Printed and bound by Nørhaven,

Viborg, Denmark

ISBN: 978-1-84391-504-1

CHAPTER ONE

It is 20th June 1940, a sunny Thursday morning in London. In Hyde Park, the birds are chirruping, and swans are gliding over the motionless waters of the Serpentine. On the deserted lawn sit a woman and a man in deckchairs. The woman is wearing a floral dress and has taken off her shoes. Absently, she considers her feet with their red paint-ed toenails. The man's sports jacket hangs over the back of his deck chair, his unbuttoned shirt is creased. The two are holding each other's hands and making low conversa-tion, without looking at one another.

'You must be strong now, sweetheart.'

She turns to him. Her eyes are big and brown. Her close-cropped dark hair falls softly onto her forehead. 'It can't be much longer. We've been separated so often, but this time it's different. I'm afraid.'

'Who knows? Maybe they'll overlook me.'

'First they classify us as "refugees from Nazi oppression", and now we're supposed to be Fifth Columnists. At least you are: I'm just a woman.'

She speaks German with a harsh accent.

'They're right, of course. Or perhaps you were in a position to plan the overthrow of the British government? But you have to admit: mutating in a single day from a pitiful refugee to an enemy alien and Fifth Columnist isn't without its funny side.'

His Viennese idiom gives a certain familiarity to the sarcastic undertone of his remarks, a familiarity which she finds irresistible.

5

'Your eyes are so blue,' she whispers.

He smiles and caresses her cheek.

'It'll all be fine. We've been through so much together.'

'Yes, but that was together! If the Germans come, and you're not with me, then what, Erich?'

'The Germans won't come.'

'You and your optimism! You know that the *Picture Post* has devoted its entire latest issue to how to behave when the Germans come. For the *Post*, invasion is quite a realistic prospect.'

'Yes, yes, and we should all stock up with Molotov cocktails! What nonsense.'

'And Churchill? If the German paratroopers arrive, it will be better for both the English and for us not to be here. That's what he said, right? I can still distinctly remember you showing me the newspaper with his speech.'

Erich cannot think of a good answer.

'Sweetheart, look how blue the sky is. But behind this tree you can definitely see a grey cloud. Right?'

'When I look at you, my dear, everything in front of my eyes turns blue. It's as if the sky shines through your eyes.'

Erich smiles. He knows what effect his eyes have.

'It's so peaceful here. We're sitting in this green oasis, this evening we'll be spreading juicy English butter on our bread, and on the other side of the Channel all hell has broken loose. It's all a bit unreal. France has capitulated. De Gaulle's in London. Who could have imagined that, just one year ago?'

'Who can stop the Germans now? When they come, only people with Aryan identity will be able to walk on the grass. Then we won't be able to sit on the grass here together.'

'Didn't you hear de Gaulle's speech on the radio?' Erich spreads his arms theatrically. 'The flame of French resistance will not go out! We must have faith.'

'The French! They've always been good at patriotic songs. Like my Poles. Just don't look reality in the face. I read in the paper that the British don't even have any more cement to carry on building the public shelters.'

'Irka! The other day I saw a group of English soldiers on the street, evacuated from Dunkirk – a splendid piece of logistics on the part of the English, by the way. They were laughing, shaking their fists and giving a thumbs up. They shouted to the passers-by, "We'll be back in France before long!"'

'They're naive, they don't know the Nazis. They don't know what that lot are capable of. We *do* know. But anyway, Emmerich: I'm happy to be *pocieszać* – how do you say it? Happy to be comforted by you. Who'll do it when you're gone?'

'Emmerich? Have things got that bad in these parts?'

'Sometimes I just have to tease you with your funny name. You're my boy, my lad, my dearest *chłopak*, and I have to take good care of you. If they send you to Canada, I'll buy you some warm underwear.'

'For the time being I'm still here, and it's warmer than it's been for ages. We mustn't let the opportunity slip. Who knows when we'll get another one? We're in England, at last. Let's go to the swimming pool! I'll buy you an ice cream.'

Hand in hand they stroll over to Lansbury's Lido. Despite her high-heeled shoes, Irka looks like a little girl next to him. The swimming area on the lake, crowded at weekends, is deserted this morning.

Erich opens the shutter of his camera, and the lens automatically pops out. Each time, Irka finds this fascinating. She places one foot in front of the other and puts on her melancholy smile, which in her view suits her face best.

It is rather risky, for an 'enemy alien' to take photos in public, as they really ought to have handed their camera in at the outbreak of war. But Erich could not be separated from his Voigtländer Bessa: he loves taking photos with it – black and white, 45×60 mm.

An elderly gentleman, observing them with a blissful smile, offers to take a picture of them. Erich puts his arm round his little wife.

'A lovely couple,' the Englishman murmurs as he looks through the viewfinder. Then he presses the shutter release. It clicks.

With a slight bow he hands the camera back to Erich. 'My pleasure.'

'Thank you.' Now it is Erich's turn to give a graceful bow. He stretches out his hand. 'I'm Erich. That's Irene. We're enemy aliens.'

Irka digs Erich in the ribs. 'Are you *meshugge*?'

'You're well camouflaged – no one can tell!' laughs the man.

'You see,' Erich says with a smile, 'the English won't let the Jerries in. They have way too much humour. And now for our dip. I'd like to see the shape of your breasts in a wet swimming costume. I'll take a photo to go with me to Canada!'

Irka gives an embarrassed giggle. She likes it when her boy makes suggestive remarks.

CHAPTER TWO

When war broke out, Irka and Erich had to register with the English police and report once a week. They were asked to appear in front of a tribunal whose job it was to decide which German and Austrian foreigners were genuine refugees, and they blissfully imagined that they would be safe in refugee category C, officially classified as 'refugees from Nazi oppression'. Irka's case seemed cut and dried from the start, since she was Jewish, but Erich was lucky, because some tribunals did not realise that so-called Aryans could also be committed anti-Nazis.

About 600 people were placed in Category A. They were viewed, whether justifiably or not, as a higher level security risk and were immediately interned. About as many fell into Category B, and were subject to certain restrictions on travel. The vast majority, about 55,000 people, were recognised as refugees and could continue to move freely.

With a sigh of relief, Erich and Irka were able to continue working as domestic workers, the only activity allowed them. They were employed on a country estate in the south of England, in the hills of Wiltshire: Erich as a butler, Irka as a housemaid. They had food and a roof over their heads, and they were together. While Irka kept the living quarters clean, Erich's job involved tidying up the billiard room and laying the table for the family of the house. As a boy from a working-class background, he had no idea where to put the fish knife and the dessert spoon. Holding a sketch that Irka had drawn for him, he just about got by.

They were not badly off in Wiltshire. Around the magnificent building there was nothing but rich meadows and herds of sheep, the family's property with lush gardens and old English cottages with thatched roofs. On their days off they took trips into Shaftesbury and Salisbury. But the very idyllic quality of their lives was hard to cope with. With increasing concern they followed the progress of the war. They had lost all contact with their relatives. Erich's father and his brothers in Vienna, and even more Irka's parents and her younger brother in occupied Warsaw, lived in another world, now out of reach.

In the spring, Irka handed in her notice and moved to London. She had an opportunity to work there as a goldsmith, a profession for which she had trained at the Vienna School of Applied Arts, and she assembled a collection of her pieces. In Vienna she had started to earn good money for her work. She mainly designed silver jewellery – a successful blend of the Vienna workshop that had been founded at the beginning of the century and was dissolved in 1932 together with influences from her homeland. So she was fond of using the red coral so popular in Poland for the decoration of stylized flowers.

However, the British jeweller she was negotiating with expected a financial advance that she could not provide, and the matter fell through. In times of war, people have other things on their mind than buying jewellery. In May, Erich joined her: the promoter of appeasement, Neville Chamberlain, had just resigned as prime minister, and the charismatic Winston Churchill had formed a national coalition government.

It looked increasingly likely that Erich would be interned, so they decided for now to live on their savings and spend their remaining time together. Then, the mood gradually began to change. The British public had so far been well disposed towards the refugees, even when in January some tabloids blackened their name, calling them spies and saboteurs. A commentator from the left-wing *New Statesman*, Erich's favourite magazine, expressed the view that the allegations had been put about by the army. The smears published in the *Daily Express* and the *Daily Herald* paved the way for a new direction in foreign policy. Erich spent his mornings reading the newspapers in the public library and making notes on whatever struck him as important.

The German army's Fourth Panzer Division reached the French coast opposite England on 10th May, and the first Cabinet meeting of the new Prime Minister, Winston Churchill, was held on 11th May. (And on 12th May the Royal Air Force started bombing German cities, the first of them being Mönchengladbach.) The item was listed on the agenda of the Cabinet meeting as 'Invasion of Great Britain'. Home Secretary Sir John Anderson was asked by the British generals to clear the coastal area of foreigners, so Anderson immediately declared the entire east coast from Inverness down to Dorset to be a protected zone. Two thousand two hundred German and Austrian men between sixteen and sixty who lived in this region were 'temporarily interned' as it was called. Among them were tourists who had the misfortune to have been taking a Whitsun weekend trip to the seaside.

When the Netherlands surrendered, all male Germans and Austrians in category B were quickly arrested and escorted by soldiers in close formation to a detention centre. 'Act! Act! Act! Do it now,' cried the title of a report in the *Daily Mail* on 24th May. Erich anxiously saw that even reputable newspapers like *The Times* were adopting the same line.

'We have to be prepared,' he warned Irka. 'And don't you place your charms at the disposal of any men working in the munitions industry during my absence!'

Irka looked at him, puzzled.

'Here, read this. I've copied it down for you from the *Sunday Chronicle*: "There is no dirty trick that Hitler would not pull, and there is a very considerable amount of evidence to suggest that some of the women – who are very pretty – are not above offering their charms to any young man who may care to take them, particularly if he works in a munition factory or the Public Works."'

She laughed. But as if the newspaper had arranged it, 3,000 women in Category B were next day interned on the Isle of Man.

After the withdrawal of British troops from Dunkirk, a night curfew was imposed on all foreigners, with the exception of the French. Racist propaganda against 'local Italians' living in England had already been published for some time: the *Daily Mirror* was particularly outspoken. In one article, it described the 11,000 Italians living in London as 'an undigestable unit of population', despite which ships would continue to wash ashore 'all kinds of brown-eyed Francescas and Marias, beetle-browed Ginos, Titos and Marios.' A storm was brewing in the Mediterranean, and 'even the peaceful, law-abiding proprietor of the backstreet coffee shop bounces into a fine patriotic frenzy at the sound of Mussolini's name'.

Erich and Irka were horrified to experience xenophobia in England too, having just escaped it in Austria.

After Mussolini's declaration of war on England and France on 10th June, Italians were arrested and anti-Italian sentiment resulted in attacks on Italian shops and cafes. British domestic intelligence put together lists of allegedly dangerous persons who were rounded up at dawn by police officers. Eventually, 4,500 Italians were arrested and interned, including many who had lived for decades in England, whose sons had been born there and were serving in the British Army. The writer George Orwell complained that you could not get a decent meal in London any more because the chefs of the Savoy, the Café Royal, the Piccadilly and many other restaurants in Soho and Little Italy had been locked up.

Cheered on by Churchill's rallying cry 'Collar the lot', that at first no one took really seriously, the authorities interned ever more innocent German and Austrian men from the second half of June onwards, without even bothering to point out that this was just a provisional measure. The public was led to believe that the detainees were persons who had aroused suspicion in some way.

This was what angered Erich the most. He knew people whose health had been permanently damaged in Dachau and were now again being put behind barbed wire. At the same time, no one thought of interning a British demagogue like Sir Oswald Mosley, whose gangs of fascist thugs had provoked riots in the predominantly Jewish East End of London. Erich had no illusions that his impeccable political background could still protect him now.

Anderson had a standard formula ready to silence any criticism of the practice of internment. 'I am afraid that hardship is inseparable from the conditions in which we live at the moment.'

Fear of a German invasion had gripped wide circles of the population. Increasingly, the call rang out, 'Intern them all!' There was a rumour going around that the royal family had fled to Canada, and children whose parents could afford it were evacuated in thousands. Although negotiations with Canada and Australia to accept refugees were secret, the news was leaked that the government was thinking of shipping 'enemy aliens' overseas.

So it is that Erich and Irka are prepared for the police to come knocking at their door. Their packed suitcase has been ready for days. They have considered how they can use the 'unavoidable measure' of internment to their advantage. If the men are to be sent overseas, they have agreed that Erich will hand himself in, provided Irka can follow him soon. In the Dominions, far away from the battlefields, an opportunity for them to be released will probably arise. After years of persecution, first by the Austro-fascists, then by the Nazis, they only want one thing: to live together in peace and freedom.

The approaching farewell is nevertheless difficult. Irka sobs: she has lived through too many separations in recent years. Her pregnant sister managed, just before the war, to emigrate with her husband from Poland to Australia. At least she is safe. Irka does not want to think about her parents and her brother in Warsaw. In England she can confide in only a few people: Erich is her mainstay. The fact that he was able to join her two months after her escape from Vienna on a tourist visa, and then was also recognised as a refugee, has restored her *joie de vivre* for some time now. With Erich she can even laugh about the way that she, the elegant daughter of a Warsaw felt manufacturer and an optimistic, enthusiastic art student from Vienna, now has to enter service as a cleaning lady.

Before Erich arrived in England, she had not been much in the mood for laughing. Her first job, one that she found through an employment agency, brought her in October

1938 to the house of a grouchy old woman whose only idea of fun was making life difficult for her young house-maid. She had no idea of the hell Irka had just escaped from, and did not care.

'Why do you have so many bags?' she asked when Irka arrived.

'I had to bring everything with me.'

The old woman shook her head in disbelief. 'I've never had a home help with three suitcases before.'

The cook of the house led Irka up to her attic room.

'Why isn't there any light here?'

'Servants don't need any light.'

The cook gave her six bottles and a handful of candles that Irka stuck into the bottle necks and set up around her. She lay in her bed as if it were her coffin, and wept.

The only advantage to this house was that her old woman rarely got up before lunch. In the morning, Irka plugged in the vacuum cleaner and made herself comfort-able with her English vocabulary lists, in one of the soft armchairs. To learn English as quickly as possible was her most urgent task now. At school in Warsaw she had had only French lessons.

When Erich arrived, she could already make herself understood in broken English. With her head held high, she gave notice to her old woman and moved into Erich's boarding house. He applied for a work permit, and as a married couple they started looking for a job. On one particular day, they had to present themselves in a draughty warehouse, and English ladies from the provinces came along to choose their servants. They were examined like horses at a fair. With his dazzling good looks, Erich held all the aces. 'I'll take him!' echoed across the hall. The lady was reluctantly obliged to take Irka along as well.

When, a few months later, she tried to force Erich to clean the windows on a Sunday, his trade-union conscious-ness was stirred. 'Up yours!' he said, and they gave in their notice.

With their suitcases they went along the road singing 'Why do we have a road? To march along, to march along out into the big wide world.' They had nothing to lose. They were young and in love. And between them and the Nazis lay the Channel.

CHAPTER THREE

On 24th June, early in the morning, there is a knock on the door of the furnished room in Paddington, where Irka and Erich made their home a few months ago.

'It's time,' whispers Irka, instantly awake, and clings to her husband.

Erich extricates himself from her embrace, kisses her on the forehead and goes to open the door.

The landlady Mrs Needham tells him that two policemen are asking for him. She wears a pink dressing gown and has curlers in her hair. He has never seen her looking like this before.

'You've come for me,' says Erich thickly.

'We have instructions to take you into internment,' drones one of the two tall men, as if he has learned his words off by heart. Their high black police helmets make them look even taller. 'Please pack toiletries, clothes and a change of underwear and other essential things. We'll give you half an hour.'

Erich feels like Kafka's Joseph K., whom two guards inform of his arrest without letting him know what he stands accused of. Unlike Joseph K., however, Erich does not make a fuss, as he has been preparing for this moment for weeks.

There is little time to say goodbye, the police are waiting outside the door. But they are polite and apologise for the early morning hour, they are just following orders. 'It's only temporary,' they assure him. 'You'll soon be back.'

With tears in her eyes, Irka bends out of the window and gazes after Erich. Before he gets into the waiting car, he turns around again and puts on the boyish grin that she loves so much. He gives her a thumbs up, copied from the English soldiers he saw.

'Don't smoke too much,' Irka calls after him and lights a cigarette.

Shortly afterwards the same morning, there is a second knock at the door. This time, the landlady is dressed, and her silver hair lies in careful waves on her head like a cap. Irka is still wearing her pyjamas. Mrs Needham brings a tray with a pot of tea, a little jug of milk and some butter biscuits on a flowered china plate.

'This will cheer you up, Irka.'

'Oh, thank you. This is exactly what I need right now.'

Still snuffling, Irka heaves a stack of newspapers that Erich was studying the night before onto the bed and invites her landlady to sit with her at the round tea table.

'I know it's hard for you, all alone in a foreign country. I'm so sorry. Let me know if I can be of any help.'

Irka attempts to put on a brave smile. 'If they send him overseas, he'll make sure that I can follow him. That's my only hope.'

'He'll manage, I'm sure he will. He's such a nice gentleman, your Erich. They'll all believe him when he says he isn't up to anything bad. Maybe they'll send him back to you soon.'

'We're used to being separated. In Vienna, we were both in prison. Unfortunately, not in the same cell.'

'In prison?'

Maybe she could have phrased it better. They had been so careful and told Mrs Needham hardly anything about their past lives. Now Irka needs to explain.

'Well, it was like this: when the Nazis came to power in Germany, a fascist corporate state was introduced in Austria. Perhaps you've heard of Engelbert Dollfuss? A tiny man. No? Well, all anyone knows about Austria is that Hitler comes from Braunau. In February of '34 the game was up. All political parties and trade unions were banned. Later, the Nazis murdered Dollfuss. Serves him right.'

Irka feels that talking is helping her to calm down. She pours herself some milk from the jug into the cup, as the English have taught her, and then the black tea, which takes on a wonderful light brown colour.

'At that time I was studying at the School of Applied Arts in Vienna. Erich wrote articles for a union newspaper, I drew the covers. The paper was typed on wax matrices and – *powielać* – what's the word? Oh yes, reproduced. You had to turn a crank, like this. It was dangerous because it was illegal, but we also had a lot of fun.'

This variant seems best to Irka because, after all, the English have a long trade-union tradition. The Communist Party, banned in Austria under Austro-fascist rule, which they had both entered out of frustration at the failure of the Social Democrats after the brief civil war in February 1934, is something she prefers not to mention.

'And that was banned?'

'Oh yes, all political activity was banned. Everything. On 1st May, we were clubbed down in Vienna by mounted police officers. When our work for the trade-union newspaper was discovered, we were sent to prison. That was in '36. Erich got nine months, I got six. At that time we weren't yet married. I was then deported to Poland as a Polish citizen, I couldn't go back to Austria. When Erich was released, he travelled to Warsaw to join me, and there we got married. By marrying an Austrian, I became

Austrian too. Look at this photo. That's us on our wedding day. Doesn't he look gorgeous?'

'A beautiful couple. And those lion cubs in your lap!'

'They gave them to us to hold, for a photo in Warsaw Zoo.'

'Drink your tea, Irka, it's getting cold. So your name – Irka – is Polish?'

'My name's Irena. Irene in English. Irka is the diminutive. It's what I was called from birth. In Polish, every name has a diminutive, sometimes there's more than one. My sister's name's Ludwika, we've always called her Ludka. Even for common words such as "bottle" or "table" we use diminutives – *buteleczka*, *stoliczek*. The language is full of them. You don't have them in English. Who knows what that says about the people who speak these languages? I've never thought about it.'

Suddenly she feels a yearning in her heart. How long it has been since she spoke Polish, and how much she'd like to lean her head on her big sister's shoulder and listen to her whispering Polish diminutives to her. She misses the warmth of her mother language. Even with Erich, she converses in a foreign language. Sometimes she cannot really tell him what she thinks and feels; with her limited vocabulary every thought is coarsened. She is never quite herself. Will they also speak English together, one day? In Canada, perhaps? Hard to imagine that anyone in the future will still want to hear the German language.

'Interesting,' Mrs Needham remarks politely after a pause, steering the conversation back to the prison. 'Was it bad there? I've never met anyone who was in prison.'

'Being separated from Erich was bad, of course. But I also met women there that I'd never have met in real life. Prostitutes for example. They just couldn't understand how anyone would let themselves get locked up for a political idea. They thought I was *szalona* – er… crazy. For them to spend time in jail now and again was quite normal. Then I couldn't understand how you can sleep with a man without loving him. A lesbian woman even wanted to convince me that the love of women is much better.'

'Oh!' Mrs Needham blushes.

'Compared with what came afterwards – the Nazis – the jail in Vienna was a *piece of cake* – Erich taught me this cheerful phrase,' says Irka, in a hurry to get away from the topic of sexuality. 'You didn't have to fear for your life. After Austria was annexed by Germany in '38, it all changed in one fell swoop. For the Jews it was pure hell, anyone who could got out of the country as fast as possible. But it wasn't easy, you needed a visa. Not a single country would take you without a visa. It took several months before I could find a housekeeping job and was allowed to travel to England.'

This is the first time that Irka has told her landlady about her escape. You can never tell how many English people are anti-Semitic.

'So you're… er… Jewish?' stammers Mrs Needham.

'Yes, I am. At least that's what Hitler says. I'm not religious, I've only been to a synagogue once. But that's not what matters for the Nazis. My blood is Jewish, they say.'

'Incredible. You know, I've never seen a Jew.'

'But I'm perfectly normal, aren't I?'

'That's not what I meant…'

'It's okay, I'm not sensitive. Without the Nazis, I'd never have thought about it. In my family, we felt Polish. But thanks to Hitler I became a "refugee from Nazi oppression". Erich too, even though he's not a Jew. I'm grateful to the English for taking us in. Only now...'

'Now they've taken your husband away from you. You're right, that's shameful.'

'Yes, it is. But I'm not afraid for him.'

This conversation cheers Irka. Her confidence returns. Somehow or other, it will all turn out all right. 'We're in a democratic country now. Nothing's going to happen to him. The government's panicking – it's understandable.'

'I hope you've have some good experiences in England too?'

'Oh yes, of course. Just think what's happening in the Ostmark now – there's no Austria any more. What we liked best was the small private school in Norfolk where we went a few months after arriving. We'd have happily stayed there. We worked as kitchen assistant and gardener. Erich even learned how to… oh yes, curry, is that right?… the three horses in the school. We lived in a large room with windows from floor to ceiling. What you call "French windows", right? So bright it was there! In the school everything was done on strictly democratic principles. Imagine: the entire staff was paid the same salary, so as a kitchen help I earned the same as a teacher. And there was a school committee in which the teachers and two dozen or so students were equal partners in discussion. The teachers had to put up with criticism. For us, coming as we did from authoritarian Austria, it was an incredible experience. And everyone was on first name terms.'

Mrs Needham looks sceptical.

'But after six months the Ministry of Labour intervened. I'd entered with a visa that only allowed me to take a job in a private household. My position at the school didn't comply with this condition, they wrote. The school board asked the Labour Ministry if they could keep me because they wouldn't find any English manpower as good as me.

That's right! As the cook was sometimes sick, I slaved up to sixteen hours a day and cooked for thirty people. It didn't bother me at all. And I couldn't cook at all when I went to Vienna after I graduated from high school – at home in Warsaw we had a cook. We even found a politician who stood up for me. But nothing came of it. "We cannot go back on our previous position," they wrote to me. Erich was also sad that we had to leave that wonderful place. He's such a *mól książkowy* – a bookworm, and in the school there was loads to read.'

The tea has been drunk, the cakes consumed. Mrs Needham gets up to clear away the dishes.

'Don't be afraid,' she says. 'We won't be beaten so easily. Just let those Krauts come. We're not like the French!'

'Don't tempt fate, Mrs Needham. That's what they say, isn't it?'

CHAPTER FOUR

'Pack of Nazis!' – 'Huns out of England!' – 'Fifth Columnists not wanted here!' – 'Down with the spies!' A hostile, howling crowd welcomes the refugees. In a long line, the men carry their luggage from the railway station to Huyton Alien Internment Camp in a suburb of Liverpool, escorted by soldiers with bayonets fixed, and repeatedly urged to get a move on. They have to run the gauntlet.

'We could have had a similar welcome in Munich,' says one.

Erich turns round: 'But not with a military escort!'

The first thing they see when they approach Huyton is barbed wire fences and watchtowers. Behind it, on open space next to a still unfinished brick council estate, an encampment has been erected.

On the wide parade ground they stand in rank and file. A respectful commanding officer informs them of their status as 'enemy aliens' and instructs them in the camp rules, while the other officers bark orders into the chaos. Roll call at 7.30 and 21.00, inspection at 10.45, lights out at 21.15, mealtimes in between. After this has all been explained, it is time to queue for blankets and tin mugs.

'Not all that different from Sachsenhausen,' mutters one.

Through a guard of men who have been in the camp for longer, the newcomers march to the reception tent where a suspicious-eyed sergeant takes down their details. Then they have to fill out a questionnaire and receive a piece of paper with scribbled instructions for a place to sleep.

Erich is lucky, he has been assigned a mattress in an unfurnished house. Those who were brought here in May only got a bag to sleep on, which they stuffed with straw. Others have to make do with one of the tents that, after days of continuous rain, are swimming in a sea of mud. The mealtimes, the newcomers are informed, will be taken in one of the large tents.

The camp was obviously set up in haste, and there is organisational chaos: every day, new refugees flood in. In the houses there is cold water, but no towels and very little toilet paper. Everyone gets a small piece of soap which has to last him a week. English food has a bad reputation, as Erich knows already: but in Huyton you eat only because a man has to eat in order not to starve.

The sixteen-year-olds can make even uncomfortable camp life enjoyable, but – contrary to Home Office instructions – many men have been interned despite suffering from diseases, including diabetes, heart problems, stomach illnesses, tuberculosis and blindness. There are even some cases of mentally and physically disabled men. An estimated forty per cent of the interned men are over fifty, many over sixty. For those who have already experienced German concentration camps, the flood lights switched on at night awaken distressing memories.

An infirmary has been quickly improvised, where insulin and stethoscopes, enemas and bedpans are all lacking. In the camp there is just a single doctor, but soon internee doctors and medical students are giving him a hand. For the doctors who have fled from Germany and Austria, it is a welcome opportunity to finally be able to work again, as the British Medical Association did not allow them to practise their profession in the UK. Once a week the camp is visited by a dentist, who cannot cope with the work that awaits him.

In Huyton, thousands of men are housed. Some have been living there for several weeks. Some are depressed and apathetic, others become amazingly vivacious. Anyone with money can eat better food in the canteen. Those who do not must offer their labour in the market place: cleaning shoes, darning socks, washing clothes. Some have even hung up a company nameplate on their property.

When Erich looks around on the camp road, he notices in the crowd a gaunt man with a long, thin neck and constantly bobbing Adam's apple. His outfit is as creased as that of all the others standing together in groups and talking. What will become of them? How long will they have to endure life in this inhospitable place? There is only one topic for discussion.

'Kurt Neufeld!'

'Erich! So we meet again. Not only is the pretender to the Austrian throne here, but you too!'

'You don't say! Him too?'

The two know each other from their time in police detention in the Vienna court, where they indulged in many a political joust with one another.

'It's much better than the grey house, don't you think?' Kurt calls out in his falsetto tones and slaps Erich firmly on the shoulder.

Actually, they do not like each other. Erich cannot stand dogmatic people, and Kurt sees Erich as an intellectual lightweight. Also, Erich does not like Kurt's smooth baby face with its small nose, which somehow reminds him of Lenin. But in this anonymous crowd, you are glad to see any familiar faces.

The familiar faces increase in number over the following days. Over six foot tall, with the stooping posture he has adopted so as not to keep banging his head on everything, Otto can be seen in the distance. Erich is really pleased to see him here. Otto Hirschfeld is a warm-hearted man, whose grey-blue eyes under their bushy brows stare attentively at the person he is talking to. In Vienna, he taught printmaking at the School of Art where Irka studied. Through her, the two men got to know each other and became friends.

In Vienna, Otto had made a pen drawing of Erich and Irka, a precious gift that Erich had left with his brother in Vienna. With a few strokes he was able to capture the essence of both of their faces, Erich's ironically raised left eyebrow and Irka's melancholy gaze and thin lips. Erich tried in vain to track down Otto through the Austrian Centre in London. Now they have found each other again. A friend is far more important than a good lunch, given the uncertainty of the future.

'What about Else?' asks Erich.

'She stayed in Vienna,' Otto replies without visible concern, 'she's now working for the underground. She didn't want to come to England. Nobody could quite understand why, but I respect her decision. Since the war began, I've received two telegrams from her, via the Red Cross. I think she's fine.'

Erich can remember Else clearly, an exceptional small woman with a sharp profile and hair combed straight back, like a man's. The fact that she deliberately chose a giant for her husband caused great merriment among her friends, as she only came up to Otto's chest. Else's political radicalism has always frightened Erich. He likes it when women are cuddly and wear lipstick. Like Irka.

Even those in the camp who play neither skat nor chess, and do not attend to their business, are not bored. Every event triggers extensive discussions: there is plenty of time for them. One man tries to escape, another ends up in the camp's jail when he is caught with a smuggled newspaper.

The Communists, of whom there are quite a few, are busy rallying their comrades and building up party groups. Erich writes – in English, to practise the language – in a small notebook, describing all the comic and ridiculous events that happen in the camp, and he reads the little book he has brought along, with plays by George Bernard Shaw, a playwright and satirist whose wit and political passion he reveres. Although Shaw always deals with social problems in his works, his humanitarian commitment is tempered by a humorous view of the world. Erich, who cannot stand the deadly seriousness of the Communists and therefore keeps away from them, likes this attitude. Even Shaw's take on women and marriage amuses him. For a wedding gift he gave Irka Shaw's *The Intelligent Woman's Guide to Socialism and Capitalism*. And if he wants to annoy her, he cites Shaw's attitude to marriage: 'The harbour of marriage is like all other harbours. The longer the ships stay in them, the greater the risk that they will rust.' Irka promptly gets annoyed and asks him irritably why, in that case, he ever married her. Sometimes Erich is not sure whether this is what he really wants from life. But he has long since not been able to have much say in his own life.

Apart from the newspapers that are occasionally smuggled in, and the information wrested from the guards, a news blackout has been imposed on Huyton, and wild rumours are going round. They are all going to be shipped off, they hear on the grapevine – and the proximity of the port of Liverpool makes this more probable. Canada, Australia and even Madagascar are the destinations aired.

However, you can never keep information away from an assembly of educated men, especially as new refugees keep flooding in, who have read the newspapers and listened to the radio. When, on 2nd July, the former luxury ocean liner *Arandora Star* is torpedoed by a German submarine off the Irish coast on its way to Canada, and hundreds of people, including a large number of German, Austrian and Italian internees, are drowned, the camp is abuzz with rumour.

What this embarrassing incident will mean for the German-Italian alliance is a question that is soon being hotly debated on the camp road. This is, strangely enough, of greater interest than the very real danger of the internees themselves being caught up in the battle on the high seas. Only Kurt, usually so eager for discussion, does not join in this time. When he was arrested at dawn he had to leave his son behind, and does not know what has happened to him since then. Was he also interned, was he perhaps on the *Arandora Star*? Maybe yes, maybe no.

Irka too must have heard or read about the disaster. Is she spending sleepless nights worrying about Erich? Surely she knows that, according to the official statements, those on board the ship were not innocent refugees but only Nazi sympathizers and Italian fascists. Erich has no way of reassuring her, because after arrival in the camp, the newcomers have to wait ten days before they are allowed any postal contact with the outside world. He can hardly wait to write to her. Only recently has stationery been handed out: two sheets of writing paper per head – a special chalk paper on which it is impossible to write with invisible ink. Those with nobody to write to sell their paper. It sells like hot cakes, although some sellers demand the outrageous sum of five shillings per sheet.

A few days after the sinking of the *Arandora Star*, quite a large group of survivors from the disaster is brought to Huyton. They wear khaki uniforms with a large red spot on the back and are assailed with questions.

'We thought we'd be taken to the Isle of Man, that's what we were told. Canada was never mentioned. But when we saw the ship at the pier, definitely a 15,000-ton vessel, we soon started to feel a bit uneasy. The ship was painted grey, and on the front and back decks we could see the outline of two guns. All portholes were closed with flaps, and the promenade deck was boarded up. The ship looked like a coffin.'

The man relating this, the words tumbling out of his mouth, is a young Italian from Bolzano, who seems to have survived the traumatic experience with no ill effects and enjoys the concentrated attention with which the men listen to his report.

'When we embarked they took everything away from us, but we thought that on the Isle of Man – or wherever – we'd get it back again. My father was a sailor, so I know a bit about ships. The *Arandora Star* was hopelessly overloaded, that was obvious right away. There were more than one thousand five hundred of us internees – Italians, Germans, Austrians, and Nazis and fascists, too, but mostly decent people like me, I can assure you. Among the Germans and Austrians there were a lot of Jews. The ship had not been painted with the Red Cross, though it should have been, as there were prisoners of war on board. But otherwise everything went fine, the food was tasty, and we even got drinks. If this continues, I thought, then it's going to be Canada all right.

'On the second day, early in the morning, the ship followed a wild zigzag course, the captain knew that we were in dangerous waters. But maybe it was just this conspicuous course that alerted the submarine to our presence. And because of the two guns, it probably took us for a warship. If the German captain had known that we were prisoners of war, he certainly wouldn't have fired at us.'

'Hm, well, I'm not so sure,' mutters one.

'And then what? Why did so many people drown? You were close to the Irish coast.'

'The Italians were herded together in the lower decks. I mixed with the Germans, who were housed above. I knew that I would have a greater chance of survival there in the case of a torpedo attack. You have to expect this in a war. The Italians down there would drown like rats. And that's what happened. Many people were still asleep when there was a big bang. We've been hit, I thought straightaway. The ship stopped immediately, so the turbines must have been struck, and the light went out. It was pitch black, there was not even an emergency light, broken glass everywhere, and stinking smoke poured out of the burst pipes. Otherwise total silence. No emergency orders, nothing. We were left to ourselves. So, best to go on deck! Our stairs were barricaded with barbed wire, but somehow I managed. Outside was an English soldier, with fixed bayonet, but he didn't dare to leave his post. "Run! Run for your life!" I shouted.

'The screams, the death agony of those trapped below is something I will never forget. Above, everyone was fighting for a place in the lifeboats and rafts. They shot at people who wanted to get into a boat that was reserved for the English soldiers. There weren't even enough lifebelts and life jackets. And wherever you looked, no officer or seaman to help us. No one told us how to put the life jackets on. Men jumped into the water and broke their necks on impact. I also saw soldiers hacking away with an axe at the ropes holding a lifeboat, as the boat was still hanging in the air. It then fell into the sea, and all those on board drowned. The Nazis were naturally more organised than us Italians. They had a captain as leader and he made them stand in two rows on the deck. Among them were many seamen who immediately secured a few lifeboats and safely lowered themselves onto the water.

'When I noticed that the ship was tilting and sinking rapidly, I clambered down a rope ladder and jumped into the sea. And I quickly swam away, so that I wouldn't be sucked back into the ship's body by the water pouring in. When I was a child, my father told me stories about the sinking of the *Titanic*, and I immediately thought about the suction. Older men just stayed at the highest point possible and waited for the water to swallow them. They probably couldn't swim, like many Italians. Later I heard that one man hanged himself for fear of the water. Some knelt down and prayed.'

The men standing around in silence are moved.

'I clung to a piece of wreckage and saw how the ship went down, the stern first, the bow sticking straight up to the sky. And from the portholes the water came hissing. It took half an hour. A tremendous roar, a gurgling noise, and that was that. For a short while the sea churned, then there was an awful silence, just a gentle murmur.

'I was in the water until the afternoon, when the crew of the Canadian *St. Laurent* brought me on board. *Mamma mia*, was it cold! Plus fog and drizzling rain. Many corpses, blackened by the engine oil drifting on the surface, floated past me, their heads propped up on their life jackets – it was gruesome. Some who were still alive were killed by falling debris from the ship. Elderly people had heart attacks. Around me were hundreds of planks and pieces of wood with barbed wire, I had to be damn careful. After about three hours a plane patrolling the coast spotted us. For hours it circled over our heads, perhaps so as to encourage us not to give up at the last minute. They threw some food into the lifeboats. The Canadians were great. They gave us hot tea and rum. I had to sip cautiously because I'd swallowed so much salt water and oil. The sailors then pulled clothes out of their duffel bags and distributed them to us. On the *St. Laurent*, we learned that our ship had not sent out any SOS and the Canadian destroyer had only received the order from London to come to our rescue several hours after the sinking. It was only an hour and a half away from us, so a lot of people might have been saved.'

'And after all that, they're interning you again. Incredible!' This from Otto.

'Too right. First they brought us to Greenock in Scotland, we arrived at half past six in the morning. Some died en route. In Greenock, they took the injured to hospital. At last I could have a wash – I was covered from head to toe in engine oil. The first night we slept in a big draughty warehouse, on the bare concrete floor. But they gave us woollen underwear and these Scottish uniforms with red spots on the back, so you can see right away that we're "enemy aliens" and not real Scots. The next day there were postcards for us to address to our families and sign. There were three words typed on them: "I am safe." We weren't allowed to write anything else. We spent a few nights in tents somewhere in Scotland, and now here we are, two hundred men.'

On the evening of the arrival of the survivors, a poignant service for the drowned men is held, and everyone participates out of respect. Most of the Italians weep, and many Germans and Austrians cannot suppress a sob, because the news has been leaked that the authorities are preparing a new transport overseas.

Soon afterwards, the internees receive questionnaires on which they have to write whether they will voluntarily travel by ship to one of His Majesty's Dominions. Australia is the rumoured destination. Erich will not be intimidated, any more than the British government. He would rather risk the dangerous crossing than spend months strolling idly up and down the camp road, speculating with Communists, Socialists and Zionists over the course of the war.

Those who are married, with wives and children in London and elsewhere, get together and hastily draw up a petition to the Home Office in which they offer to sign up for the journey, provided the other members of their family in England can come with them. 'Do not take from us the last thing that sustains our will to live,' they write.

With amazing speed, the promise is made. Apparently the authorities, faced with ever more arrivals, are eager to get rid of them. The commander of the camp promises that overseas – he leaves it open as to which country it will be – the personal liberty of the internees will be limited only slightly and they will be allowed to work in a career of their choice. He predicts a great future for all those who are still hesitant. Erich and Irka are dreaming of this future. They would like to emigrate to Australia to join Irka's sister and brother-in-law – at least part of the family would be together again. Erich makes a quick decision and awaits whatever will come.

The tantalizing prospect of freedom and work spreads like wildfire through the camp, and hundreds of men sign up. Most people think Australia is their destination. Kurt cannot bring himself to leave Europe without news of his son. Otto will risk it – Erich's rapid decision has encouraged him. After the war, he can return to Else, or she can join him wherever he has by that stage got to. There's no point thinking about it until then.

Less than a week after the torpedoing of the *Arandora Star*, things have already moved forward: on 10th July, an 11,000-ton vessel will put out to sea. Everyone is entitled to eighty pounds of baggage, to which he will have access during the trip: so they are assured.

'Are they trying to pull our legs?' says Otto in annoyance. Like many others he brought only a small suitcase with a few bare essentials to Huyton.

That evening, it is remarkably quiet in the sleeping quarters. They are all writing farewell letters.

I have decided, on condition that you can follow me in the shortest possible time, to go overseas, probably to Australia

writes Erich in his curved handwriting, slanting to the right. It is his first letter since he arrived at the camp.

Despite our earlier discussion, this decision has been terribly hard for me to make. I hope it will mean happiness for both of us. My dear, the hardest separation lies before us, and I beg you not to despair. It's the only way that perhaps promises a better future. I would have been happy to set sail with at least one letter from you, but it's already too late, because we start tomorrow morning. My dear, sweet child, I take my leave and kiss you many thousands of times. I hope we meet again in a few weeks, maybe two or three months, but in happier circumstances.

Your Erich

CHAPTER FIVE

While the internees await their uncertain fate, a lively correspondence is being conducted at government level. On 15th June 1940 the High Commissioner of the United Kingdom in Australia, Sir Geoffrey Whiskard, writes an 'urgent and confidential' letter to the Australian Prime Minister Robert Gordon Menzies. The total number of male German internees in Great Britain amounts to over 12,000, of whom 2,500 are clearly supporters of the National Socialists and therefore constitute a source of danger, as in the case of a parachute landing or an invasion. Also, 1,500 Italian males, members of the National Fascist Party, should be interned, along with some 800 other male Italians, who should probably not be allowed to roam around freely. Moreover, there are already 3,000 German prisoners of war, including German sailors who were taken from sinking ships.

'The detention of such a large number of dangerous or potentially dangerous persons represents a considerable burden on the authorities responsible for their internment and commits a considerable number of military personnel to the task of guarding them,' writes Sir Geoffrey. It is therefore urgent to intern them outside of the United Kingdom. The Canadian government has already agreed to accept 4,000 internees and 3,000 prisoners of war. Might Australia take some in, and if so, how many? All costs incurred for transportation and living expenses would be borne by the United Kingdom. A similar request is also directed to the government of South Africa.

On 1st July Canberra informs the Minister for Dominion Affairs that Australia is prepared to accept 6,000 internees and prisoners of war, and requests more detailed information regarding the classification of the persons concerned. 'If we could receive adequate information concerning the first four thousand men, we would be able to take the necessary steps within the next six weeks.'

'Might not these internees pose a serious problem?' Menzies is asked in the Australian Parliament. 'However much of a problem they may be,' he replies, 'in Britain they would pose a far greater problem.'

The British public does not know anything about the government decision to deport internees until the evening of 3rd July, when the BBC reports that at six o' clock in the morning of the day before, the former battleship *Arandora Star*, on its way to Canada with 1,500 German and Italian internees on board, had been hit by a torpedo from a German U-boat and sunk off the west coast of Ireland. The population is given the impression that only German Nazis and Italian Fascists had been on board.

The British press soon finds an explanation for the large number of Italian victims. 'Foreigners fight each other in a wild panic,' reads the *Daily Herald* headline on 4th July. In the battle between Italians and Germans to grab a place in a lifeboat, many men had fallen into the water, writes *The Times* the next day. 'To separate them, the English sailors and soldiers had to waste valuable time from their real rescue work.'

Four survivors of the disaster, Germans and Italians, are so dismayed by the reports in the British press, all of them blaming the victims for their own deaths, that they draft a memorandum in which they report their experiences. The claim that German prisoners had pushed the Italians off the lifeboats was untrue, they firmly state. The large number of Italian casualties is due, rather, to the fact that the Italians were accommodated in the lowest deck and could find no room in the lifeboats when they finally made it to the top.

The debates following the sinking of the *Arandora Star* reveal that the ship had left the port without military escort and the families of the victims would not be paid compensation because it was sunk by enemy action. The British cabinet is primarily concerned with the question of whether, after this disaster, they should continue with the other planned transports to Canada. The proposal put forward by Sir John Anderson, to examine the composition of the groups to be shipped more closely before sending them across the oceans again, is completed rejected as too time-consuming. Thus it is that the *Ettrick* and the *Sobieski* embark on their journeys as planned, from Liverpool and Glasgow, this time with a military escort. By 15th July some 6,750 German, Austrian and Italian internees and prisoners of war have reached Canada.

Much to the surprise of the Canadian officers and soldiers, who had been expecting a dangerous cargo of spies and saboteurs, the internees include a remark-able number of doctors, lawyers, pianists and Talmudic scholars.

CHAPTER SIX

On 10th July 1940, a rainy day with leaden skies and occasional claps of thunder, Erich takes leave of Europe. That day marks the beginning of the Battle of Britain. The Luftwaffe will attempt to force Great Britain to surrender or, if the British refuse to yield, the Germans will prepare for the invasion of the island. But the 500 or so men who around noon get on board the train and by about three o'clock have reached the pier at Liverpool are henceforth cut off from all information.

Erich does not have much time to ponder how things are going with Irka in London, his father in Vienna and his in-laws in Warsaw, because the embarkation of the 2,500 internees, including many who are boarding the ship quite unwillingly, is a chaotic process: the crowds jammed into the sooty departure hall dating from the time of Queen Victoria, the infernal noise of hundreds of men's voices, the increasing press of internees streaming in from the platform, and the soldiers vainly endeavouring to impose order on the hubbub. And between the columns moving in different directions come the vociferous cries of welcome from friends, relatives and comrades-in-arms who have lost touch with one another in the various internment camps and have now, for a short time, found each other again.

The column of men from Huyton makes its way out of the hall out into the cold damp air of the pier in Princess Dock. They gaze in astonishment at the vessel looming before them, His Majesty's Transport *Dunera*, a gloomy dark grey troop vessel. At least a 12,000-tonner, some say:

no, a 15,000-tonner, say others. The crowd on the pier blocks the view. Some of them are struggling with their allowance of forty kilos of luggage. Erich is glad he has just a small suitcase and a briefcase. The gas masks which everyone was supposed to carry with them are collected in, as they probably will not be needing them wherever it is they are going – this at least is good news. They are also relieved of their heavy luggage, to be loaded separately: the suitcases should be accessible to their owners later.

A larger group of men, whose horror can be read in their eyes, is immediately separated from the others. Word quickly gets around that these are survivors of the sunken *Arandora Star*, who have been promised that they need never again go on board a ship. They are the first to be driven up the gangway, by fiercely staring British soldiers who have just piled out of buses.

It will be a long time until they are all on board: that much is certain. Time to listen to the different stories of the interned men brought in boats, trains and buses from camps across the country to Liverpool, mainly from the Isle of Man. They relate that the whole island has virtually become a prison island, and the owners of hotels and bed and breakfasts have earned a fortune. Within days of arrival, the internees had set up a People's University in Onchan, a visibly thrilled professor of classical philology called Weber tells anyone who will listen, with courses in different languages, telegraphy, advertising and First Aid.

'On the Isle of Man there are also Walter Freud, grandson of Sigmund Freud, Robert Neumann, the founder of the Austrian PEN, and the Dadaist artist Kurt Schwitters,' Weber continues. 'And Kurt Jooss, the German choreographer who emigrated to England in 1933 because he didn't want to continue working without his Jewish employees.

You must have read *Germany Jekyll & Hyde, 1939 – Germany from within*? A splendid analysis of the emergence and success of National Socialism. Yes, the very same man – Sebastian Haffner! He's been interned too. A collection of wonderful people. I felt honoured to be one of them.'

The detainees from the Isle of Man have been told that Canada is their destination, and even given an address en route. But Australia has never been mentioned. Married men were promised that their wives and children would come along in convoy. However, women and children are nowhere to be seen. There are just men, many of them still half children with smooth, rosy faces and an irrepressible excitement about the coming adventure.

Many who had been waiting in England for their visa to emigrate to the USA have been advised to sign up voluntarily for transport to Canada, from where they can more easily arrange to cross into the United States. In addition, they will then save on the ship's passage. Like Erich, they are full of confidence as they wait for their embarkation to freedom.

'It's a mistake, it's a mistake,' cries one remarkably well-dressed man with a hat, who has been delivered to the pier by taxi. He waves a piece of paper. 'I have a passage for the Isle of Man!' No one pays him any attention. Like all others, he is driven onto the *Dunera*. Erich has the vague feeling he has seen him somewhere before. A film actor, perhaps?

A larger group of men in red and khaki uniforms climbs up the gangway with stony faces and is whisked onto the rear deck. 'German prisoners of war', the rumour goes round like wildfire through the crowd. One man named Anton, about forty years old, with horn-rimmed glasses, thinks he recognises a Gestapo boss he knows personally, from Mannheim. 'What's he doing here? What's he after in England? And now we're both being deported together!' Anton shakes his head in disbelief and mutters angrily.

Urged to get a move on, Erich's big Huyton group is now stumbling along the wooden planks of the pier and is driven up the steep entrance gangway, beset on all sides by soldiers in brand new British Army uniforms. A few still have considerable amounts of luggage with them, from which they refused to be separated. Again and again the throng comes to a halt as the men climb the narrow bridge that leads through an iron door into the ship. Now the huge transport vessel looms even more menacingly over their heads. Erich and Otto lose sight of one another in the crowd. Back on the pier, a few pairs of broken glasses remain.

Behind the door, there is a double line of British soldiers waiting. They do not mess about. With their rifle butts, they push the internees onto the deck, where they are met by soldiers who tear the luggage from their hands and frisk everyone. Anybody who defends himself is kicked and punched. Some of the baggage flies straight into the sea, where it breaks up as soon as it bounces into the water. Documents and items of clothing bob on the surface. Some bags are slashed open with bayonets. Whatever the men are carrying in briefcases, backpacks and on their bodies, everyday items as well as things that are of particular value to them, is randomly thrown into a pile: gloves, pyjamas, pipes, slippers, wash bags, lighters, pens, bibles, prayer shawls and documents. Jewellery, watches and money are dropped into bags held open to receive them, or casually disappear into the soldiers' pockets.

Minute by minute the mountain of empty wallets grows. Important documents – identity papers and emigration documents, certificates, notebooks and Nansen passports for stateless refugees that have cost a fortune – are taken from them, thrown to the ground or shredded before the horrified eyes of their owners. 'You won't be needing any of this, you lot of Fifth Columnists: it's back to Germany after the war for you,' grins one of the guards.

An elderly man with a wide-brimmed hat is carrying a violin case with him. When they want to wrest even this from him, he hugs it like a child and pleads with the guards to leave him the violin, it's valuable and belongs to his son who is still interned in England. He cries out in pain as a rifle butt comes down on his foot. Lieutenant Colonel William Scott, commander of the escort troop composed partly of prisoners on parole, stands by with arms crossed like Admiral Nelson and watches the scene with a smug smile under his carefully trimmed moustache. When he and his assistant Lieutenant John O'Neill have derived sufficient amusement from the scene, O'Neill snatches the violin case from the old man and leaves him to hobble around on deck with a bleeding foot.

Erich's Waterman fountain pen, a gift from Irka from better times, has been confiscated. He demands a receipt: he is, after all, an accountant. For once the soldier is speechless. You've got to trust a member of the British Army, he eventually roars with a red face: they are not Nazis! Erich secretly congratulates himself that he shoved his passport into one of his shoes in good time. From the front of the queue, the news is passed to the back: 'Hide everything you can: there are *goniffs* at the front.' Erich has watched a man next to him stuffing two pounds into the lining of his tie.

'Well, everything's getting off to a really nice start,' says Otto in his familiar bass. 'Did you see the way they just chucked that man's manuscript into the sea? He'd been working on it for years. It broke my heart to see it.'

43

'He'll write a new book,' says Erich shrugging. 'It's war, everything's different. The main thing is he's alive.'

'Yes, but these men are British!' protests Otto.

CHAPTER SEVEN

'Fifth Columnists, Nazi pigs, move it, *now*?' shout the guards as they herd the passengers, dazed by this harsh welcome, prodding them on with the barrels of their guns, shoving them in no discernible order in groups onto the forward part of the quarterdeck, the afterdeck, and amidships. From the corner of his eye Erich can see another area on the deck, fenced off with barbed wire, apparently where the survivors of the *Arandora Star* are gathered. He recognises the young Italian among them. He prefers not to remember his story right now. He grabs Otto's hand and pulls him along. Because of Otto's girth, a source of constant teasing, he is sometimes a little slow and clumsy.

Through a heavy iron door with a high threshold, they go through a fenced-off corridor just a few planks wide into the vessel. Between barbed wire and railings stand the guards. Erich is transfixed with horror when he realises that this is the only way to get off the ship or gain access to other parts of it. There is no time to think about what would happen if the ship is torpedoed. With rifle butts and yells they are pushed through a narrow iron staircase down into the belly of the ship. A stale smell drifts upwards. If anyone slips, the men behind fall on top of him. They are all confused, in a state of shock: no one has ever seen an Englishman acting so brutally, it just does not fit the image they have of them. The Englishmen, even the British soldiers, whom they have met before have been likeable, restrained people who even apologise if you tread on their toes on the bus.

'Get a move on, pack of Nazis! At the double!'

In the first lower deck they are awaited by soldiers with guns at the ready. An officer is leaning on the banisters and swinging his stick in a stylish circular motion. Down they go, ever further down. The press of men is indescribable. And then it is over. They have arrived on the second lower deck in a large, dimly lit room: tables and wooden benches have been secured to the floor. Perhaps they will be given something to eat in this dining room, they think, and then be assigned to their sleeping quarters.

One of the soldiers rudely orders them to grab one of the grey bundles piled up on the tables. They contain a hammock and a felt blanket. Soon it becomes clear that this 'dining room' is their terminus. Erich has quickly recognised that they would do well to secure hooks to hang their hammocks from.

Gradually the room fills: soon it is almost bursting. There must be hundreds, each of them trying to get a place, any place. The first battles are joined. 'Shut your traps!' shout the guards. You could cut the air with a knife. Through the vents in the ceiling, just enough oxygen gets through to stop the internees suffocating. Behind the portholes, barricaded with steel plates, you can dimly hear the lapping of the waves. On the side walls are coarsely timbered shelves with plates and cups made of metal and lights that cannot be switched off: these cast a dim light over the hodgepodge of confused men.

Then the wait is over. Again they need to step up to clear the last of their belongings from the pockets of their trousers and jackets. Those who do not voluntarily do so are rudely frisked. Watches, fountain pens, wedding rings and wallets disappear as before into uniform pockets and bags.

No sooner have the robbers cleared up than a barrage of abuse is unleashed. All that is left to the humiliated internees, robbed of their belongings, feeling hungry and thirsty, is rage, cynical wit, or impotent threats to get back at the criminals one day. The nature of their response varies with their characters. The smarter ones, who managed to hide their valuables from the crooks in their clothes, feel a secret sense of triumph. At 9 p.m. there is at least something to eat. Then the landlubbers clumsily try to hang up their hammocks, and their failed attempts to clamber into their swinging berths for the night arouse laughter. At least this calms them down.

For a long time, the floating prison sways, its engines humming quietly, in the port of Liverpool. Not until midnight does the *Dunera*, escorted by a destroyer in convoy with another ship carrying the evacuated children, move out onto a sea so still that the men do not notice they are moving. When he finally realises they have started, Erich feels a mixture of nostalgia and wanderlust. Once, he went on a boat trip from Genoa to Dubrovnik, but this is something of a completely different order.

Whatever may happen, for the time being they are prisoners, and literally incarcerated on this, their first night. For emergency purposes, black tarred buckets have been placed around the room, and it is not long until the waves in the notoriously wild Irish Sea start to rise, and the first men grow seasick. 'Stay in your hammocks and try to get up as little as possible,' warns one man who clearly knows what he is talking about. 'As long as you keep still, you're swinging with the movement of the ship.'

'Was that something about hammocks you just said?' comes an angry voice.

Not everyone has been able to get a hammock, and due to lack of space even the lucky possessors of one have not always been able to find somewhere to hang it up. They have no choice but to settle down on the floor or on the narrow benches and tables. Soon the buckets fill up and spill over, vomit, urine and faeces pour out onto the floor and soak the blankets of those who have the misfortune to be lying on it.

Voices with accents from every part of Germany and Austria flutter through the darkness.

'Welcome aboard.'

'Can you believe it? The swine have housed the Nazis on the rear deck. So they're closer to the fresh air and can be out in the open quicker if we sink.'

'Do you know what one of the officers said? "If any of you are survivors from the *Arandora Star*, I can reassure you it won't happen again. We've taken precautions to ensure that no one gets off here." Can you imagine?'

'That's what I call the British sense of humour.'

'The ship's a floating grave. We only have a narrow staircase – for us and for the men above, who'll be able to get out quicker. And in front of the door there's barbed wire, did you see? Before we drown, we get torn to shreds. I'm an old hand when it comes to barbed wire: first Sachsenhausen, then Dachau. Three long years. And now this.'

'They haven't even provided us with life belts.'

'You can forget that. We're enemies to them. Enemy aliens. No one's going to shed a tear for us when we all get sucked down. They'll write in the papers that we were to blame because we attacked each other, instead of climbing into the lifeboats in an orderly way. That's what happened in the *Arandora Star*.'

'The next one of you to mention the *Arandora Star* gets a punch on the nose from me. Understood?' This from a Berliner.

'Okay, okay. What's the point? Let's try to sleep.'

'They chucked my visa for America into the sea,' sobs one man, unmistakably from Saxony.

'They swiped my PhD certificate, my birth certificate, my marriage certificate and the photos of my children.'

'Will I get back my grandmother's jewellery? It was all I had left in the world. The officer wants to keep it for me. So he said.'

'In Sachsenhausen, at least they wrote down everything they took away from us. When they released me, I got my stuff back.'

'I'm diabetic and had two packets of insulin. They threw them in the sea. Imagine that!'

'They trod on my glasses. Now I'm practically blind.'

'Oh God, I feel sick.'

'Just don't puke on my neck.'

The soldier, who sat for a long time on the stairs to prevent any movement between the decks, has cleared off. Soon, none of the men has any more desire to add his own adversities to the rest. The seasick gaze apathetically at the ceiling. Erich closes his eyes and enjoys the rocking of his hammock. He is in good shape, and not the slightest bit sick. And he loves to travel. As a child, he never got beyond Windischgarsten, the picturesque village in the mountains of Upper Austria where his grandparents lived. After he became politically undesirable in his home country and lost his job as an accountant, he found employment as a tour guide. True, it was an insecure job for just a few months a year, but he enjoyed it enormously. He much preferred being a tour guide to being an account-ant. Whenever he appeared for dinner in the hotel, in white trousers and a white shirt, with his suntan and his blue eyes gleaming with *joie de vivre*, women just lay at his feet. And then came England, where everything was different from Vienna: transport, politeness, even the doorknobs. He likes England very much, he could have stood life there for a good while longer. The public libraries in particular met with his approval. In Vienna he had worked in his spare time for a workers' library. Everyone is talking about Canada, when he was convinced they were going to Australia. That was what he eventually applied for. For Irka's sake it should be Australia. Besides, that is the country farthest away from the European hell. The only thing is that he will then not see his father for a long time – who knows whether he will survive the war?

Irka. They have known each other for ten years. Elegant, petite Irka from Warsaw. Warsaw, yes, he has been there too. To get married. Another world, the house with the two clocks on the main floor flanked by two cherubs, the high ceiling with the stucco rosette, the plump cook, a Christian woman who served the food, the mother who spoke perfect French, Russian and German, the fine silverware. He, a worker's son who never graduated from school, who had never used a napkin as a child, made a good impression on the Jewish gentlefolk, especially on Irka's mother, a fine, well-groomed lady with rosy skin and white hair. She took him aside and told him not to hesitate to box Irka's ears if she kicked up too much of a fuss. He still does not know what she meant: with him, Irka is as tame as a lamb. And extremely tough. Just a little edgy – which you cannot blame her for, given the situation. He even got on well with his father-in-law, an elegant rascal with round glasses and a moustache, a chap with a similar temperament to Erich. Perhaps that was why Irka fell in love with him.

He is already feeling a little guilty because he is filled with pleasure at the prospect of the journey and everything that awaits him over there, while poor Irka has had to stay back in London all alone and survive on temporary jobs as a domestic. She is not really cut out for this, even if she has learned to cook quite surprisingly well in England. But she will come over to join him, that much is sure. He knows her: she will move heaven and earth to achieve her goal. She is more assertive than he is, a real fighter. Over there they will start a new life, and all will be well. Above all, he needs to improve his English: maybe one day he will be able to work as a journalist, for that is his dream. He does not want to spend his life as an accountant. Can anyone of his age learn a foreign language well enough to express himself like a native? Joseph Conrad could.

The men snore, each in his own tone. The sour air is disgusting, but fortunately the fans at least are working. What time is it? The bastards have even taken his watch off him, his Doxa. At least he still has his wedding ring – they swiped Otto's. Because of his size he is conspicuous wherever he goes. Erich hears Otto stirring next to him in the hammock. 'Goodnight,' he whispers, 'it's definitely going to be interesting.'

Soon he will fall asleep, hear nothing and smell nothing more: how delicious is the moment just before, in these difficult conditions. This is how one ought to be able to die. In his mind he embraces Irka's charming girlish body and tries to keep everything else at bay, just summon to his memory the sound of her slightly brittle voice with its hard Polish accent and incorrect grammar. He smiles.

CHAPTER EIGHT

In the morning, volunteers have to report to fetch breakfast from the galley – an opportunity to escape from the
stinking lower deck up towards fresh air. A soldier leads
the squad of food orderlies over the narrow passage to an
entrance fore and then down to the lower deck where the
galley is located. There they meet men from the deck above
them. Information is exchanged. The German prisoners of war, the food orderlies report on their return, are
sailors from the German merchant ship *Adolph Woermann*,
captured before their East African campaign and like the
other internees taken to a British camp.

Not all feel like having any breakfast, they are too tired
to move after their night. But Erich is starving and enjoys
his food. There is traditional English porridge, a small cup
of lime juice and something to prevent rickets. You eat
with a spoon, as knives and forks are prohibited.

The first day the men spend trying to clean up the excess-
es of the night from the deck, and trying to find their way
round in these novel conditions. As in Huyton, there are
rules that must be adhered to: get up at 6.15 a.m., breakfast
at 7, snack at 4 p.m., dinner at 7, sleep at 10.15. During
the day the hammocks are rolled up and used as pillows or
cushions against the hard benches and the floor. The room is
hopelessly overcrowded. The men doss down wherever they
can, even on the stairs; if there was an attack, it would trigger
a stampede, and they would be in a perilously narrow spot.

Anyone who wants to go to the toilet has to clamber over
his fellow sufferers and, given the high waves, be careful

not to tread on them. For a total of some 1,600 men there are about two dozen doorless toilets, and every time they are flushed, such a strong surge is produced that a mixture of salt water and excreta pours over the toilet seats and floor. The men queue up for the toilets: most of them are seasick and tell those ahead of them to get a move on. Soon a 'toilet police' forms, shouting 'Next, please!' and sharing out the toilet paper. There are two sheets per head per day. The paper is white and smooth and is suitable for writing and drawing. Some people hoard it.

Only a very few can work up much interest in this first day's poor and meagre food. Even a possible torpedo attack loses its terror as most of them are preoccupied by their stomachs. Bodily discomfort blots out all other thoughts. A restorative resignation starts to spread, now that they are ultimately helpless in the face of events. Better to be drowned in the Atlantic Ocean than croak in a German concentration camp: this is the prevailing opinion.

As soon as it becomes apparent that the English have no intention of improving their conditions in the dim half-light below deck, the politically minded among them start to organise the men. First, they set about reclaiming their lost property, especially the essential things like toothbrushes, soap and razors. Three men are chosen to be spokesmen for the second deck – a priest, a Jewish law attorney and Erich, who speaks good English. Their complaint about missing toiletries bears fruit, and a guard with one of the bags full of confiscated property comes down and empties its contents onto the table. The men scrabble round for their personal belongings. When the soldier decides the procedure is taking too long, he gathers everything back into the bag and walks off without a word.

The atmosphere reaches its nadir. Hardly anyone has any clothes apart from what he is already wearing. Filth and stench are not part of the everyday experience of most of those on board. Is the whole trip going to be like this? How can they live without shaving and brushing their teeth? How will they survive the boat ride in these cramped conditions without tearing each other to pieces?

A few people are brought up on deck to help with sorting the luggage. 'My luggage is over the ocean, my luggage is over the sea, oh bring back, bring back, oh bring back my luggage to me,' they sing on their return.

'They're still looting,' they report. 'They've broken the locks on the suitcases open with their bayonets, ripped open parcels and helped themselves. Like when we came on board. They've chucked documents, books, manuscripts and notes into the water.'

'And then the empty suitcases followed after.'

From now on, all those whose luggage has not already been thrown into the sea before their very eyes have to live with the question of what they might find left in their suitcases by the time they reach their destination.

The politically organised look out for comrades, and gather to discuss the situation. What they do discover is that a group of 320 internees from the camp at Lingfield Racecourse who were meant to be taken to Huyton have mistakenly ended up coming along on the *Dunera*. No wonder that the ship is overloaded.

On the evening of the second day Erich is just standing under the hot saltwater shower at the open hatch where you can escape the stench for a while and enjoy the feeling of cleanliness. Salt water is the only thing of which there is enough and to spare on board. They are off the north coast of the Irish Sea. Suddenly, a loud bang is heard, like metal striking against metal. 'Sounds like we're being torpedoed,' says Erich jokingly to the naked man showering next to him. But then he hears the sound of breaking dishes and the shout 'Torpedo!' rising from many throats.

Erich pulls on his trousers. On his deck, there is dead silence. Then there is another bang, this time muffled and further away. Now the men start to emerge from their fright and rush to the stairs – just one set of stairs leading upwards for two decks with a total of about 800 people. A Berlin Communist, a great hulking man, directs one group as it rams the locked door with a long bench. A soldier with a life jacket open to the waist aims his rifle at the men and threatens to shoot.

'Shoot then!' roars the Communist, 'it ain't gonna do any good. We ain't getting out of here in a hurry.'

'You bastards!' yells another. 'You'll save yourselves and leave us to croak down here.'

They all start yelling at once. The young soldier looks scared and cannot bring himself to fire. Then, a shot is heard from the rear deck.

The men respond differently. A priest pulls out his prayer book and starts to pray aloud. Some Jews do the same. Erich is gripped by an ice-cold composure. He is a good swimmer and convinced he will be safe in any danger. He has memorized what the young South Tyrolean told him: quickly swim away from the ship. Otto is near him, that's the important thing. Erich watches what the others are doing and decides that, later on, he will write it all down exactly. One resignedly shrugs and climbs into his hammock as if to await his end.

The ship starts zigzagging. The engines are still working, and the *Dunera* seems to have registered no impact on its side. Also, the lights are still on. The all-clear siren sounds, and at the top of the stairs appears an officer. He calls on two men to check that nothing has happened.

Everything is in order, report the two men: the escort destroyer has turned away and is sailing off at top speed. Does this mean that the *Dunera* is finally out of the danger zone? Only the Lascars, the Indian sailors, have not yet calmed down and are running around like headless chickens, the men report. From the Italians' quarters you can still hear occasional 'Ave Marias'.

'You can understand them reacting that way when the shit hits the fan,' grunts the Berliner.

No one can explain why the German submarine has not followed up the other two attacks. At just the same place where the *Arandora Star* sank, the *Dunera*'s captain executed a clever manoeuvre that meant the first torpedo struck the rear hull of the ship lengthways without exploding. The second reached the *Dunera* at the bottom of the hull and shot away under the keel when the ship was lifted by a wave in the air. The rough sea and the captain's zigzagging had saved them. Accompanied by the destroyer dropping depth charges, the convoy ship with the children on board is sailing quickly away from the *Dunera*.

Why the U56 did not pursue the *Dunera* is never clearly established. According to one version, the German commander, Lieutenant Otto Harms, saw men jumping into the water through his periscope, and suspected a mutiny. So he did not fire any more torpedoes but as night fell he sent sailors in rubber dinghies out across the sea to collect any survivors. However, all the sailors found were suitcases bobbing around on the surface: Lieutenant Harms orders that some of them be brought on board. They contain, among other things, German-language manuscripts and letters addressed to internees in British POW camps.

Harms transmits a message to all other German submarines in the preferred area for attack in the Irish Sea and informs their commanders about the POWs on board the *Dunera*; they are not to be attacked, but rather escorted out of the danger zone. He will not risk a repeat of the embarrassing incident with the *Arandora Star*.

The *Dunera* can continue its journey unmolested.

CHAPTER NINE

Even before Erich's departure, Irka had moved out of Mrs Needham's. Dr Pollak, the wife of a dentist interned in Huyton, has offered her a room. Her luxurious apartment in a Victorian brick house with the euphonious name Primrose Mansions already houses four other women from Vienna: Dora, Gusti, Käthe and Lizzi. On the other side of the road, opposite the gently curving line of identical terraced houses, lies Battersea Park, one of London's most beautiful green spaces, where the government is just about to build shelters in case of necessity.

To begin with, Irka enjoyed the company of these women who shared her predicament. All, including their hostess, are waiting: to travel overseas, to receive a letter from the camp or news from Vienna or even, though they know this is unlikely, news from Warsaw and a turning point in the war. Only the German scholar Dora has a job, working as a German teacher and governess to a couple with a German background, who in spite of the current situation want their children to learn the language of Thomas Mann. It's a golden opportunity: you can hardly get away from cheap German teachers in London – there is a large supply, but the demand is dwindling to almost zero. Dora is happy to have found a job, even if she has her hands full with the two children; they hate everything German.

The other women are trying to make themselves useful round the house. When it is not raining, they take long walks in the park and talk incessantly about what they have experienced and what might happen. Irka talks mainly about Erich.

Lizzi is a colourful character, she met Dr Pollak at the Austrian Centre, at the opening of the Austrian Labour Club, the first independent organisation for Austrian Social Democrats and Socialists in Britain, which since January 1940 has regularly organised discussions on cultural issues. At the end of the twenties Lizzi, still almost a teenager, had converted to Catholicism, not out of opportunism (there was as yet no need) but as a fervent devotee of Thérèse de Lisieux, who at the end of the nineteenth century, aged twenty-four, died of consumption and, just before Lizzi's conversion, was canonized by Pope Pius XI. None of the women can understand her inexplicable passion, and Lizzi knows that it is useless to explain to her atheist friends what led her to take this step; she hardly knows herself. Thérèse offers her support; that is all she knows. Following Thérèse's example – she preached devotion to God and her fellow men – Lizzi had trained as a nurse. As panic over Fifth Columnists rose in England, she lost her job at a London hospital. The fact that she has had to flee from the Nazis as a Catholic and has been dismissed by the English as a Nazi sympathizer puts her faith to a severe test.

'You think you're superior,' Lizzi hears Irka telling her. Irka has no patience for her crazy belief. 'Haven't you ever heard of the Nuremberg Laws? You're a Jew like all of us. We didn't choose it either. Do you think I value being Jewish? The whole of Jewry can get lost as far as I'm concerned.'

'Leave her alone!' beseeches Gusti gently. It is not the first time she has tried to calm down the hot-headed Irka. 'Why do you always have to start a fight?'

'If we get Communism one day, no religions will be needed any more,' intervenes Käthe. 'They're all the same anyway, just there to blinker people and distract them from the essential.'

'And what is the essential?' asks Lizzie, who has made a vow to avoid any discussion with her miscreant friends. 'Human beings – they're the essential thing.'

'Society is the essential thing,' retorts Käthe, 'the structure that should allow each individual to live a full life in the context of his abilities and needs. Even as a God-botherer, if you ask me.'

'So you two aren't so far apart,' says Gusti, still trying to maintain harmony.

Like Irka and Erich, Käthe had been active in an illegal Communist cell in Vienna. On 12th February 1934, the day when Viennese workers rose against the fascists and were immediately and completely routed, they got together in Käthe's apartment in Karl-Marx-Hof to worry about their men, stranded in the city and unable to reach them.

Now Käthe's partner is interned on the Isle of Man. With her thick curly hair and slightly slanted dark eyes, she is the most beautiful of them all, although she does not care about her appearance and always wears men's clothes. But when she sits on the sofa with one leg tucked under her, gesturing wildly in the heat of conversation with her slender hands, she is a picture of inimitable elegance. Irka envies her for her slender body, which allows her to always wear comfortable flat shoes. Since the age of fifteen, Irka has never left the house without high heels. It is hard work, but she has become accustomed to it. As a teenager, it was her dream to be at least five foot three but she stopped growing at an inch and a half too short.

The women are united in their rejection of Dr Pollak. They always call her Dr Pollak, although it is only her husband who is a doctor – an Austrian habit. But this means they can express their distance from the thin dry woman who has indeed taken them in without asking for rent, but who never allows them to forget who is in charge in the house. Dr Pollak has a deep voice that brooks no argument. Everything she says sounds like some final sentence in a court of appeal, or as if she is issuing an order. Her slightly stooped demeanour emphasizes her aggressiveness. In Vienna the two of them – she, the daughter of a wealthy textile merchant from the city centre, and the real Dr Pollak – had moved in so-called high society. On the basis of her father's business connections, they were able to save much of their wealth and bring it back to England, though this still did not save the dentist from internment. That he is now forced to starve with the have-nots in Huyton is something that Dr Pollak's wife takes as a personal insult.

Irka it is not accustomed to living with other people. Having to share a kitchen and bathroom soon gets on her nerves, especially since the women can never agree on a common mealtime. One of them always wants to cook just when another is starting to get busy in the kitchen. Irka is rarely alone in the house: there is always another of the women standing at the door and prattling on at her. And the conversations go round and round in circles.

Irka feels the need to be alone more often than before, so that she can indulge in her memories. She misses Erich, more than she could ever have imagined. She longingly thinks back to their time together in Wiltshire. She would love to clean the silver cutlery again and make the beds, even get yelled at by her boss, if only she could be with Erich. When, filled with illusory hopes, she came to

London to find a job that would suit her education, he held on to his job at the stately home for another two months – a separation that she now bitterly regrets. Had she known how soon they would be torn apart again and how much she would miss him, she would not have put up with it.

Two weeks after Erich's embarkation, Irka receives a telegram from the commandant at Huyton, informing her of Erich's departure on 10th July. She already knows about this, as Erich's farewell letter has arrived. The package she sent to him in the camp shortly before his departure never reached him. It contained things that would have been useful to him on his travels. For days she sorted through his clothes, and went round London buying the things he still needed: shirts, trousers, underwear, socks, sheets, shoe polish and shoe brushes, thread and sewing needles, scissors, soap, soap flakes, ink, cheese, jam, tinned milk, sardines. She had wrapped everything lovingly. Will they now return the package to her or forward it to him?

Irka is glad that, at the last moment, she urged Erich to take the winter coat he had wanted to leave behind because it was now summer. Sometimes he fails to think ahead, that beloved dreamer of hers. How will he cope without her? How long is the trip to Australia – if it really is Australia? In any case, they are cut off from one another for an indefinite period. She even wrote her last letter to him after he had already left. Who knows when it will reach him?

Primrose Mansions, 12th July 1940

Erich, my love, since Monday I've been living in Battersea, where I do some of the housework and am glad to be among people. Life is very quiet here, and we have this beautiful park just opposite. I'm just worried about you and about our future. If you have to leave

England, let me know, I would definitely want to go with you. It's awful for me to think I might have to stay alone in this country. Why must we be separated? I just don't understand it. What a waste of my young years! I know I shouldn't complain, after all it's a fate we all share, but after so many years of persecution in our country we long for a little peace and security.

Your Irka

That she had written 'in our country' comes as a surprise even to her. Twelve years have passed since she left school and went to Vienna to continue her studies. She wanted to be independent, free, to shake off the control of parents, uncles and aunts. Actually, Paris had been her dream destination, Paris, where the artists live. But to her parents' eyes, the capital of France was a den of iniquity, into which their already wayward daughter would dive head first: they were fully aware of this, and wanted to avoid it. In Vienna, after all, there lived a Jewish aunt of hers, who was given the task of keeping an eye on her niece. But Irka tolerated the surveillance for just a week, before fleeing. So she was free in Vienna, but did not feel at home there: xenophobia and anti-Semitism were ubiquitous. She felt lonely. She was never invited home by a fellow student. It was as if there was something threatening in her accent, her un-Austrian temperament.

But then came Erich, and all was well. By marrying him, she became an Austrian national, but 'her country' did not want to keep its new citizen. Now Austria no longer exists. England is their country now, it is England that has taken her in. And taken her husband away, too. Is there an airmail service between Australia and England? An ordinary letter probably takes forever to get there.

Two days after the telegram, something happens: a letter from the Germany Emergency Committee of the Quakers arrives, in which she is registered as a refugee. Official notification has been received that her husband is en route to Australia, and she is to follow him within a few days. Australia it is then: Irka is satisfied. She is also told in the letter to take her luggage – up to forty kilos – to the refugee office of the Interior Ministry. The attached labels for her bags are to be filled out and attached to the luggage. She can take five pounds in cash, and as jewellery she is allowed her wedding ring, a brooch and another piece also worth five pounds. On 31st July she must arrive in London where a room in Newlands Hotel has been booked for her. She will need warm clothes for the journey, so she should pack for both summer and winter in Australia. If she has any financial resources in England, they will ensure that her money is transferred to her in Australia. Even luggage in excess of the allotted forty kilos will – 'in certain circumstances' – be sent on to her, and she needs simply to give an address in England from which it can be picked up.

'On the 31st! So soon! Lucky you!'

Instantly, all resentment evaporates. Dora, Lizzi, Gusti, Käthe, and even Dr Pollak hug Irka and all start talking at the same time.

'Australia! Where the sun always shines!'

'You have to send us a photo of a kangaroo! What are they called in Polish?'

'It's almost the same: *kangur*.'

'And a koala too!'

'Did you know that koalas sleep all the time? And do you know why? It's because they only eat eucalyptus leaves and so mustn't expend much energy. Interesting, isn't it?'

'Oh, you just know everything, Dora!'

'And there's masses of convicts there. You won't stand out.' Käthe's contribution. Laughter.

The summer night is chilly. The women sit cross-legged on the carpet in front of the fireplace and warm their faces by the flames. On their backs they feel the cold draught from the hallway. Only Dr Pollak sits enthroned in one of her flowery chintz armchairs, knitting. Since her husband has been interned, she has taken up knitting to calm her nerves.

'And I'll be seeing my sister again! My clever big sister.' Irka beams. 'Our Warsaw relatives couldn't believe it when she and her husband decided to emigrate to Australia. And Ludka was still pregnant. What do you want to go there for, they asked? With a newborn child as well. *Kangury* and convicts, they said – just like you lot! No culture. Actually I can't stand her husband, Ludka is far too clever for him, but he was the one who insisted they emigrate. After the Munich Agreement he was the only person who realised that Poland was doomed. And the Jews even more so. Shortly before the war started, they left Warsaw, and Ludka's son was born in Sydney. They called him Sydney. Rather funny, don't you think?'

'You've really misjudged your brother-in-law. You should kiss his hands.'

Over the next few days, Irka is seized by a nervous restlessness. She sells off her jewellery at far less than its value, to a jeweller's where she had tried to get rid of her finery a few months ago. Dr Pollak takes her delicate gold necklace with onyx stones, one of her finest pieces, which she hands over with a heavy heart. Since she is only allowed to take five pounds' worth of cash on the journey, Irka immediately begins to use their money to buy commodities. She buys a watch for herself and, for ten pounds, a baby Empire typewriter for Erich, the passionate letter writer and amateur journalist.

With her own luggage and a suitcase with Erich's things, she takes a taxi to Bloomsbury Street, where the British government has set up a central contact point for organisations aiding refugees from Europe. This is Bloomsbury House, a magnificent red and white building in the Flemish Renaissance style, located in the heart of London.

So excited is Irka that she cannot sleep at night: not until the early hours of the morning does she manage to doze for a few hours. Soon she will be in Erich's arms and she will never let go of him again. She would so much like to write to him and tell him how much she misses him and is looking forward to seeing him again, but she has no address. Erich is on the high seas and with any luck he is safe and sound. Then she remembers the news of the torpedoing of the *Arandora Star*. Erich could have been on that ship! Strange that she has never thought of such a possibility. The idea would have been unbearable. Apart from him, now on his way to Australia, and her older sister who is already there, she has no one in the world. Her parents and her brother are out of reach, imprisoned in occupied Warsaw. Her hometown lies in ruins. Two and a half weeks of non-stop bombing. She wonders whether the house where they grew up is still standing? Maybe her family is no longer alive?

Her mother could easily have saved herself, if she had only stayed in England and listened to her daughter. In August 1939 she had visited London with her daughter-in-law Marysia. Before they left, she and Erich had spent half the night trying to persuade them. 'Stay here and get your men out of Poland! First Austria, then Czechoslovakia, then Poland. That's how it's going to go.' But her mother would not hear of it. Decide to stay, during a holiday, just like that, with nothing but the dress she was wearing, her hat, handbag and a small suitcase? Leave her husband, son, apartment, everything...? It was more than she could possibly imagine. For her what happened was like an accident that, a few seconds ago, you would never have expected. And then, all of a sudden, the whole world changes.

So it happened: the German attack on Poland. Erich and Irka had foreseen it, as had Ludka's husband. Why would her mother not believe them? It would not have been easy for her, at her age she would not have found a job, but she would have been safe, and still alive. The refugee aid organisations give money for upkeep, even Irka receives regular support. Janek, her brother, and her sister-in-law would have been able to work. Her father and brother could have entered the country on a tourist visa. Erich too. Everything else would have been sorted. Somehow. After the outbreak of war, the English would not have been able to send them back. Even Marysia, the efficient one, could not imagine just staying put. She was too dependent on all of the beautiful things she had left behind in Warsaw, the elegant gowns, the jewellery, the perfumes.

And now? The trap has been sprung. What are the Germans doing to the Jews? Better not think about it. Just think of Erich.

CHAPTER TEN

The *Dunera* carries on its journey without further incident, but the tension remains, although the physical discomfort overshadows everything else. You can tolerate it only if you fall back on a certain degree of apathy. The portholes with their heavy flaps remain closed, no daylight penetrates through to the stifling underworld, and air from outside reaches the lower deck only through the air vents. All day long, the dim emergency lights glow and the fans whir.

Lieutenant Brooks, the Scottish military surgeon, is one of the few Britons sympathetic to the prisoners. He warns the internees to wait until they arrive before they complain about the shameful treatment by Scott and O'Neill, since mutiny can be punished with death on board ship. The two commanders have absolute command over the internees in their care, and there is nothing to be done about that. O'Neill is known to be abusive when drunk. Quite a few of the passengers enjoy the privilege of being abused by him as a 'German Jewish swine' and 'son of German Jewish dogs'.

Brooks is fighting to get more air into the lower decks, and together with the captain, a warm-hearted Cockney, and the latter's First Officer, he manages to create a shaft through which additional fresh air can get down. Most of his efforts to try and improve the situation, however, are blocked by the military on safety grounds. Even his attempt to get fresh clothes out of the internees' luggage is rejected. All the same, he does manage to ensure that soap is handed out to the men once or twice a week – one bar of soap for twenty men. Later they also get towels, mostly from the plundered luggage.

Although there is a lack of basic medical care on board, essential drugs are thrown overboard as soon as they are discovered on any of the internees. The soldiers mete out the same treatment to false teeth, and there are quite a few pairs of dentures, as British dentists are notorious for preferring the pliers to the drill. At night, it sometimes happens that the guards show up without warning to rummage round for valuables they have not yet pilfered. They pull one young man's wedding ring off him so brutally that he needs medical attention. Brooks writes a report on the incident and sends Scott a sarcastic note: 'If one of your soldiers wants to remove a ring, let him do it in my practice, under surgery and in sterile conditions. Do not let him tear the skin off with it.'

The queue outside the doctor's office is almost as long as the queue outside the toilets. The sick wait patiently, leaning against the wall, as there are hardly any seats. Brooks, with just one assistant, has to look after a poorly equipped health department amidships: it has a hundred beds, and they are always full. But, as in Huyton, there are several doctors among the internees, such as the renowned heart surgeon Dr Paul Schatzki and several medical students who are happy to give Brooks a hand.

The hospital also offers the opportunity to exchange information between people who are separated by barbed wire, as the fore and aft of the ship are hermetically sealed off from each other. The route to the amidships area goes partly over the upper deck, so that those who visit the hospital can breathe some fresh air and enjoy the sunshine for a few seconds. Being ill is a privilege, so many of the men turn up saying they are ill even when they are as fit as a fiddle, just so that they can trot along behind a corporal, escape from the lower deck and in the hospital enjoy the luxury of a bed protected by a half-height grille and clean sheets.

In the kitchen, in the washrooms and the latrines, the hatches are open during the day and constantly surrounded by a dense crowd panting for a chance to pump fresh air into their lungs. So the toilets become a meeting place, a place for a smoke, where you can pinch some toilet paper and pick up the latest bog gossip – even though many suffer from diarrhoea and seasickness, and in heavy seas the floor is one big sewer. But at four in the afternoon, even in the shower stalls the hatches are closed. After that, the air gets particularly bad in the washrooms, where the water vapour mixes with the sweat of the men crammed in there.

Actually, neither cigarettes nor matches are allowed, and if they are discovered on an internee, he is put on a diet of bread and water in the vessel's bunker for twenty-four hours. Internees, who are, according to the final analysis, dangerous spies could set fire to the ship – or so it is feared. But the ban is difficult to enforce. Between sailors and internees, a brisk trade soon develops in the Waverley brand of Virginia cigarettes in beautifully painted tin boxes that find their way to people through an elaborate system of wholesalers, middlemen and small retailers. Needless to say, 'fraternisation' with the internees is strictly forbidden. Even money that managed to evade the British soldiers (despite their repeated searches through items of clothing) is in circulation. Everyone has his own secret stash. For smoking, two detainees take it in turn to keep watch. If the agreed warning signal 'Eighteen!' is heard, the cigarettes are hastily stubbed out.

'Did you used to have a secret smoke in the school toilet?' Erich asks Otto.

'I wasn't brave enough.'

One lucky case is Hein Heckenroth, a painter and stage decorator, who taught at the Folkwang School in Essen before 1933. When the officers learn that he is an excellent painter, they get him to paint their portraits and pay him with cigarettes that Heckenroth shares out between his table companions. Not everyone is as generous as he. Under the more stringent conditions on board, people's character traits appear in sharpened form – for better or for worse.

Fresh water for washing is available only two to three times a week. Since the men's shaving kits have been taken away, many suffer from itchy eczema. Anyone with a nice clean shave, because he has somehow managed to save his blade, is threatened with a spell in the bunker. Since most only have the clothes they are wearing, they have nothing to put on when they wash their clothes with saltwater. Pretty soon the clothing gets torn. With the sole pair of shoes they are wearing on their feet, the men have to wade through faeces and urine.

But however dirty and ragged they are, the internees manage to build up an internal organisation. The sea has calmed down, their stomachs are getting used to the regular moderate swell of the Atlantic, and energy starts to flow back into their bodies. Three men, one of whom is unmistakably a lawyer, draft a constitution laying down self-management for the internees. Since the only paper available for writing is toilet paper, this goes down in history as the Toilet Paper Constitution.

On board there are many doctors and psychiatrists. Although they have neither medicine nor bandages to care for their comrades with, they still get involved, calming people down or shaking them up, depending on when apathy and despair threaten to spread. First they try to convince the men with appeals to their reason: 'Don't be a fool. As long as a man lives, he can't give up hope.' If this gentle method does not work, they try severity: 'Do you think you're the one only one who's suffering here, the only one who's worried about his family?' If even that does not help, they reassuringly lay their hand on the arm of the person concerned, put on a gentle smile and tell a story in order to elicit a smile in turn from the melancholy patient. Most doctors are Jews, so they tell Jewish stories. They are mainly concerned with preventing mass psychosis breaking out.

One day, a shocking scene occurs. A middle-aged Jew squats under the stairs on the coat he has rolled into a bundle and rocks back and forth as if in prayer. In between, he pauses, presses his hand to his heart and laughs like a *meshuggener*.

'Have you got a pain in your heart?' a doctor asks. The man looks at him as if he has not understood the question. With his face buried in his hands, he begins to cry bitterly.

'Let him cry for a while, maybe it will do him good,' advises a grey-haired psychiatrist.

The general mood is melancholy. While the Jew weeps, none of the men dares to make a sound. Some have tears in their eyes. Erich feels ashamed and does not know why. Maybe because he has not suffered enough in his life or because he has a loving wife who will soon be following him. Because he still has most of his life ahead of him. This man, as you can see straightaway, has nothing left that is worth living for. Erich would like to hand him a glass of water, but where to get one? Except for the few sips they are granted at mealtimes, drinking water is not available.

Suddenly the man stops crying, takes his hands from his face and mutters a few words.

'What did you say?' asks the psychiatrist when the man does not respond, and then again: 'What did you say? Talk to me, I can help you. We all want to help you.'

The man unlaces his right shoe and pulls the sock off. The men stare, transfixed, as the psychiatrist strokes him and repeatedly asks what the matter is. Then the Jew gets up and swings his right leg until a small package falls out of the trouser leg. 'There, there,' he calls.

The psychiatrist picks up the packet, unties the string and unfolds the newspaper in which the article is wrapped. A broken chunk of brick appears.

'What's this?'

For a long time the man is silent and gazes into the distance, as if trying to remember an event in the distant past. Then suddenly he starts to speak, even if only in snatches.

'Lauterbach... Synagogue.'

'Yes, Lauterbach,' one man says into the silence, 'it's in Hesse.'

'Grandfather... Torah scroll.'

'Your grandfather donated a Torah scroll to the synagogue,' the psychiatrist says, helping him along.

'Then...'

'Then the Nazis set fire to it. And the Torah scroll was burned. Is that what happened?'

'Our synagogue, beautiful and big... they blew it up... father, grandfather, great-grandfather, they all prayed there... destroyed.'

'Calm down,' said the psychiatrist soothingly. 'We've all been having a tough time. In Aurich, where I come from, they set the synagogue on fire too.'

'Everything broken... lost... wife, child, house... concentration camp... dead... heart failure.' The Jew's face is bathed in tears. 'And here, on this ship, robbers, thieves... all stolen, the wedding ring, my wife's gold necklace... both dead.'

'We'll make sure you get it back. Erich will look after it, won't you?'

Erich can only nod mutely.

'And the brick?' The psychiatrist will not stop probing. 'What's that about?'

'From the synagogue... the only thing.'

The man takes the stone, stares at it for a long time and puts it in his jacket pocket. Then he utters his first coherent sentence: 'I'll take it with me to my grave.'

In the dead silence, the ship's engines suddenly sound really loud. The men have lowered their heads. Many are weeping.

Erich now knows why he is ashamed. He is not a Jew. He has a Jewish wife and feels a bond with the Jews, he likes the humour and cynicism of his Jewish friends. So, as things stand, cynicism is a healthy way of life. He was a Jew by choice, Erich previously liked to say. Since the Nazis such an expression is frivolous. How many Jews would now be happy not to be Jews? Irka's family. The family of this inconsolable man has been in the synagogue community of his city for generations, they at least know why they are being persecuted. Irka has been to a synagogue just once in her life – when one of her girl friends got married. She found it absurd that this friend deliberately selected a pious Jew for a husband, but for her sake Irka went. Like Erich, Irka rejects all religion: in her opinion, it is only there to stop people working for a better life on earth. 'Opium of the people', indeed. Her family agrees. They wanted to be law-abiding Poles, not Jews.

Erich became aware of the role of religion when he was fifteen. He realised then how deeply the Catholic Church reaches into the most intimate areas of people's lives and how much it is mainly concerned with power. He left the church and swore eternal enmity on it. His father, a Social Democrat, and far from being a believer, was still horrified.

His father, yes, even for his sake Erich is ashamed in the face of this unhappy man. His father is anti-Semitic. Not rabidly so, but laden with enough prejudices to want his son to marry a nice Catholic girl and not some foreign Jewess. Erich did not even answer back when he tried to persuade him not to marry Irka with the comment that, 'Out there in Germany', intermarriage was prohibited. 'Fortunately, we don't have any Nuremberg Laws yet,' was all that Erich could think of. He is not used to quarrelling with his father. Erich and his two brothers were brought up to obey. If they did not jump to it, they got 'a good hearty belting'.

'Do you know what my father said when I came out of prison and went for a walk on the Kahlenberg with him?' Erich suddenly asks Otto, who is sitting on the floor with his knees bent and his head hanging between his knees. Otto looks up. 'We always went for a walk if there was something important to discuss, and my father wanted to know what my plans were. So I told him that I was going to Warsaw to marry Irka. "For God's sake! The Jews have already brought disaster on our family once," he said.'

Otto's grey-blue eyes are sad. He is silent.

'I am ashamed of my father. I don't even know what he meant. We had no contact with Jews.'

'You're an admirer of George Bernard Shaw,' says Otto. 'I have a quotation from him for you: "The more things a man is ashamed of, the more respectable he is." There is no shame in feeling ashamed. Quite the contrary.'

'Do you ever think of Else?' asks Erich. 'She's now surrounded by them.'

'Yes, of course,' replies Otto. 'It's not easy having no news from her at all, but she'll be fine, I know her.'

CHAPTER ELEVEN

A week later, there is still no land in sight. But it is getting warmer by the day. The men gather around Uwe, the mathematician with experience in navigation. 'When are we going to get there?'

'Now we're veering south,' he announces. 'If it's Canada we're heading for, we should see land tomorrow.' It sounds even less convincing two days later. 'Now we should soon be turning west if we're still supposed to be going to Canada.'

The men have grown used to the regular movement of the sea. In the eternal twilight that reigns in the belly of the ship, one day flows uneventfully into the next, and in the midst of chaos a certain routine settles in. At meal times they have different sittings, as there are not enough tables for everyone. Some fifteen to twenty men gather as a 'family' to eat at each table. The tables have numbers that the designated waiters in the galley have to call out. No number means no food. Mostly they get smoked fish, sausage, potatoes, and a spoon of melon or lemon marmalade. Not infrequently they have to fish white maggots out of the soup. Even the bread is often maggoty, the butter rancid.

The family that Erich eats with is a mixed bunch: a scion of the old Austrian aristocracy from Prague, a Communist from Dresden, a baron from Salzburg, a Dutch merchant navy sailor from a working-class district in Vienna, and a Belgian travelling salesman are among the more prominent members of the group that chance has thrown together. And Otto.

There is always a good deal of squabbling when rations are distributed, since there is never enough food. Those lucky enough to have managed to get a job in the galley or pantry can look forward to extra rations. The barbed wire in front of the galley, where the stairs lead up to the deck, is called the Wailing Wall, and men often hang around here clutching a bowl in the hope of a charitable gift from the other side. The bigger and stronger a man is, the more he suffers from hunger.

'Apart from our hatred of the Nazis, we have nothing in common,' notes Erich wryly. 'People behave just as if they were still in Vienna or Berlin.'

'Yes, it's striking,' says Otto. 'Some of these business-men know all the tricks of their trade and really rip people off! And the industrialist from the next table is only out to feather his own nest. Solidarity and empathy would be of much more help to us in the circumstances, but this lot have never heard these words.'

Erich laughs. 'The only thing they agree on is that the ship will go under if the left-wingers win.'

As one of these left-wingers, Erich is trying to act as a spokesperson in as neutral and diplomatic a way as possible, smoothing over the blazing disputes that sudden-ly break out between people of different backgrounds, education and belief. The incredible injustice they all feel they have fallen victim to sometimes does not create any solidarity, but an aggrieved mood. The real prison-ers of war, some of them Nazis and fascists, enjoy respect as enemies among the English, while in the view of Lieutenant Scott and his accomplices, Erich's compan-ions are nothing more than dirty Jews, Bolsheviks and Jerries who deserve no better treatment. So they've set up a barbed wire fence enclosure on the aft deck, where the prisoners of war can spend all day out in the fresh air. This is hard to stomach.

'From Scott's point of view you can actually understand it,' says Otto. 'He wants his peace and quiet. And Jews can be unbearable troublemakers. Of course we're in the right, but what good is that on the high seas?'

'If you're a Nazi or just a very ordinary German sailor, you know that you're a prisoner of war and not likely to be treated with kid gloves. But what about us? We're allies, dammit!'

'Since we're always grousing, we're not really allies for Scott, but enemies that can harm him. And – you mark my words – when we finally end up where we're going to live, harm him we will, that much I'm sure of. It makes no sense to complain. Scott made it abundantly clear that he doesn't want to be bothered with letters in which we complain about stolen property. "I'm not an amateur detective," he said.'

Otto was talking just this morning to Simon, one of about 200 pious Jews on board who usually keep away from the secularists and atheists as if they were afraid of contagion.

'Imagine: the pious eat practically only dried vegetables, onions and fruit – and as we know, there's not much of this about. Chief Rabbi Ehrentreu decides what's kosher and may be eaten. The bread is baked here in tins smeared with lard, so the Orthodox can eat it only if they remove the crust. And only people who are very ill are allowed to eat ship's biscuit. The rabbis decide which of the sick can eat something to stay alive. And yet they tirelessly study the Bible and the Talmud, mostly from memory: only the fish can read their books now. That's what I call discipline. The few sets of tefillin they managed to salvage get passed round from one to another. Their behaviour deserves respect, whatever you may think of them. We should learn from them. We mustn't let ourselves get beaten down.'

But there is no danger of that, of course. In spite of all the stresses and strains, those who aren't completely jaded cannot help but be infected by the effervescence of communal life on board. Just about every profession is represented: there are hairdressers, cooks, mathematician, rabbis, composers, lawyers, poets, doctors, bankers, teachers, butchers, psychoanalysts, linguists, journalists, tailors, shoemakers, and of course lots of merchants and artists. If only out of boredom, if not a sense of responsibility, many of them try to contribute their skills and abilities. But amidst the many intellectuals, hairdressers, shoemakers and tailors are most needed.

'I'm a member of a chess club now!' Erich announces with flashing eyes. Since childhood he has been an avid chess player. 'Someone's crafted a chess game from bits of stale bread.'

Another cobbles together a dashboard from the fruit boxes in the pantry and opens a driving school. Those who have managed to save their pack of cards play bridge, rummy and Tarot, all day long. Someone has given a boy called Siegfried some postcards, on which he starts drawing caricatures and scenes of life at sea that the internees find deliciously amusing. More and more people want Siegi to do a portrait of them. 'If you can rustle up the paper for me, I'll be happy to do so,' says he. And by some miracle they manage. Of course, Otto draws too, sometimes they sit side by side and see who can draw the best – though occasionally Otto goes off to the debating society where the world situation is discussed as well as the situation on board.

Erich is in his element and tries to take the floor as much as he can. He seizes the chance to make up for what he missed out on in Vienna because his father didn't send him to the high school where, according to his teachers at least, he actually belonged. A working-class child did not need high school, his father decided: after all, *he* had not attended one and had still managed to rise to the rank of fire captain. All the same, his son was allowed to attend a technical school, where he learned the solid career of an accountant. On board the *Dunera* Erich never misses an opportunity to learn something new, attends a lecture on astrophysics or Renaissance art, a performance of Schubert songs by an opera singer or a French lesson. He attends the philosophy lectures given by Gerd Buchdahl who has managed to smuggle a copy of C.E.M. Joad's standard work *Guide to Philosophy* on board ship and reads out to an enthusiastic audience excerpts from Plato and Aristotle. Buchdahl also teaches English and is one of the authors of the *Dunera* constitution.

The wealth of knowledge concentrated here is inexhaustible. Walter Heine talks about modern shipbuilding. Walter König, a Catholic priest, talks about Goethe's *Faust*. Dr Richard Ullmann talks about Oswald Spengler's *The Decline of the West*. When Kurt Cohn from Vienna, who appeared in England under the name of Ray Martin and has by some mysterious means kept hold of his guitar, sings in his clear, bright voice, 'South of the border, down Mexico way', the men first listen reverently, but many of them are soon joining in. Erich just listens – he would like to sing along, but he does not dare. At home, they never sang, and unfortunately Irka is no good at it either. The only thing that would emerge from her throat is a croak, she says, and keeps her mouth shut tight when friends start up a song: she will not even join in when they sing 'The Internationale'. Erich envies the people who have set up choirs on board. When they sing, they seem to forget all their sorrows and beam with enthusiasm.

Gustav Heinrich Clusmann, a handsome man of Erich's age, sings unaccompanied spirituals. Peter Meyer composes a '*Dunera* Mass', and Boas Bischofswerder, a Chief Cantor from Berlin who has been deeply shocked by the mistreatment on board, composes a 'Phantasia Judaica' for four tenors. His son Felix writes the score out on toilet paper. It is the first time that Erich has heard Jewish prayer music.

'I'm an agnostic – can I still think that the music is beautiful?' he asks his confidant Otto.

Otto shrugs. 'It's art. You can always think that art is beautiful. Isn't it wonderful just how little it means if you take material things away from people like this? Their culture, their education, their art – you can never take that away from them. They'll always get by with that, anywhere in the world.'

On the ninth day of the journey, in a corner of the crowded room in which articles of clothing of every shape and colour have been hung out to dry on ropes and banisters, a cluster of young people gathers around a small, delicate man wearing thick glasses. Erich and Otto hang around nearby. The man is describing a volcanic eruption on the island of Stromboli.

'On the morning of 11th November 1930, the entire island was covered with a fine layer of black ash, and since many islanders still remembered the eruption of 1919, they advised the farmers strongly against going out into their fields. But since many people had at that time left the island in a panic, quite a lot of farmers had been recruited from elsewhere and were not familiar with the signs of an impending volcanic eruption. So while the old inhabitants stayed put in the village, the newcomers went out to work their fields as they did every day.'

'How do you know that in such detail, sir? Were you there?' asks a blond boy who sounds as if his voice is still breaking, but this cannot be true, since after all, the youngest on board must be over sixteen.

'Yes, I was there,' replies the narrator. 'Call me Arnold by the way, we're all equal on board ship.' He pauses, then resumes, with a hint of embarrassment in his voice. 'It was like this: my parents were rich, very rich, my father ran a ball-bearing factory in Düsseldorf. And after I graduating from high school, they sent me on trips, as usual in middle-class families, saying I should first see the world before taking over my father's factory later on. Well, back then we did not suspect anything yet... everything was Aryanised...' Arnold blinks behind his glasses, and then continues, with a firmer voice. 'One of the mandatory visits on this trip was Pompeii, and in Pompeii...'

'Pompeii? What's that?' asks the blond boy again.

'Pompeii is, or rather was, a city, a city of the ancient Romans, not far from Naples, a beautiful, rich trading city with luxurious villas and a harbour. Two thousand years ago it was destroyed by a terrible volcanic eruption.'

'But for *that* one you weren't there at the time,' adds another listener.

'No, I wasn't. The Romans had built Pompeii right at the foot of Mount Vesuvius. And Vesuvius... You've heard of that, right?'

'I might have seen it on a postcard. Before I was born, my parents travelled a lot. I used to play with those postcards when I was a kid.'

More and more young people join in the conversation.

'If you saw a picture postcard of Naples, Vesuvius was in the picture for sure. Vesuvius and its billows of smoke.'

'And Vesuvius destroyed this city?'

'Yes, it happened all of a sudden, a terrible catastrophe. You can still see the petrified corpses in the position in which death suddenly overwhelmed them. There's a dog, too. So you can imagine it all really vividly.'

'And if Vesuvius once destroyed a city, couldn't it happen again? Couldn't it destroy Naples?'

'I don't know... For a long time now, there have just been weak eruptions that are not dangerous and don't frighten anyone.'

'And why was it so violent two thousand years ago?'

'I don't know. From time to time a volcano gets really angry, like a man. Don't you ever get really angry?'

'Yes. But a volcano isn't a human being!'

'I'm a writer. So I can't answer all your questions, unfortunately. It's just that volcanoes fascinate me, because I myself have experienced an eruption. And I'll never forget it. Sometimes I dream of it.'

'Ah, Stromboli. High time we returned to the topic. So do tell us about Stromboli.'

Erich nudges Otto in the ribs and points with his chin to the boy, a tall dandyish fellow with an Oxford accent.

'I could strangle people like that,' whispers Erich.

'All in good time,' counters Arnold and waves his hand defensively. He clearly enjoys keeping the young people in suspense. 'A good story requires adequate preparation. So: after I'd visited Naples, Pompeii and Mount Vesuvius, I went to Stromboli. In a boat, as it's a small island, a volcanic island, which I was curious about. There are always small eruptions going on, thousands every year.

For the ancient Romans, the flames that sizzled up from Stromboli's crater at night were like a lighthouse.'

'Are there still... erup... erup...?'

'Eruptions. Yes, I think so. But when I was there... Anyway, together with a farmer, later in the afternoon, I climbed the volcano to see the crater. Black lava every-where. Not a single plant, not a blade of grass. It was scary, but beautiful too. The whole night I stayed up there and couldn't get enough of the little explosions and the red glow of the lava that spewed from the crater. It was a grand spectacle and not at all dangerous. So I thought at the time.'

Arnold takes a break to increase the tension.

'And then?'

'The next morning, I returned to the village, Piscità it's called. It was November and for the villagers already winter, but I was enjoying the warmth and decided to stay for a few more days. I even went swimming. And two days later...'

It's really become quiet, the boys' eyes are wide open.

'When in the morning I left the house where I'd taken a room with some nice people, I saw this black layer of ash, and suddenly a really violent gust of wind knocked me over, it felt like I was being squeezed down. A quick glance at the summit, and I saw the mushroom, an impressive cloud of ash and stones, accompanied by an infernal noise, a roar of thunder like a moving pile of rubbish. Later I heard that the whole island had risen almost thirty feet.'

'Why? It was a volcanic eruption and not an earthquake.'

'I'm no expert, but I think it was because of the pressure inside the mountain. Let me tell you how it ended: I rushed down to the house, maybe thirty or forty yards. As soon as I was inside, I could hear stones pattering on the roof, at first small ones, like a downpour, then bigger and bigger ones, making an incredible racket. And at the same time there was a hissing noise like with a bomb attack.'

'Weren't you afraid the roof would collapse?'

'Yes, I was, but my hosts reassured me saying the house had already survived the eruption of 1919. They shouted to me to stand at the door jamb. The walls there were ninety centimetres thick, to keep the house cool in summer, but also to protect the residents during a volcanic eruption. Even the roofs were thick, but at the same time different materials had been used, elastic enough to withstand the rocks. After about twenty minutes of continuous bombardment, darkness sank over the village, and fires broke out everywhere, fanned by strong gusts of wind. Under my feet I heard a noise like a hammer, first it was under the ground, and then it came from the crater. The next day we found some huge boulders several feet across.'

'Were there many deaths, like in Pompeii?'

'Official reports said there were eight deaths, but many farmers from abroad weren't registered, and almost all the residents fled in panic after the eruption. How many returned later after this traumatic experience on the island, I do not know. For myself I can only say that I still dream about it sometimes. It was a feeling of complete helplessness.'

'Can't they predict a volcanic eruption?'

'I'm not so sure about that. The residents say you can tell if there's something brewing from the way the surface of the water in a fountain behaves.'

Satisfied with this answer, the group disperses.

'Now you know what to do in a volcanic eruption,' says Otto. 'Stay under the door jambs. That's also true for earthquakes. We might need to know this in Canada – if that's where we're heading.'

'The Canadian Shield is one of the oldest rock formations on earth. No earthquakes or volcanic activity have been recorded in the whole known history of Canada,' says Erich, sounding like a lecturer. 'A phrase I learned off by heart for a geography exam. Funny that it should still pop into my mind.'

CHAPTER TWELVE

At noon of the tenth day at sea there appears a Dr Grünberg, a lawyer who after a rather unclear selection procedure has been made the representative of all the internees. It is his unpleasant task to pass on the instructions of the commander to the internees. Grünberg informs the men on Erich's lower deck that they have to go up several times a week to endure a kind of prison-yard walk, in the fresh sea breeze. The ten- to fifteen-minute exercise has to take place barefoot, so the wooden floor of the deck will not be damaged. In addition, two men must be willing to regularly scrub the deck. This demand triggers spontaneous outrage.

'That's out of the question!'

'What the hell are they thinking! We're not convicts!'

Grünberg departs to tell the commander that the group will think it over. Eventually there are two who, having given the matter due consideration, volunteer to take on the job, and out of a sense of solidarity they are not left to carry out this task alone.

Given the stench and the oppressively cramped conditions in the lower deck, the men are looking forward to their short stay outdoors. But the 'prison yard' reminds them even more intensely that they are prisoners without any rights, and have been delivered over to a pack of hostile sadists.

'Fifteen minutes' exercise! Everyone up on deck! Keep in step!' The shouts ring out through the entire ship, and masses of men are soon pouring out of all the doors onto the deck. Manned machine guns are pointed at them, and the soldiers look as if they were just longing to feel their weapons vibrating in their hands again.

The men are obliged, under constant scolding, to run round in circles, and anyone who cannot keep up the pace is granted a closer acquaintance with the butt of a rifle. 'Hurry up! Faster, faster! Move it!' the soldiers yell, and make a joke of chucking their empty beer bottles in front of the men's feet. If they shatter, the internees are forced to walk barefoot on broken glass – even the Catholic priest and the rabbi in his black suit, as no exceptions are made. The Indian sailors who are used to being pushed around by whites now grin with satisfaction: for once, they're on the other side. And on the top deck the officers sit, sipping whisky and watching the undignified spectacle with amusement.

Erich recognises the soldier who stole his Waterman. As he runs past, he tries to talk to him, but he just gets pushed back into the circle. On the next round, Sergeant Brown hauls him out. The burly, brutal man, who walks around with a loaded pistol always at the ready, is nicknamed the 'Lion Hunter' by the men.

'What did you want to talk to that soldier about?'

'I wanted to give him my name and my deck so he can give me back my fountain pen. I can live without a watch, but not without a pen.'

'What kind of fountain pen?'

'A Waterman.'

Erich says he believes that he has recognised the soldier who stole it. Now he is wearing a helmet, but on the day they embarked he had been wearing a cap. The soldier had assured him that he could trust a member of the British Army.

'Just you watch it! Don't chatter so much, otherwise it's the bunker for you. Now fuck off, you filthy pig!'

Otto tries to help Erich to understand. 'They're poor fellows, Dunkirk veterans bitter about their defeat. They hold us responsible and now they're taking their revenge. Although it's difficult for us to imagine, they might view some of us as paratroopers. But in any case, for them we're prisoners of war, in other words enemies. They can't distinguish between Nazis and us anti-Nazis, we all speak German. They can't know how loyal we are to England, how grateful that they've given us refuge. Maybe they even see us as traitors to our own people. Everything is possible. And in any event they're anti-Semites.'

'A devils' brew,' growls Erich. 'The Lion Hunter is hardly a poor fellow. With ordinary soldiers you could try to strike up a conversation.'

'That's really not worked today.'

The guards use the exercise period to slink unobserved down into the empty lower deck and rummage round in the stuff that has not yet been confiscated. Only the rings dangling from the inside button of the flies of a pair of trousers are safe from them. They have no respect for anything, and even religious garments, prayer books and bibles disappear without a trace. When the spokesmen of the different decks complain to the officers, the latter defend the actions of their subordinates. They are simply following the instructions of the War Department, all property will be returned to the internees at the end of the trip. If they are requested to put this commitment down in writing, the English get angry and threaten the spokesmen with the bunker and say they will be handed over to the authorities in handcuffs when they arrive.

Arrive where? The ship has taken a southwest course. Now it is clear to the man of experience, Uwe, and not just to him: their destination cannot be Canada. The wildest speculations start flying around: perhaps they are headed for the Bahamas? From the rear deck, the rumour is spread by the German seafarers that they are going to British Guatemala. No, that's wrong, it soon transpires: the course has changed. Jamaica and Bermuda are also possible destinations. Meanwhile, the crew unpack their pith helmets and appear wearing their shorts. Many of the younger internees cut off the legs of their trousers.

On 22nd July, an internee throws a message written on a piece of fabric and attached to a wooden spoon out of the latrine window. Instead of falling into the sea, it lands right in front of an officer and results in the crew's temper turning really rather nasty. Word gets around that the message was a cry for help meant for the enemy. The spokesmen are given an ultimatum to track down the culprit by noon, otherwise there will be serious consequences. The guilty person is never found, and the matter is settled once the spokesmen have given their word to the officer that they are loyal to England. For a time, the officers are even more watchful during the 'prison yard' routine than usual.

Two days later everything is groaning under the unbearable midday heat. After two weeks at sea – land ahoy! A queue of impatient men forms outside the toilets. Everyone has twenty seconds to peek through the hatch. Freetown, Sierra Leone, Africa! A palm-lined, gentle bay. Palm trees in the wild, something that none of them has seen. Colourful canoes with half-naked black people. 'Negroes!' the younger men cry out in excitement. But after just twenty seconds the order comes, 'Next, please!'

An adolescent who is pretending he has stomach pains manages to stay for a short while on the upper deck on his way to the ship's hospital. Full of excitement, he comes back, saying that the harbour is full of ships and black workers lowering crates, barrels and sacks through the hatch into the depths of the ship. On the quayside all is hustle and bustle, Englishmen in white suits with tropical helmets and native children dressed in rags. But mostly, he raves about the bright light and the flawless blue sky.

There is no longer any doubt: they are sailing around Africa and across the Indian Ocean to Australia. Erich is satisfied, others are appalled – and say so.

'We'll never get away from there. It's the other side of the world!'

CHAPTER THIRTEEN

Irka's euphoria does not last long. You must not come to the hotel now, it says in the telegram. The departure will be delayed, they must be patient.

Her world collapses. The fever of the last few days cools and leaves a lump in her throat, which prevents her from swallowing. She cannot eat a thing. A wave of hopelessness overwhelms her. Suddenly everything has changed. In her mind she was already in Australia and burying her face in the chest of her beloved boy.

Only yesterday she had stood for a long time in front of the mirror, inspecting herself. Is she still good enough for her husband, when even the English sun has conjured an exotic tan into his face? What will he look like in Australia? She has a bulbous nose, and the clothes pegs she used to stick on it when she was a teenager have not been of the slightest help. This is what she is going to look like for the rest of her life. This flaw in her appearance is offset by her big brown eyes that always look a little sad. 'Your Jewish eyes', as Erich has teased her several times. She is as exotic for him as he is for her with his blue eyes. Where she came from, nobody ever had blue eyes. Only the Polish woman teacher at the Catholic school, who had received Irka, a Jew, with sorrow and distress, had blue eyes. Irka has always been fascinated by blue eyes, they seem so foreign to her, even intimidating. One look into Erich's eyes, and she was done for. She had never fallen in love so fast.

They had plenty of time to think about this at leisure, in the milk train between Innsbruck and Vienna. The train stopped at literally every barn, to load the full milk jugs. Erich was gorgeous. His cultivated Viennese accent enveloped Irka like a silk scarf. His voice was soft and flattering. He talked and talked and smiled and beguiled her. In reality, she was a prickly person, but she succumbed to Erich's voice without any resistance.

Their first separation was terrible. They were both held in detention. She was in police custody for six months before being deported to Poland. Before their departure, they were allowed to see each other briefly. Erich had to serve another few months, but in the end they released him earlier than expected because Chancellor Schuschnigg, under pressure from Hitler, had issued an amnesty for jailed Nazis, and the Reds benefited too. It was a very emotional moment, the reunion in the visiting room of the grey house. And then it happened. Erich made her a proposal of marriage, quite in the old style. He even kissed her hand. That was how a Polish woman needed to be treated, he said.

And now she is his wife. Maybe, under other conditions, it would never have come to this, as Erich is a charmer who loves his freedom, his freedom and women, too. Even after all these years, Irka cannot believe it: such happiness. A happiness that is constantly threatened. First prison, then deportation, then their escape to England and now the worst: Australia, where it does not seem likely she will be able to follow him. A larger distance you could not even imagine.

Irka looks in the mirror again. The gleam has gone from her eyes, her boundless sense of hopeful anticipation. She has let her hair grow and piled it up with hairpins into a roll that frames her round face. Her hair and her eyes, the two strong features in her face, her 'assets', as the English say. And now?

She thinks back to the time in Vienna when the Nazis were getting bolder by the day. They sat stiffly in the tram and looked straight ahead when three young men with close-cropped hair started growling 'When Jewish blood spurts from the knife' without needing to fear they would be hauled up before the courts. And Hitler had not even marched into Austria yet. But the men were targeting Erich, the so-called Aryan, not the Jewish Irka with her round face and her dirndl. No, Erich has what the Nazis imagine as a Jewish nose, big and curved. Of course Irka had been scared then, but not much, because Erich was at her side.

Now she has no choice but to wait alone in a foreign country. All of a sudden, everything seems unreal to her. Only the written confirmation from the Home Office that her suitcases have been in Bloomsbury House, in storage and ready for departure, since the second week of August is a proof that her travel fever was not just imagination, a dream, a mirage.

What is she supposed to do all day? She has hardly any money, as it has all been turned into goods. She cannot start looking for a job when, at any moment, she might be summoned on board. She is living a provisional life. Like that time in Vienna, waiting for the British visa. Or any visa: she would happily have gone to Colombia. But you never get used to it. Separation from Erich, and the uncertainty of her situation, are a nagging pain that will not go away.

With Gusti, who is even smaller than her, but still wears flat shoes, Irka goes for long walks in Battersea Park. True, Gusti is apolitical, sometimes even annoyingly naive, but she can be a real friend in need, one who can listen and does not irritate you with well-meaning advice. Her husband, who suffers from severe asthma, is interned in the camp at Warth Mills in the town of Bury, near Manchester. Irka recalls how each time he visited her Vienna apartment, he had to take a break on the landing to inhale. Half a glass container filled with a brownish liquid, together with a hose and rubber pump. Without this device he cannot live. Of course, Gusti worries about him. They agree that anyone as ill as Oskar should never have been detained. How can you be a danger to the country when you have severe asthma? It's absurd.

'MI5 couldn't care less about the fate of Oskar Tisch,' says Irka drily.

'Do you really think that internments are run by the secret service?'

'Well of course Anderson has repeatedly tried to stop them. But against the War Office and MI5, he was powerless.'

'How do you know?'

'I read the papers, my love, and I also read between the lines.'

'A secret service would actually be able to distinguish between Nazis and Category C refugees.'

'You'd think so, but maybe the people working in the secret service are just plain stupid. They have a schematic view of the world. Germans are Germans, full stop.'

Gusti is probably not as apolitical as Irka has always thought. Just because she is a good person does not mean that she has to be naive. True, Irka tries to rein herself in, but her spontaneous, visceral judgments always move faster than her brain.

'And do you have any idea why we haven't been interned?' asks Gusti. 'Women have been locked up too.'

'As far as I know, only women in Categories A and B have been interned. But they must have made several mistakes.

Anyone who doesn't know the situation in Germany and Austria really can't assess it properly. I've always thought that Erich was interned because he isn't a Jew, and that they haven't interned me because I am.'

'That just can't be right. Oskar's a Jew, isn't he? Jewish men have been detained en masse, we know that. In the case of women, there's no discernible pattern.'

'Probably they can't imagine us women being politically active. It's always like that. Women are taken less seriously. I noticed that myself, when they interrogated me in Vienna.'

'You suffragette! Perhaps our turn will come, who knows? The war isn't over yet.'

'You can say that again. The Germans are bombing British ships in the English Channel right now, and who knows what'll happen to us if they invade? I'm pulled in two directions. On the one hand, I'm glad Erich is safe, on the other hand I'd be less worried if he was with me. That's selfish, I know. And it's an illusion, too. What on earth could he do if the Germans put us Jewish women in a concentration camp?'

The wait drags on. Irka can take it no longer and writes to the refugee office to find out when she can expect to depart. After a few days she receives a letter signed by the Director in person.

I do indeed realise how difficult it is for you and all other wives in similar predicaments to plan your life from day to day and indeed, it is a matter which is occupying my mind constantly, and I can assure you that I am doing everything I can to hasten arrangements for you and others to rejoin your husband. One thing however is definite: the Government will reunite you to your husband – do not have any doubts on this point. The only question is how soon, and there I

cannot yet let you have a definite answer, much as I regret it, but I
am striving ceaselessly towards this end. As soon as I know, I will
write you at once.

Irka sits for a long time and stares at the words until the
letters start dancing. She does not know what to think.
No travel dates, but also no definitive rejection. So she
must wait and keep hoping. Such inactivity is torment
for someone used to tackling problems directly. Although
she has no idea where Erich might be, she writes to him
at an address that she has got out of Bloomsbury House:
c/o Prisoner of War Information Bureau, Melbourne,
Australia.

Primrose Mansions, 7th August 1940

Dearest, I am writing to this address and hope you will get this card
upon your arrival. It's a shame that my letters have not reached you.
About three weeks after your departure, I thought that I too would
be leaving soon, but now everything is uncertain again. I'm waiting
and getting quite desperate already because you're so far away. Now
I'm living with Kätchen and the others, but they don't have much
space for me. Perhaps this time we'll have to wait for ages before
we meet again. I have only one request to make of you: don't forget
me, because I'm very lonely, and my family is scattered all over the
world. Try to contact my sister Ludka, she will help you if you need
anything. Can you send me a telegram when you arrive?

Your Irka

Meanwhile, the air battle over Britain is raging, known as
'Operation Sea Lion'. Every day there are new reports of
terror. On 19th July, Hitler made a speech to the Reichstag

in which he offered the United Kingdom a 'peace proposal', appealed to the reasonableness of England and invited the British government to prevent further bloodshed. Three days later, on day thirteen of the Battle of Britain, Lord Halifax rejected this with the words: 'Germany will get peace when it has vacated the occupied territories, restored the liberties it has suppressed, and provided guarantees for the future.'

Irka can breathe again. Halifax, who in his efforts to prevent a war has been duped by Hitler more than once, has finally grasped how much the promises made by Nazi Germany are worth. He follows the guidelines of Churchill, who when he came to power spoke of 'winning at all costs'. Do these costs include the senseless deportation of men like Erich?

CHAPTER FOURTEEN

While the boys crack jokes and refuse to allow the fun of this great adventure to be spoiled by a few drawbacks, the older men, especially those who have survived concentration camps, slink away in fear whenever a man in uniform comes by. Some express suicidal thoughts. Those who have lived a life in safety and comfort before being interned find it difficult to cope with the daily struggle for 'living space', a hunk of bread, a half-smoked cigarette or a place on a toilet bowl.

On 19th July, Lieutenant Colonel Scott, who usually avoids contact with the detainees, summons the spokesmen of the forecastle and gives a short speech.

'I must speak with you,' he barks, 'but will not be answering any questions you may have. I have received detailed instructions regarding your treatment from the Ministry of War. The security of the transport is my primary concern. I must fulfil this task. You will be treated in accordance with these instructions. As for your property, you will be getting it back.'

The next day he gives a notably longer speech to the internees of the aft deck, ending with the words: 'My officers have complained that they are being harassed by your demands, requests and complaints. If this does not stop, I will have to think about taking appropriate measures.'

He addresses his troops in the tone of an old soldier: 'I know that British Tommies take an opportunity like this to help themselves to little things that get left unattended. When I recently inspected your company, I couldn't help seeing small objects that I'm sure you didn't bring on board, and I've heard that some chaps have begun to loot suitcases. This must stop, but I'm damn well not going to punish any man unless he really deserves it.'

While the internees were puking their guts out on the high seas, a young British soldier was writing a letter home, just a day after their embarkation. This letter kicked up significantly more dust than all the hopeless complaints of the *Dunera*'s passengers. Merlin Scott, no relation to Lieutenant Colonel Scott but the son of a senior staff member in the Foreign Ministry, was in charge of guarding the Italian survivors of the *Arandora Star* in Birkenhead, Cheshire, and subsequently accompanying them to Liverpool, from where, he was informed, they would start on their journey to Canada.

The young man expressed his shock: 'I thought the Italian survivors were treated abominably – and now they've all been sent to sea again to Canada. The one thing nearly all were dreading, having lost fathers, brothers, etc. the first time.' He described how the Italians were forced up the gangway and robbed of their belongings that were then chucked, soaked by the rain, on a disordered pile. Many telegrams had arrived, he wrote, in which family members told the survivors of their relief. But none of the addressees had set eyes on these telegrams. 'As the ship has now sailed, I know they will never get them. Some of them said they had no mail for six weeks.'

When Merlin's father laid the letter before his colleagues in the Ministry of Foreign Affairs, it turned out that neither that Ministry nor the Home Office had been informed of the deportation of the survivors of the *Arandora Star*. The trail led to MI5 which, in turn, passed the buck back to both the Home Office and the War Office. During Erich's internment in Huyton, doubts had already arisen among the British public as to whether interning the 'refugees from Nazi oppression' had been the right way of protecting themselves from the Nazis. On the very day of embarkation, a heated six-hour-long debate on the issue was held in the House of Commons.

'It has been the historical policy of this country for many centuries to give asylum to refugees,' the Conservative MP Major Victor Cazalet declared. 'As a result of the tremendous influx of refugees in recent months, coupled with fears of invasion and Fifth Column activities, there had been a tremendous public demand for the internment of practically everyone whose family had not lived in England for 100 years, in complete disregard of the individual merits of the cases concerned – a totally un-English attitude to adopt.'

'What attempts has the government made to correct the impression that the stories in the press have created?' asked the MP Wilfrid Roberts. 'As I perceive it, the Home Office and the Government have been all too ready to use press propaganda and the public mood as an excuse to pursue a policy that would not meet with approval throughout the country.'

Cazalet demanded the release of all whose loyalty was unquestioned, and laid the blame for the deportation of the internees from the *Arandora Star* at the feet of the Chairman of the Home Office Cabinet Committee, Neville Chamberlain, who himself was not present, although he must have been informed of the debate. Since politicians had spoken out against the army, MPs demanded to know the reasons for the detentions. But the Minister of Home Security, Anderson, was evasive: the aliens had been interned for reasons 'for which we are not responsible'.

The State Secretary at the Ministry of War, Sir Edward Grigg, in turn tried to excuse the debacle by referring to the fact his Ministry was being overstretched. 'I should like to say here in the clearest terms that the business of looking after the internees is not the business of the Army, and I very much hope that the Army may, in due course, be relieved of it.'

Knowingly or unknowingly, members of the Government repeatedly misled Parliament. Thus, on 16th July the War Minister, Sir Anthony Eden, stated that all persons present on the *Arandora Star* had without exception been Italian Fascists or Category A Germans. And the Secretary of State at the Home Office, Osbert Peake, still expressed his conviction on 13th August that all the internees sent to Australia would have volunteered for service – a blatant falsehood that he would repeat on 22nd August.

The heated cabinet debates place the question of the detention and deportation of refugees on the public agenda. Neville Chamberlain is 'greatly disturbed' about the 'large number of complaints'. Since, on Churchill's instructions, he had resolutely been pushing ahead with the internments and deportations, his change of opinion proves to be a breakthrough. The Cabinet decides to withdraw the internal management of the camps from the control of the Ministry of War and to hand it over to the Home Office.

All in all, the detention of the men in Category C, which began on 25th June, lasts just three weeks and ends as suddenly as it began. Three White Papers regulate the release of all detainees in Britain who are known to be opposed to the present regimes in Germany and Italy, or whose continued detention for other sufficient reasons does not appear desirable. So the number of internees reaches a peak at 27,200, just under the number of 29,000 people interned during World War I.

This is of no help to the 2,543 internees, eighty percent of them Jews, who are now on the way to Australia on board the *Dunera*, as the Australian government is in no circumstances willing to release the men after their arrival. When, in the House of Commons, MP Eleanor Rathbone asks Herbert Morrison, who has replaced Sir John Anderson as Minister of Home Security, whether he agrees with her that it is a waste of highly qualified men to shut them away in Australia, Morrison replies: 'That would be a proper question for the Parliament of Australia. I would not like to give an answer to it.' And on the question of whether it would be inconceivable for Morrison to turn to the Australian government with a similar suggestion, he answers: 'Naturally, there was a clear understanding that the immigration policy of the Australian Government was their business, and I do not feel it is possible for me to intervene in the way suggested.'

On 19th August, the British government recommends that the Australian government should accommodate men from different categories in different camps and intern the Italians separately, if possible. In well-chosen words, the British government also advises the Australians to keep potentially dangerous 'enemy aliens' under strict surveillance, while a less stringent security is required for the 'refugees from Nazi oppression'.

This broad hint is greeted with indignation by the Australian government, which on 13th September retorts that the British government is suggesting, according to a telegram, that some internees could be released by Australia under certain conditions.

The Commonwealth Government only agreed to accept prison-ers of war and internees for internment in Australia. To release certain persons on arrival here would be undesirable on grounds of national security and would also involve questions includ-ing employment, sustenance and ultimate repatriation of such persons even though it is assumed that any expenditure in respect of them would be borne by the United Kingdom Government.

The Australian Government considers it important – continues the telegram – that only such persons will be allowed into Australia as will continue to remain interned until they can be sent back to the United Kingdom to be released. Australia is 'not prepared to accept for intern-ment in Australia any aliens who would not, in the ordinary course of events, be considered sufficiently dangerous to warrant internment in the United Kingdom.' Similar conditions will also apply to the wives and families of the internees.

The Commonwealth Government is not (repeat not) prepared to receive non-interned wives and families of internees even though prepared to come to Australia at their own expense.

In reality, the British government was intending for the 188 wives and 204 children of the men from the *Dunera* to follow them to Australia, especially since it has now become known that several refugees volunteered only because they were promised that their families would be sent on after them. One family has actually made its way there at its own expense.

What the mother country has clearly not reckoned with is the 'White Australia' policy, which dictates that at least half of these immigrants have to be British. People from Germany,

Austria, Italy, Japan and Hungary are considered 'enemy aliens' and are – unless they are locked away in camps and funded by the British government – undesirable. There are also, among the Australian population, significant prejudices against Jews. It is assumed there is a lack of willingness to integrate them, and there is fear of increased competition on the already overstretched labour market.

CHAPTER FIFTEEN

When the *Dunera* reaches the tropics, shoals of flying fish glide alongside the ship. The climate is bearable only in the shower. Even at night, the damp heat is relentless. The men wallow in their sweat as they sleep. During the day, they try to move as little as possible. Around the toilets and washrooms hangs a greasy cloud of steam. Many internees are suffering from colic. The journey seems endless. People recite poems and ballads to pass the time away. One actor recites Schiller's poem 'The Bell' by heart – Erich likes to listen, it is a good opportunity to refresh his knowledge of German literature.

The men are allowed to sit near the openings to the long corridors, to breathe the fresh sea air and watch the waves beating against the hull. They may now occasionally visit other parts of the ship and make the acquaintance of the disciplined German prisoners of war who avoid any confrontation with the Jews.

On the morning of 27th July, the *Dunera* approaches reddish earth and a pier projecting into the water with palm trees in the background. It is drizzling and suddenly turns cold. The black longshoremen are shrouded in heavy raincoats. 'Takoradi' reads a sign in the dock. And then a miracle happens: for the first time, the guards open the flaps of the portholes, and sea air flows into the stuffy area below decks. Everyone rushes to the hatches. There is not much to see. Takoradi. The men look at each other, perplexed. 'British Crown Colony, Gold Coast, West Africa', one man drily states. But you can tell that he is eager to tell them everything he knows.

'Did you know that Gross Friedrichsburg in Princess Town was a Brandenburg fortress in the seventeenth century? A brief Prussian colonial interlude.'

The historian's moment has come. When Arthur Ascher boarded the ship in Liverpool, he was a neatly dressed academic with carefully parted hair, which he kept in shape with pomade. He wore an English-style brown-green check tie, a tweed jacket and a pair of neatly creased trousers. Because he comes, like Erich and Otto, from Vienna, the two have made friends with him – the native Viennese accent is music to their ears and their souls. At the time of landing in Takoradi, the immaculate Arthur looks a little '*zernepft*', or so his friends tease him. He is keeping up his baggy pants with a cord around the waist, and the absence of brilliantine, of which the soldiers have relieved him, along with his other possessions, makes his brittle hair stick up like jagged mountain peaks.

'This is where the European powers built a denser network of fortresses than in any other region of Africa,' he lectured, obviously pleased to finally have an audience. 'The Portuguese, the Dutch, the Swedish, the Danish, the Brandenburgers, they were all there. And the English, of course. The fortresses were lined up right next to each other along the coast.'

'Why was that? What is there, here?'

'Gold, my sweet, gold! As the name suggests: the Gold Coast. Until the development of the California gold fields in the nineteenth century, the Gold Coast was one of the major gold producers in the world. Gold, cocoa, precious woods. If you had a mahogany table at home, then the wood was definitely from the Gold Coast.'

'My father was a fireman,' growls Erich with a certain class resentment. 'There were no mahogany tables at home.'

'I'd have been glad not to have had any. I just hope the Nazi swine choke on them. The thought of an SA family sitting round our dinner table right now makes me feel sick. At Kristallnacht they soon saw what they could pinch from us.'

'Oh, Arthur,' says Otto, trying to appease him. 'That's half a world away. Don't think about it. We're in Takoradi! Did you ever think you'd come here?'

'I'd love to get off the boat. There must be some lovely beaches here. I'd also love to have a look at the fortresses, they were the pillars of the slave trade until the middle of the nineteenth century. They must be pretty impressive.'

'A dark chapter of our European civilisation,' comments Erich. 'And then we get all worked up over the Nazis.'

'Our guards have preserved some of the old spirit of the British slave traders,' says Otto. 'Maybe we'll be sold in Australia.'

'Look at us! Who'd want to buy us?'

In fact, the men have started to look quite dangerous, with their hollow, unshaven cheeks, some covered in scabs, their tattered shirts and their shoes thick with grime. Like Arthur, many of them have lost so much weight that they have to hold up their trousers with belts, if they have one, or just with string.

'Bedraggled – that's the English for *zernepft*,' says Erich, making good use of a word he picked up recently from an English teacher.

For two days the ship lies at anchor in the apparently lifeless port of Takoradi, while oil and water are hauled aboard by workers. None of the internees is allowed on the upper deck.

Hardly anyone notices when, shortly after leaving Takoradi in a tropical rainstorm, they cross the equator.

Gradually, the diarrhoea sufferers begin to recover, and the temperatures become bearable again.

Ten days later, the floating prison is heading for Cape Town. All the men are driven up on deck, where Jewish immigrants and fervent Nazis mingle. The internees housed in the aft deck had already had frequent contact with the German sailors, which had the advantage that they soon knew what course the ship was bound on. They had the opportunity to correct their prejudices, since not all the prisoners are Nazis. Only if their self-proclaimed 'Führer', a jagged Gestapo chief, approaches, does the mood between the two groups turn hostile. Otherwise they are welded together by their common fate, whether they want it or not. Guarded by armed soldiers, they are now waiting for a half-naked, thickset Italian to cut their hair and trim their beards with a hair clipper. Are they due for an inspection, or is the trip going to end here? South Africa has not been mentioned at all – but why not? Isn't Cape Town near the Cape of Good Hope?

Huge albatrosses with black-rimmed wings of enormous wingspan accompany the ship into the harbour. Erich is disappointed because the famous Table Mountain is shrouded in mist, but the next morning it reveals its full beauty and now looks the same as in the geography book from his school days – as flat as a gigantic table. While the ship lies at anchor in Cape Town, the desire for solid ground under the detainees' feet becomes a terrible itch. Ships are loaded and unloaded. Cranes swing round, trucks drive back and forth, a hubbub of voices drifts across the harbour. A big city with houses, cars, cinemas, restaurants. How long ago it has been since they saw anything like it. Cape Town lies there at night, all lit up, and the glittering lights are reflected in the black water. The men cannot get enough of the sight.

The sailors go ashore and come back drunk. Then it's best if you keep out of their way, but in general the non-military occupation is more sociable than the gang of half-criminals led by Scott and O'Neill. Many sailors slip them a piece of bread or a cigarette when no guard is in sight. In Cape Town, they can sometimes persuade a crew member to smuggle a newspaper on board. From his hammock, Arthur reads bits out of the newspaper and comments on the events. This much they know now: an air battle is raging over Britain. A depressed mood starts to spread: many of them have friends and relatives in England. Erich is worried about Irka.

In Cape Town, the Gestapo boss is taken off the ship, together with a German from Africa. He bids goodbye to his comrades with a Nazi salute. In exchange for a British diplomat, they are both being repatriated to their homeland, or so the rumour goes: no more details are available. The men shake their heads. It is so unfair that *he* of all of them should be set free, but who wants to be transferred to Germany?

In the late afternoon of the second day, the *Dunera* sails from the port of Cape Town and rounds the rocky southern tip of Africa. Before them lies the crossing of the awe-inspiring Indian Ocean.

One night, the men are shaken awake by shouting and the acrid smell of smoke. Someone had hung a towel on the emergency lights. The guard on duty notifies the officer, and the event is interpreted as a malicious attempt to set the ship on fire. The man believed to be responsible – he was lying closest to the lamp – is immediately sent to the bunker. Once he has managed to convince the commander that it was an accident, he is allowed to return to his deck the next day. After this incident, the internees start organising a night watch.

Soon a poem is doing the rounds, whose author prefers to remain anonymous. Maybe he normally writes philosophical treatises and is ashamed of producing doggerel. The men like the poem: it captures everyone's mood exactly.

Here it comes, the golden coast
Of Africa, that land of sun!
And here comes Lion Hunter, too,
Our sergeant, and the desert's son.

What's that then, in the waves down there?
A great big shark? Upon my word!
But don't lean too far over, as
The shark's already come aboard.

Sailing off to Aussie land?
Better be a kangaroo.
Learn to hop and skip all day
And flap your pouch. That's empty too.

Far from home and quite unshaven,
Far from home, ah so it goes,
Off we sail on the Dunera,
Export goods for the land of Oz!

Deportees on the Dunera,
Off to mighty Oz we sail,
Our suitcases are all bust open,
Our shirts are worn by John O'Neill.

The soldier bellows 'Hurry up!'
On walks we have no time to lounge.
He's off to shop in Cape Town, and
He's snaffled all of our spare change.

With shiny gun and rotten teeth,
Our English Tommy stands right there:
But just to keep our hero safe
There's also plenty of barbed wire.

Thanks be to you, oh noble cooks,
You try to keep us properly fed.
But if we actually ate it up,
We'd very soon, alas, be dead.

After Cape Town, everyone gets an apple, an ice cold apple called Granny Smith, the first fresh fruit since Liverpool. It is the best and most beautiful apple that Erich has ever had in his life. For all of them, this apple is something special. The men roll it round between their fingers, back and forth, and marvel at its shape, as perfect as a work of art. They hold it for a long time, sniffing it; they cannot make up their minds to bite into it, even though their mouths are watering. Those for whom there is something more important in life use the green apple as a means of payment. Three cigarettes for an apple. Or a hunk of bread. Or a pair of underpants. From now on, there is a weekly fruit day, with apples and oranges. Sometimes even a piece of cheese appears: people immediately start fighting to get a share of it.

As if the alleged danger from the Fifth Column were diminished solely by the distance from Europe, tension on board starts to drop and some of the guards show a hint of friendliness and allow the detainees to wrest information about the course of the war from them. That the German invasion of England has so far failed to materialize is a relief for the English and the internees alike. The political exiles suffer from a lack of information. When they sit together and talk, which is what they most like doing, they can hardly do more than speculate. How will the Battle of Britain end? Will the Americans enter the war? How long will it last? What will happen to Germany after the war?

The amateur astronomer born in England and mistakenly brought on board cannot speak a word of German and so is isolated, but he is actually better off. As he stares through a hatch and marvels at the Southern Cross in the sky, he forgives his countrymen for the absurd misunderstanding that has led to his deportation. For him, the trip was worth it, he says. When they sail into a huge gust of wind, he may change his mind. The boat lurches as if the waves were playing ball with it, and many are seasick again.

On 11th August the Catholic priest is allowed to celebrate Sunday mass on deck, and a good number of men attend. The sixteen-year-old Christian Donnerstein, from an ancient Austrian noble family, is allowed to act as server. After the Nazi annexation of Austria, his father sent him along with his three brothers to England to spare them heroes' deaths at the front. Christian is so moved that tears pour down his cheeks. 'A mass in the middle of the Indian Ocean,' this student of the Jesuits murmurs, and shakes his curls that have grown almost down to the shoulder.

A few days later, internees are for the first time allowed to wear shoes for their exercise session. But as the sea is extremely rough, the men cannot really appreciate this new perk and would actually rather have stayed below deck in their hammocks.

On 21st August, at 9.38 during the walk on deck, Jakob Weiss manages to break out of the ranks performing the goose step and jumps over the railing. 'Man overboard!' cries a sailor, and the ship's siren rings out, amazingly fast.

Sailors come running from all directions. The engines are stopped and run full steam astern. There is a brief rumble before the ship comes to a halt. The subsequent onset of silence is eerie. They are all staring into the water. Lifebuoys are thrown into the sea. The waves are too rough even for a boat to be lowered. The sailors sweep the sea with their binoculars, nowhere among the waves can a head be seen. Weiss cannot have survived for long, as sharks are spotted nearby.

At 10.30, as Jakob Weiss has still not surfaced, the three lifebuoys are hauled back up, and the *Dunera* continues its journey.

Weiss had fled from Austria to England, the men tell each other, and after twelve months he had finally obtained the coveted visa for Argentina, where his family is waiting for him. Instead of heading off to join them, he had been arrested, interned and forced to board the *Dunera*. On 21st August his visa had expired.

'Only yesterday he told us he did not want to live any longer,' says one to the shocked men gathered round, and another claims to have learned that both Weiss's father and grandfather had taken their own lives in similar ways.

'Actually, it's surprising that so far only one man has killed himself,' says Otto, when the engines are running again and they are squatting down in their usual corner.

Some days later, a memorial service is held for Jakob Weiss. All the men are saddened, including the guards and some officers, though few knew him personally. Many internees are startled by the realisation that in a period of intense depression, they too could have fallen prey to the same fate.

The Indian Ocean is wild. The night after the service, gigantic waves heave the ship like a nutshell into the air, it creaks at every joint, and the decks rise and fall sharply.

Anything not nailed firmly down starts flying everywhere. Some men are thrown out of their hammocks by the ship's lurchings.

It is quite a spectacle, observing the stormy sea through the hatches of the shower rooms. For a short time the ship clings to the crest of the wave, only to plunge with dizzying speed down into the valley. None of the men have ever experienced anything like it. The deck is drenched in sea water, and slippery. Fetching the food turns into an almost impossible balancing act, and porridge pours out over the stairs. The cook has roped himself to the galley for safety's sake. At Erich's and Otto's table, the men eat with carved wooden sticks, as after washing up, one of them has chucked the rinsing water along with the spoons into the sea.

The youngsters enjoy the tugging of the wind on their hair and the salt spray in their face. It will be something for them to talk about one day. Later. Where will they be, later? In Australia? In America? In Germany? Anywhere is possible. Even Erich, obsessed by his worries over Irka, laughs in the wild wind.

On this journey, battered by elemental forces, Otto finds the artist from whom he sometimes gets paper huddled on the stairs.

'What's up, Siegi?'

'It's my birthday today. I hadn't imagined my eighteenth birthday would be like this.'

'Happy Birthday! I bet your parents wish they could celebrate it with you. Do you know how they are doing?' asks Otto, maybe not the most intelligent thing he could have said, as his question finally makes Siegi burst into tears.

'That's just it. I have no idea, I went to England by myself. My emigration was organised by the ORT school – do you know what that is?'

115

'No, tell me.'

'It was a private Jewish vocational school in Berlin where teenagers were prepared for their emigration to Palestine. Many of us lads on board came to England via this school. It took me forever to finally get out of Germany. At the end, it was still hanging in the balance, August '39, I finally got the exit permit, a week before the war broke out, though I didn't know that then. I can still see my parents in the Charlottenburg station, my mother had red eyes from crying. I was embarrassed. And I said: "You shouldn't have come." Imagine, what a stupid thing to say! And now I'm going to Australia, and that's the last sentence they heard me say. When will we meet again? How are they managing to live now? My father had to sell off his cardboard box factory dirt cheap. The money won't last long.'

Otto sighs. With the best will in the world he cannot think of anything comforting to say. 'I don't know what's happened to my wife, either,' he says.

In the fourth week of August, the rumour starts going around that Australia cannot be far away, because salt water soap and razor blades are suddenly being handed out again. After basic repair work to their appearance, many of the men have bleeding cuts on their faces. They are also given a variety of garments from the plundered suitcases: they do not fit at the front and the back, so that many of them look even shabbier than before. Men over fifty-five and the sick are now allowed to spend two hours daily on the upper deck. They are given red ribbons so they can be recognised by the guards. Someone has the bright idea of cutting the fabric to make more ribbons. There is not enough for Otto and Erich .

Suddenly, word starts going round that all the detainees will be released in Australia.

'Of course you won't be released,' sneers the Lion Hunter. 'In a few months maybe.'

When Erich dares to remind him that the men expect to retrieve their valuables upon landing, he spends a few days on bread and water, locked up in a prison cell. He sleeps on the bare ground. In the evening he looks through the bars, as two youths are knocked about by a dead drunk O'Neill, with the help of two equally drunk soldiers. When O'Neill is drunk, he is dangerous, everyone knows that. 'You're a *Schwein*, and your father is a *Schwein*,' he mumbles repeatedly in German. He punches the younger of the two in the pit of the stomach so violently that he folds up like a jackknife.

When Erich returns from prison, he is shaken. 'Now I have to say this for the Austro-fascists, they never hit me like that.'

Life on board becomes more unbearable the longer the trip lasts. The smuggled money has long since run out, so that smokers can no longer buy cigarettes and turn surly and quarrelsome as a result. The food is monotonous, there is less and less of it, and its quality is diminishing: weak tea, dry bread with rancid butter or margarine, maggoty porridge, a watery soup without any nutritional value, canned food, and the occasional onion and on better days kippers, sausages and rotten potatoes. The men have no energy for cabaret evenings as in the early days, and they are getting more and more apathetic. For over two weeks there has been nothing to see on the ocean.

One internee dies from a heart attack brought on by wrangling over a bar of soap; not even Dr Schatzki can save him. For the burial at sea, O'Neill orders all hands on deck. Sailors carry the wrapped corpse in a hammock and lay it on the deck planks next to the railing. The ship's engines are stopped. The captain walks up to the dead man and says a short prayer. Then the sailors commit the bundle to the sea.

On the morning of 27th August, the propellers suddenly start turning more slowly, there is a rattle of chains and the constant sound of the sea fades. The *Dunera* is audibly preparing to land. 'Land ahoy!' the men shout excitedly. Can they have finally reached Australia?

'Australia!' they yell, joyfully.

'The port is called Fremantle and belongs to Perth, the capital of Western Australia. Doesn't look so bad,' says Otto, staring keen-eyed at it. 'Trees, sun, cars, all brightly lit like in peace time. What more could you want?'

In Fremantle, doctors, inspectors and customs officials board the ship and are shocked at the sight of the emaciated men and the stench that wafts up from the lower decks. The ship is disinfected, and the internees vaccinated. The inspectors remain on board until Melbourne and try to improve the conditions in the few remaining days. Immediately the hatches are opened. Those who are most emaciated are prescribed an extra ration of milk and eggs by the doctors. One of the inspectors writes a handwritten letter in which he describes his personal impressions: 'If you could only see these Huns and Wops after two months at sea, most of the time in stormy weather! Makes you wonder how in the world they've survived it all. There were only two deaths en route, a natural death and a suicide. It's amazing there were no more deaths.'

Well knowing that his charges will not mince their words when they step onto Australian soil – after all, they are already complaining constantly – Lieutenant Colonel Scott considers it necessary, before landing in Melbourne, to write a memorandum addressed to the Information

Bureau for Prisoners of War of the Australian Armed Forces, in which he attempts to justify the loss of the internees' luggage and valuables.

As there are over 2,000 bags and a like number of document cases, all unlabelled, it is absolutely and completely impossible to sort out the property of any internee going ashore in Port Melbourne. This will be appreciated when I inform you that embarkation at Liverpool was made in such inadequate time that to tabulate this baggage was out of the question. Moreover, as the voyage progressed, bags had to be forced open in order to obtain linen and clothing which after fumigation and washing, was distributed piecemeal to the internees. This was an urgent necessity owing to large numbers becoming lousy.

It will be a simple matter for detention authorities at Sydney to distribute baggage on identification by internees when the balance may be returned to Melbourne.

Then Scott turns to the question of valuables:

Valuables have been placed in a sack and sealed. Two valuable items of jewellery are under separate cover. I have already pointed out, search was commenced on shore by the Dock and Military Police in conjunction with my command, but there being such urgency to sail owing to escort and convoy anxiously waiting, that it had to be continued to the best advantage on board ship.

It will be appreciated that in the difficult circumstances of sorting out internees in their respective groups, that certain articles are possibly missing, but in my opinion this of course is unavoidable. I have asked Australian authorities to support my urgent request to the British authorities that they should in no circumstances permit internees to have more than one kit bag per head and that all valuables should be handed over by

119

conducting officers in a sealed parcel for which receipt may be demanded.

As if an idea of how incredible his defence is has stolen over Scott as he writes, Scott adds a few pertinent remarks on the composition of the human cargo supervised by him:

I would now like to give my personal views on (a) Nazi Germany, (b) Italians and (c) German and Austrian Jews.

(a) Having warned this group prior to sailing of my methods should trouble arise through them, their behaviour has been exemplary. They are of a fine type, honest and straightforward, and extremely well-disciplined. I am quite prepared to admit however, that they are highly dangerous.

(b) This group are filthy in their habits, without a vestige of discipline, and are cowards to a degree.

(c) Can only be described as subversive liars, demanding and arrogant, and I have taken steps to bring them into my line of thought. They will quote any person from a prime minister to the president of the United States as personal references, and they are definitely not to be trusted in word or deed.

Between Fremantle and Port Melbourne, the men can recover. The sea is as smooth as glass and the sky is blue. The houses on the shores of Port Phillip Bay are pretty and peaceful. On deck, a makeshift office is set up. A major from military intelligence allows selected internees to come in for questioning, though all he asks for is their name, last place of residence in Britain and last internment camp. Then, with a furrowed brow, he leafs through the documents that have been brought along and scribbles notes. No one knows what any of this means. It is equally difficult to understand why they all have to show their hands with their palms facing upwards. Maybe to see if they are carrying something dangerous? All the internees have their fingerprints taken, they are photographed, and each receives a Certificate of Registration with his Internment Number that he has to hang around his neck. Erich gets the number 54323. It takes hours, but an optimistic mood starts to spread. Most have come to terms with their involuntary destination, and are curious about Australia. At last, they are again being treated as people, and they can enjoy fresh water showers on board for the first time since Freetown.

In Fremantle some out-of-date newspapers managed to find their way on board, and were distributed freely by the soldiers. The news revolves around the Battle of Britain and the negotiations with the USA about providing fifty destroyers in exchange for naval bases. The internees learn that even Australian fighter pilots are taking part in the Battle of Britain and the Australian navy in the Mediterranean is fighting the Italian navy.

On 3rd September the *Dunera* glides over the motionless waters of the Bay of Melbourne at Australia's southern tip and drops anchor at Prince's Pier. The soldiers have built an enclosed area with slats and barbed wire fence round it, so that the internees can watch the spectacle of landing from the deck. Now the journey is coming to an end, they think with longing. Instead, the Major takes up his position in his makeshift office again and reads names out from a list. The persons named must hold themselves in readiness to be taken off the ship together with the Italians and the survivors of the *Arandora Star*.

The Port of Melbourne is full to the last berth. Police officers with white berets guard the disembarkation site.

On both sides of the gangway that has been set in place, soldiers from the *Dunera* guard line up. Two hundred and fifty-one Category A Germans and Austrians, whom the British Government has classified as dangerous or potentially dangerous disembark, ninety-four Germans with 'dubious' political affiliation and two hundred Italians, most of them survivors of the *Arandora Star*. The Nazis and sailors march in front. Behind come the Italians and the political prisoners, apparently in a hurry to leave the ship. Before they disappear towards the warehouse, they turn around again. The young South Tyrolean waves at them and grins. Will they ever see each other again?

'They'll be glad they managed it,' says Otto. 'And what about us?'

Three decks are now orphaned, the ship seems almost empty. After twenty hours the *Dunera* sets off again. Soon she is swinging into the Pacific Ocean, the fourth sea since leaving.

Another three days in cooler temperatures. The men dig out their rumpled coats. The portholes are opened. The ship sails along the east coast of Australia, which leaves behind a welcoming impression with its golden beaches, the towns and farms. The sea remains calm. Lighthouses at night throw their light onto the men who can now at last sleep free of anxiety, as if welcoming them to this distant continent.

On 6th September there is already, by 5 a.m., a throng of men crowding into the washrooms. At 10 o'clock, a panorama of breathtaking beauty reveals itself. Past countless small bays with shimmering white sandy beaches, villas, attractive detached houses and luxuriant gardens, the ship glides into Sydney Harbour Bay. And then, like on a picture postcard, against the bright blue sky: the elegantly curved steel arch of Sydney Harbour Bridge, the landmark of the city. At 11.25 the *Dunera* passes under the bridge, and they all strain their necks to admire this miracle of technology from below. On the other side, the ship is towed to its berth at Wharf 13 in Sydney Docks.

The bridge, the sky, the sun, the greenery, the beach villas and the glittering skyline of the city with its skyscrapers are, after fifty-seven days at sea, after fifty-seven days of oppressive narrowness, stench and dirt, so astoundingly beautiful to look at that at first, nobody can utter a single word.

'Sydney! The most beautiful port city in the world!' says Erich, finally able to give vent to his feelings.

'We've made it!' breathes Otto. 'We're alive and on the other side of the globe.'

'Spring has come at last.'

Erich has tears in his eyes. He wishes he had Irka with him now.

'In primary school, did you ever draw children standing upside down on the southern part of the globe?' asks Otto.

'I have a different recollection. I was about twelve years old, sitting reading a book with an essay on the construction of the Harbour Bridge. So I'm staring with admiration at the photo. Then my father, the old spoilsport, leans over my shoulder and says: "What are you looking at that for? You'll never go there!"'

CHAPTER 16

List of the German and Austrian internees landing in Sydney

A

Hans Abarbanell
Fritz Nachmann
Veit Abel
Hans William Abel
Theodor Aberbach
Leo Abraham
Kurt Abrahamsohn
Peter Abrahamson
Richard Abrahamwicz
Siegbert Abrahczyk
Siegfried James Adam Alfred Adler
Emmanuel Israel Adler Fritz Adler
Georg Jakob Adler
Hans Adler
Harry Adler
Herbert Adler
Josef Adler
Louis Adler
Max Adler
Adolf Abraham Aftergut
Leo Israel Albert
Paul Albert
Rudolf Hermann
   Heinz Albrecht
Heino Alexander
Josef Almas
Herbert Alpert
Peter Kurt Emil Alsberg
Ludwig Altbach Günther Altmann
Heinrich Altmann
Paul Altmann
Franz Altschul
Heinz Altschul

Bert Andjel
Herbert Ansbach Hans Ansbacher
Joseph Ansbacher
Otto Anspach Benjamin Antmann
Beno Antmann Ernst Appellbaum
Gerhard Kurt Max Arendt
Walter Arje
Hans Amdt
Hans Günther Arndt
Herman Arndt
Alfred Amsdorf
Max Amsdorf
Max Arnsdorf
Selmar Arnsdorf
Hans Robert Friedrich Arnstein
Waldemar Wolf Aron
Benzion Aronoff
Kurt Casper Aronsfeld
Fritz Max Aronstein Arthur Ascher
Ernst Ascher
Josef Ascher
Emil Auer
Georg Auer
Paul Auerbach
Robert Aufrichtig
Hersch Aug
Michael Austern
Helmut Aufricht
Hans Gustav Axelrad
Josef Axelrad

B

Rudolf Erwin Israel Bach
Lothar Bacharach
Fritz Hermann Bachmann

Hans Abraham Israel Bachrach
Jaques Bachrach
Fritz Bachwitz
Erich Bader
Arthur Badt
Rudolf Bäcker
Robert Friedrich Wilhelm Bälz
Georg Bändel
Hans Bär
Herbert Bär
Walter Samul Israel Bär
Werner Bärwald
Kurt E. Baier
Karl Baldermann
Emanuel Baldierer
Raphael Israel Ball
Berthold Bamberger
Rudolf Bamberger
Wilhelm Bamberger
Walter Balnemones
Joseph Moses Bandel Lothar Bank
Max Bank
Herbert Barber
Max Erich Baron
Otto Barosch Franz Joseph Bartes
Erwin Theodor Basch Robert Bass
Horst Israel Bassman
Heinz Ludwig Baswitz
Herbert Baswitz
Max Bauer
Otto Bauer
William Bauer
Julius Baum
Max Baum
Leon Baumer
Günther Baumgarten
Horst Herbert Baumgarten
Gotthard Baumwollspinner
Karl Rudol Bazant
Egon Bazar
Franz Beer Frederick Beer
Josef Beerwald
Klaus Eberhard Begach

Felix Adalbert Behrend
Jakob Behrendsohn
Werner Behrendt
Alex Kurt Behrens
Bernhard Behrens
Alfons Heinz Bellak
Bernhard Belocerkowski
Walter Benedikt
Heinz Adalbert Benjamin
Jakob Alfred Benjamin
Stefan Benjamini
Wilhelm Baumann
Otto Bennemann
Fritz Bensinger
Manfred Berend
Fritz Berg
Richard Elias Berg
Robert Otto Berg
Bernhard Isidor Berger
Martin Berger
Sigmund Berger
Theo Berger
Walter Hermann Berger
Hans Hermann Bergfeld
Bernhard Bergmann
Ferdinand Bergmann
Walter Bernliner
Lutz Bernhardt
Paul Berlin
Heinrich Adolf Bernstein
Hellmut Michael Bernstein
Max Bernstein
Gerhard Besch
Martin Bettlheim
Eugen Emil Betzer
Salomon Aaron Beutel
Kurt Bial
Wolfgang Bial
Ernst Biber
Louis Biber
Arnim Bick
Leo Bieber
Erich Bienheim

Günther Heinz Bier
Victor Bild
Anton Wolfgang Billitzer
Boas Bischofswerder
Felix Bischofswerder
Geord Blank
Otto Blau
Friedrich Otto Blauhorn
Paul Bledi
Adolf Bleichröder
Normann Bleiweiss
Adolf Bloch
Arthur Leopold Bloch
Günther Bloch
Heinz Bloch
Kurt Bloch
Erich Walther Blumenfeld
Gerd Adolf Blumenfeld
Hans Blumenthal
Heinz Joachim Blumenthal
Horst Blumenthal
Karl Blumenthal
Wolfgang Blumenthal
Bruno Boas
Chai Bobker
Ludwig Boch
Heinz Joachim Bock
Menasse Bodner
Gerhard Moritz Böhm
Heinrich Samuel Böhm
Leib Abraham Böhm
Ralph Albert Böhm
Gottwald Böttcher
Josef Hugo Bondi
Markus Max Borchardt
Leo Borger
Friedrich Franz Peter
Iwan Borinski
Julius Bombaum-Birnbaum
Gerhard Boronowski
Victor Boronowski
Alexander Ulrich Büschwitz
Leo Botknecht

Walter Adolf Brach
Morduch Brainin
Jürgen Fritz Brandeis
Erich Brandt
Gerhard Israel Brandt
Zwi Hans Brandt
Alfred Brandweiner
Martin Brasch
Lothar Brat
Erwin Braun
Paul Braun
Hans Braunberg
Simon Breifwechsler
Egon Breiner
Alfred Breitman
Adolf Brenner
Heinz Breslau
Moshe Bretier
Wolf Juda Brettholz
Jacob Breuer
Rudolf Manfred Britzmann
Alfred Broch
Martin Israel Broch
Herbert Bruch
Heinz Werner Bruck
Günther Bruckmann
Hans Georg Brühl
Egon Brüll
Kurt Brüll
Leo Manfred Brummer
Gerhard Alfred Brunn
Alfred Brunner
Günther Buch
Gerd Buchdahl
Hans Adolf Buchdahl
Arnold Buchtahl
David Buchen
Wolfgang Buchthal
Walter Buchwald
Otto Büchenbacher
Alfred Bürger
Stefan Bukowitz
Erich Bunzl

Ludwig Burkart
Günther Busse

C

Franz Robert Cahn
Fritz Cahn
Richard Otto Cahn
Andreas Carlebach
Walter Hugo Callomon
Günther Werner Carstens
Ulrich Cassirer
Max Chaskel
Johann Chlumecky
Moritz Chlumecky
Georg Chodziesner
Fritz Chone
Herbert Chone
Werner Chotzen
Bernhard Cinander
Gustav Heinrich Clusmann
Alfred Cohen
Erich Cohen
Friedrich Cohen
Max Cohen
Erich Adolf Cohen
Gerhard Cohn
Gerhard Norbert Cohn
Hans Hermann Cohn
Joachim Werner Cohn
Klaus Peter Cohn
Kurt Ernst Cohn
Robert Julius Cohn
Sally Cohn
Siegbert Cohn
Siegfried Cohn
Siegfried Salomon Cohn
Siegfried Serog Israel Cohn
Hans Otto Cohn-Oppenheim
Fritz Cossen
Gerhard Cossmann
Edwin Cromwell
Emil Culmann
Fritz Culp
Horst Günther Czarnikow

D

Edward Dahl
Hans Joseph Dahl
Rolf Berret Daltrop
Heinrich Damm
Gerhard Noah Daniel
Otto Erich Daniel
Norbert Dankowitz
Alfred Dannenberg
Gerhard Danziger
Heinz Georg Danziger
Peter Danziger
Rudolf Walter Danziger
Felix Hellmut Darnbacher
Herbert Gottlieb Darnbacher
Karl Dattner
Josef David
Moritz David
Hans Davids
Otto Davidsohn
Hans Davidsohn
Hans Defieber
Heinz Dehn
Erwin Dengler
Pietro Mario Depangher
Alfred Deutsch
Eduard Johann Deutsch
Friedrich Michael Deutsch
Heinrich Deutsch
Heinrich Josef Deutsch
Josef Deutsch
Leo Deutsch
Leo Diamond
Walter Joachim Dick
Herbert Dietzch
Hermann Dietrich
Walter Dietrichstein
Max Direktor
Georg Dollinger
Hans Ernst Franz Domsch
Paul Robert Morgen Doring
Wilhelm Dorn
Georg Drach

Otto Drach
Heinrich Drechler
Hans Drexler
Walter Dreyfuss
Hans Jürgen Driels
Jonas Driels
Norbert Driels
Klaus Peter Dschenffzig
Kurt Alfred Dudek
Joachim Dümmler
Georg Erich Dürrheim

E

Bernhard Ebel
Bruno Ebstein
Peter Perez Eckerling
Frank Eckes
Reinhold Eckeld
Waldemar Eckfield
Erich Eckstein
Friedrich Edelhofer
Rudolf Edelhofer
Hans Edelmann
Leib Edelstein
Ludwig Edelstein
Heinrich Joachim Ferdinand
    Eggebrecht
Ernst Ehrentreu
Hermann Hersch Ehrenwert
Anton Ehrenzweig
Berthold Ehrlich
John Josef Ehrlich
Karl Wolfgang Ehrlich
Walter Ehrlich
Kurt Ehrmann
Hans Eibuschitz
Ludwig Eichbaum
Ernst Eichengrün
Emil Eichler
Fritz Eichner
Hans Eichner
Max Einbinder
Friedrich Eirich

Justin Eisemann
Adolf Eisenberg
Paul Franz Wilhelm Eisenklam
Karl Eisenstädter
Konrad Eisig
Erich Eisinger
Jacob Eismann
Edgar Elbogen
Robert Elbogen
Otto Elefant
Albert Ellner
Gunter Elting
Walter Heymann Emden
Kurt Enderl
Leopold Engel
Theodor Engel
Werner Adolf Engel
Hans Robert Engelmann
Max Julius Hermann Israel
    Engelmann
Eduard Alexander Ephraim
Kurt Ephraim
Andreas Eppenstein
Richard Eppenstein
Martin Eppstein
Kurt Epstein
Walter Waldemar Epstein
Erich Karl Erdös
Franz Erlanger
Leo Ernst
Herrmann Ettlinger
Heinrich Eule
Arnold Hans Ewald
Jean Ewald

F

Erwin Friedrich Fabian
Günther Fabian
Peter Alfred Fabian
Hans Heinz Fachon
Wolfgang Amadeus Fackenheim
Sigbert Falk
Heinz Siegfried Falkenburg

Hans Falkenstein
Karl Falter
Oskar Fass
Hugo Fassel
Walter Fast
Rolf Werner Feber
Hans Werner Feder
Markus Abraham Federbusch
Heinz R. Federer
Peter Ilman Karl Federn
Paul Fehl
Emil Feichtmann
Hans Georg Feidelberg
Hans I. Feige
Siegfried Feigelstock
Heinz Peter Feistmann
Siegmund Feldan
Adolf Felder
Henry Hansheinz Felder
Erich Horowitz Feldmann
Hans Feldmann
Leo Feldsberg
Jakob Felsenstein
Paul Fent
Alfred Festberg
Oskar Feuchtwanger
Franz Wolfgang Feuerstein
Hanns Gerhard Feuerstein
Hans Fichmann
Ernst Fink
Salomon Finkel
Samuel Finkel
Leo Fisch
Max Fischbach
Alfred Fischer
Alfred Joachim Fischer
Anthony Fischer
David Josef Fischer
Emil Fischer
Emmerich Fischer
Erwin Raimund Fischer
Franz Fischer
Hugo Fischer

Isucher Fischer
Kurt Fischer
Max Hermann Fischer
Robert Fischer
Rudolf Fischer
Eugen Fischl
Ferdinand Fischmann
Heinz Siegfried Flachsmann
Gert Flatan
Walter Josef Fleitsch
Hans Ernst Fleischer
Hermann Fleischer
Paul Fliess
Walter Fliess
Kurt Flussmann
Erich Förster
Fritz Fokschaner
Gotthold Karl Forell
Heinz Martin Fränkel
Herbert Max Fränkel
Karl Fränkel
Martin Fränkel
Emil Frank
Lorenz Frank
Paul Max Frank
Rudolf Adolf Walther Frank
Werner Frank
Erich Franke
Ludwig Heinrich Franken
Walter Franken
Hans Frankenstein
Hans Frankmann
Friederich Franz
Eli Freier
Fritz Israel Freier
Walter Freiberger
Karl Friedrich Freilich
Elisa Freind
Fritz Karl Freitag
Karl Frenz
Walter Freud
Erich Gabriel Freudenstein
Georg Gerson Freudenstein

Carl Freund
Emil Freund
Friedrich Freund
Günther Freund
Haller Hans Heinz Freund
Heinrich Alexander Freund
Walter Freund
Gerhard Freuthal
Peter Hans Frey
Erwin Gustav Freye
Klaus Georg Friedeberger
Felix Friedemann
Paul Kurt Friedenheim
Heinrich Oskar Felix Friedheim
Arnold Friedhofer
Karl Friedhofer
Erich Friedländer
Kurt Friedländer
Bruno Ernst Friedlander
Hermann Friedlander
Ignaz Friedlander
Paul Friedlander
Arnold Friedmann
Ernst Hans Friedmann
Kurt Friedmann
Max Friedmann
Ulrich Georg Friedmann
Walter Friedmann
Rudolf Frimer
Ernst Friedrich Frohlich
Georg Hans Fröhlich
Peter Emerich Frohlich
Edgar Fromm
Felix Frommer
Max Joachim Fruchling
Haim Simche Frymerman
Arthur Fuchs
Ernst Martin Fuchs
Josef Fuchs
Max Miksa Fuchs
Walter Fürst
Paul Phillip Hans Fürstenberg
Robert Fürnberg

Hans Georg Fürth
Richard Fürth
Jakob Fuks
Harry Fuld

G

Arnold David Gabler
Werner Bär Gabriel
Isidor Gadiel
Rudolf Geiringer
Hans Hermann Geisenberg
Hersch Geister
Erich Julius Geismar
Gustav Israel Geismar
Paul Gelb
Paul Gelbein
Hans Georg Geiler
Ludwig Geiles
Max Gellis
Leopold Gerber
Walter Ger ber
Helmut Gemeheim
Herbert Gerstel
Richard Gerstel
Leo Gerstein
Alfred Gersti
Heinz Geyer
Alexander Wilhelm Giepen
Horst Giesener
Walter Ginsberg
Hans Gerson Glaser
Hermann Glaser
Karl Glass
Paul Georg Glass
Max Meier Glatt
Max Glesinger
Alex Glogan
Berthold Glogauer
Ernst Glücksmann
Ernst Gold
Joseph Gold
Isaak Goldberg
Hans Goldberger

Friedrich Goldenberg
Bernhard Goldfarb
Bernhard Goldmann
Ernst Ludwig Goldmann
Franz Goldmann
Friedrich Joachim Goldmann
Günther Goldmann
Jacob Goldmann
Leo Werner Goldmann
Wilhelm Goldmann
Alfred Israel Goldschmidt
Erich Goldschmidt
Hans Eberhard Goldschmidt
Herbert Goldschmidt
Kurt Edwin Goldschmidt
Kurt Max Goldschmidt
Max Goldschmidt
Walter Peter Goldschmidt
Werner Goldschmidt
Friedrich Goldschmitt
Werner Fritz Goldstaub
Fritz Goldstein
Hans Alfred Goldstein
Herbert Goldstein
Joachim Goldstein
Martin Goldstein
Otto Goldstein
Werner Nathan Goldstein
Leo Goldsticker
Hans Wolfgang Gonsenhauser
Heinz Gonsior
Max Gonsiorowski
Abrascha Gorbulski
Hugo Gottlieb
Martin Grabowski
Friedrich Grätzer
Ignatz Grau
Leo Grau
Oswald Grauer
Felix Graupner
Walter Greif
Hans Greilsheimer
Adolf Grielhaber

Julius Grieshaber
Pinkas Chaim Grindlinger
Josef Groch
Hans Werner Grodszinski
Leo Grodszinski
Josef Grondziel
Erich Wolfgang Gross
Hugo Gross
Jacob Grossbard
Julius Grossbard
Siegfried Grossbard
Herbert Grossmann
Robert Carl Ludwig Grothey
David Grün
Fritz Grün
Kurt Grün
Kurt Grünbaum
Kurt Gerhard Grünbaum
Moses Chaim Grünbaum
Kurt Grünebaum
Paul Grüneberg
Siegfried Grüneberg
Fritz Grünberger
Ignatz Andor Grünhut
Otto Grünhut
Simon Grünhut
Felix Grünpeter
Kurt Grünpeter
Friedrich Günser
Ernst Gumperz
Hans Heinrich Gurland
Victor Bernhard Gussmann
Leo Guter
Paul Gutfreund
Gerhard Gutmann
Hermann Gutmann
Fritz Guttenberg
Hans Guttmann
Karl Guttmann
Rudolf Guttmann
Simon Guttmann
Wilhelm Leo Gutsmann

H

Manfred Haarburger
Walter Paul Haarburger
Werner Haarburger
Henry Haas
Bruno Israel Haase
Robert Haase
Hans Haber
Otto Haber
Joseph Hackenbroch
Wilhelm Leon Hackenbroch
Kurt Hagenow
Gustav Alfred Hager
Albert Hahn
Georg Haim
Felix Isaak Halberstadt
Hermann Halberstadt
Samuel Halle
Siegfried Hallgerten
Benjamin Halpern
Leon David Halpersohn
Friedrich Hamberger
Gerhard Lothar Hamburger
Ulrich Wilfred Hamburger
Theodor Hammel
Jakob Josur Hammer
Arthur Hammerschmidt
Hans Herbert Hammerstein
Alfred Hanf
Erich Hannach
Kurt Paul Hannach
Bruno Salomon Harrens
Günther Hartwich
Josef Otto Hecht
Hein Heckroth
Abraham Heftler
Arthur Moritz Heichelheim
Wilhelm Heidorn
Milton Heilberg
Bruno Heilborn
Adolf Heilbronn
Max Heilbronn

Siegfried Heilbronn
Sigmar Heilbrunn
R.M.G. Heilbut
Wolfgang Heilner
Erich Israel Heimann
Friedrich Albert Heimann
Josef Heimann
Max Heimann
Albert Heine
Walter Paul Rudolf Heine
Karl Heinz Heinemann
Hugo Heinsheirner
Manfred Heli
Samuel Heller
Walter Heller
Werner Alfred Heller
Siegfried Hellman
Nikolaus Georg Peter Hemer
Ludwig Hemmerdinger
Kurt Siegbert Henle
Herbert Heppner
Peter Herbst
Philip Günther Herbst
Heinz Robert Hermannsohn
Wilhelm David Herr
Gangolf Herrmann
Josef Herrmann
Kurt Herrmann
Arthur Herrnstadt
Emil Emanuel Hesch
Hans Joachim Herschaft
Paul Herschan
Alexis Ralph Vernon Herz
Hermann Herz
Kurt Herz
Sophoni Herz
Georg Herzog
Gustav Herzog
Herman Herzog
Herbert Herzog
Josef Hess
Israel Heszel
Walter Julius Heumann

Fritz Heymann
Hans Peter Heymann
Jim G. Heynemann
Alfred Hillet
Egon Hirsch
Ernst Herman Hirsch
Fritz Maximilian Hirsch
Heinz Hirsch
Hugo Hirsch
Josef Hirsch
Kurt Hirsch
Leopold Hirsch
Siegfried Hirsch
Walter Manfred Hirsch
Walter Max Hirsch
Gerdt Hirschberg
Günter Hirschberg
Hans Ulrich Hirschberg
Arthur Kurt Hirschfeld
Hans Julius Walter Hirschfeld
Ludwig Hirschfeld
Werner Hirschfeld
Willy Hirschfeld
Sander Joseph Hirschhorn
Gustav Hochberg
Isaak Hochberg
Siegfried Hochberg
Simon Hochberger
Emil Höchster
Heinz Hermann Hönicke
Fritz Hofbauer
Hans Ernst Hoffmann
Herbert Hoffmann
Paul Heinz Hoffmann
Peter Hofmann
Robert Hofmann
Walter Hofstädter
Robert Hogen
Simon Hohenberg
Adolf Hohenstein
Siegfried Holländer
Julius Homberg
Oskar Hony

Peter Horst Horn
Philipp Horowitz
Heinz Alfred Hulisch
Rolf Humberg
Harold Huppert
Peter Huppert
Siegfried Huss
Wilhelm Huss
Pavel Husserl
Alfred Heinrich Huttenbach
Ernst Heinrich Hutterer
Hugo Hutzler
Frank Huzenlaub

I

Rudolf Inländer
Louis Isacsohn
Max Arthur Isay
Franz Israels
Curt Italiener

J

Alfred Jablonsky
Ferdinand Jacob
Georg Johann Jacob
Heinz Jacob
Otto Jacobs
Heinz Jacobius
Horst Jacobinski
Josef Jacobowitz
Erwin Jacobsen
Harry Jacobsohn
Hans Jacobus
Franz Victor Günther Jacoby
Fritz Jarecki
Gerhard Jaskulewicz
Paul Jeenek
Harry Jeidels
Georg Tobias Jessel
Fritz Siegfried Joachim
Friedrich Johne
Harry Aron Jontofsohn
Bernhard Joseph
Ernst Joseph

Karl Joseph
Otto Moritz Aby Joseph
Wolfgang Josephs
Franz Josef Josten
Hans Josephy
Kurt Judell
Heinz Werner Judenburg
Franz Juliusberg
Werner Leopold Jung
Pinkas Jungleib

K

Gerhard Kaczynski
Gerd Kadden
Julian Kadisch
Leo Kadritzki
Paul Frank Kämmerer
Karl Kafka
Siegfried Kahan
Jakob Isak Kahane
Heinz Kahn
Josef Kahn
Julius Kahn
Rudolf Anselm Kahn
Gert Kaiserblüth
Mendel Kalb
Norbert Kalb
Tibor Kaldor
Harry Kalimann
Erwin Kaller
Richard Kallmann
Richard Kandelmenn
Manfred Kantorowicz
Walter Heinz Edgar Kantorowicz
Albert Vincent Kapitzki
Alfred Aron Kaplan
Josef Kappius
Rudolf Henry Karbasch
Berthold Kardegg
Albert Ferdinand Karolyi
Heinz Manfred Karpowitz
Emil Karter
Arthur Kassel

Fritz Karl Georg Kassel
Edward Kassner
Max Herbert Kassner
Hans Kastelan
Heinrich Katschke
Walter Katschke
Albert Katz
Alfred Felix Katz
Artur Katz
Ernst Katz
Gerhard Katz
Manfred Katz
Rudolf Katz
Werner Hans Katz
Abrahàm Israel Katzauer
Heinz Egon Katzenstein
Georg Moisius Kaufmann
Georg Eduard Justus Hugo
  Kaufmann
Hans Werner Kaufmann
Paul Kaufmann
Rolf Kaufmann
Walter Kaufmann
Willy Kaufmann
Paul Kaufteil
Hans Paul Eduard Kaul
Karl Ernil Kayser
Hans Jürgen Keil
Adolf Kellner
Hermann Kempe
Bernhard Kempner
Willi Wolf Kerber
Adalbert Bela Keresttes
Erich Hugo Kernek
Leopold Kerpen
Ludwig Kerpen
Alfred Hans Egon Kessler
Heinz Peter Kessler
Julius Kirchhausen
Gunter Kirschner
Hermann Kirstein
Siegmund Kirstein
Ernst Kitzinger

Emil Klak
Fritz Klarsfeld
Stephan Hans Klausner
Albert Kleeberg
Georg Israel Klein
Julius Klein
Julius Israel Klein
Manfred Martin Klein
Max Marcus Klein
Peter Klopffleisch
Herbert Karl Kluger
Hermann Knechtel
Hans Knonower
Siegfried Knopp
Hans Walter Knothe
Fritz Koblitz
Helmut Kobrak
Bernhard Koch
Walter Koch
Leo Maria Köllner
Matthäus Kölz
Hans Peter König
Walter Hermann König
Paul Königsberg
Heinz Martin Königsberger
Rolf Erich Königsberger-Maassen
Robert Köstenmann
Adolf Kohn
Hans Kohn
Josef Kohn
Kurt Kohn
Leopold Kohn
Walter Kohn
Hermann Kohner
Felix Kolben
Rolf Kollar
Fritz Emil Kolm
Leo Komorner
Karel Josef Konig
Hans Clemens Konigsberg
Hans Peter Konigsberger
Ladislaus Kopfstein
Erich Maria Koppel

Heinz Koppel
Fritz Korn
Benjamin Korngold
Heinz Moritz Kossmann
Alexander Kowalik
Peter Koziol
Leo Kramparski
Bruno Hermann Johannes Krantz
Günther Kranz
Karl Ludwig Krappel
Ernst Krause
Fritz Krausz
Rudolf Krautter
Adolf Krebs
Gustav Friedrich Karl Krentler
David Krieger
Herbert Kriegsmann
Karl Krips
Kurt Kriszhaber
Hans Kronsberger
Walter Mayer Kruk
Heins Ksinski
Ulrich Charles Hermann Kubach
Ernst Kuczynski
Heinz Kühlenthal
Isak Künstier
Steffan Kuffner
Georg John Erich Ed Kunick
Paul Kupfer
Fritz Kupferberg
Gerhard Kupperheim
Ernst Kurz
Paul Kurz
Hermann Kuzrok
Hans Kutscher

L

Paul Erwin Ladewig
Erwin Lamm
Wolfgang Willy Lampl
Eduard Lanczi
Alfred Landauer
Rudolf Landauer
Wilhelm Landberger

Heinrich Landesmann
Ferdinand Lang
Johannsa Carl Langmeier
Peter Jürgen Heinrich Langstein
Robert Lanzer
Rudi Siegfried Eduard Laqeur
Peter Laske
Ernst Laufer
Kurt Laufer
Moritz Laufer
Ulrich Sigmund Laufer
Georg Julius Lederer
Gustav Lederer
Rolf Severin Leeser
Erich Leffmann
Ernst Peter Dietrich Lehmann
Ernst Elias Lehmann
Max Lehmann
Siegfried Lehmann
Hans Peter Ernst Lehner
Siegmund Lehnert
Arthur Lehr
Dagobert Lehr
Norbert Wilfred Helmut Leicht
Peter Leicht
Wolfgang Josef Leidert
Hans Georg Israel Leiser
Kurt Leiser
Hans Leitner
Walter Leschnitzer
Ernst Leser
Hans Siegfried Lessmann
Albert Leufer
Kurt Jakob Levenbach
Ernst Justin Levi
Hermann Levi
Max Levi
Rudolf Samuel Henoch Levi
Max Levin
Jakob Michael Levin
Kurt Levin
Leonhard Israel Levin
Bertold Levistein

Adolf Levy
Ernst Levy
Fritz Levy
Hugo Levy
Kurt Levy
Max Levy
Werner Lewen
Bruno Lewin
Erich Lewin
Georg Lewin
Ilbert Lewin
Manfred Lewin
Oskar Lewin
Rudolf Martin Lewin
Salomon Lewin
Kurt Bernhard Lewinski
Alfred Lewinsky
Max Werner Lewinsky
Hans Lewinsohn
Max Lewinsohn
Siegmund Lewinsohn
Arnold Lewiny
Juda Leo Lewinzon
Hans Lewkonja
Moses Lewkowicz
Artur Lewy
Egon Lewy
Ernst Lewy
Hans Lewy
Hans Lichtenstern
Ludwig Lichtheim
Eduard Liebel
Leser Liebschütz
Felix Liebesny
Alfred Liebster
Erich Liffmann
Alexander Lind
Josef Lind
Johannes Hans Fritz Otto Lindan
Alfred Lindemann
Wolfgang Karl Gustav
  Lindemeyer
Kurt Benjamin Lindenberg

Bela Lindenfeld
Paul Theodor Lindheimer
  alias Peter Land
Walter Lindheimer
Artur Lindner
Manfred Lindner
Walter Linz
Ernst Max Lion
Siegfried Lion
Bruno Lipmann
Erich Lipmann
Heinz Lippmann
Karl Lisewski
Moritz Lissauer
Franz Georg Litwin
Walter Lob
Paul Lobt
Hermann Lock
Hans Walter Löb
Emerich Löbl
Ludwig Israel Löb
Martin Hugo Löb
Eli Löbenstein
Heinsmann Löbenstein
Martin Ludwig Löhr
Klaus Günter Löwald
Arnold Joachim Löwe
Egon Theo Israel Löwe
Hans Hermann Adolf Löwe
Gustav Löwenhart
Peter Karl Löwensberg
Fritz Karl Heinz Löwenstein
Hans Löwenstamm
Hans Löwenstein
Helmut Löwenstein
Max Löwenstein
Robert Leopold Löwenstein
Werner Löwenstein
Ernst Moritz Löwenthal
Georg Kurt Alexander
  Löwenthal
Siegbert Löwenthal
Arthur Löwinsohn

Alfred Israel Löwy
Moses Löwy
Schalom Lomas
Menko Lomnitz
Peter Wolfgang Lomnitz
Heinz Herrmann Lopatka
Klaus Lopatka
Friedrich Lorge
Renato Lowenstein
Werner Julius Lowenstein
Karl Lowy
Hans Günther Luca
Wilhelm Ludwig
Siegmund Luka
Walter Lustig
Hans Heinz Lutterkort

M

Ludwig Maas
Herbert Maas
Max Machcsow
Helmut Machol
Alfred Magaziner
Herbert Mainzer
Josef Mainzer
Herbert Malinow
Edmund Mandl
Peter Leo Mandl
Otto Mandler
Johann Mang
Julius Mann
Leopold Manhart Manna
Gustav Manasse
Hans Mannheim
Ernst Mannheimer
Julius Mannheimer
Siegfried Mannheimer
Walter Wolfgang Mansfeldt
Edwin Manzoni
Erwin Marcus
Fritz Marcus
Hans Wilhelm Marcus
Heinz Hermann Marcus

Siegfried Marcus
Julius Margules
Heinz Werner Margules
Leonhard Marienberg
Lothar Hermann Markiewicz
Max Markus
Oskar Markstein
Heinz Marowilsky
Alexander Israel Marx
Karl Marx
Moses Marx
Otto Marx
Walter Israel Marx
Hermann Maschke
Fred Robert Maschler
Hans Mases
Ernst Mass
Robert Mass
Franz Massarik
Oskar Masur
Reinhard Ernst Matzig
Friedrich Willibald Matzner
Friedrich Ignatz Mautner
George Mautner
Leo Max
Gerd May
Edfried Mayer
Heinz Adolf Mayer
Henry Mayer
Karl Georg Mayer
Kurt Mayer
Josef Wilhelm Mayer
Otto Hans Mayer
Wolfgang Mayer
Zacharias Mayer
Kurt Mehlhausen
Edmund Arthur Mehlmann
Wolfgang Bernhard Mehrländer
Bernhard Meier
Bertold Meier
Gerhard Hermann Meier
Josef Meier
Bernhard Meisels

Walter Melhausen
Michael Mellinger
Abraham Arno Mendel
Victor Menschel
Franz Menzel
Kurt Menzer
Hans Martin Merzbach
Dalbert Menssias
Karl Rudolf Heinrich Meth
Max Ludwig Meth
Albert Ernst Meyer
Erwin Walter Meyer
Friedrich Meyer
Hans Meyer
Hans Meyer
Hans Joachim Meyer
Hans Josef Meyer
John Hans Meyer
Klaus Meyer
Kurt Meyer
Max Meyer
Nikolaus Meyer
Otto Martin Meyer
Walther Meyer
Erich Meyerhof
Gerd Meyerson
Solly Israel Meyerson
Hans Hermann Meyerstein
Paul Mezulianik
Alfred Michaelis
Ernst Günther Michaelis
Jakob Michel
Werner Michels
Arno Michelsohn
Joseph Millet
Joseph Minz
Leopold Mischkowski
Horst Mittoch
Paul Modern
Jesaja Mohr
Rudolf Jacob Mohr
Martin Bernhardt Mohrenwitz
Alfred Monath

Ernest Mondschein
Kurt Morgenroth
Bob Wolfgang Morgenstern
Isak Morgenstern
Peter Curt Morgenstern
Siegfried Morgenstern
Arthur Moses
Georg Moses
Gerd Moses
Gerhardt Moses
Viktor Moses
Karl Adolf Mrak
Georg Muchlig
Kurt Münz
Robert Francis Mugdan
Elias Munk
Carl Murrnann
Ludwig Carl Mysa

N

Hans Georg Nadel
Harry Nagler
Isidor Nagler
Leopold Nassan
Walter Nathan
Hans Gerhard Nathansohn
Walter Nathansohn
Hans Nauen
Max Israel Naumberger
Max Nawratzki
Fritz Nebel
Kurt David Nebel
Otto Neitzel
Martin Nethaus
Eduard Nelken
Gerhard Heinz Nell
Karl Heinz Nerichow
Heinz Günther Neubar
Ernst Nenfeld
Rudolf Nenfeld
Wilhelm Neufeld
Paul Neugebauer
Samuel Wolf Neugeboren

Jakob Israel Neuhans
Erich Neumann
Kurt Neumann
Leo Neustadt
Hans Neuwahl
Heinz Peter Newmann
Helmut Hermann Albert Niendorf
Abram Nieporent
Walter Nissels
Josef Hosias Nissenfeld
Siegfried Nothmann
Henry Nowottny
Adolf Nussbaum
Ozias Nussbaum

O

Alfred Oberländer
Leopold Oberländer
Hans Joachim Österreicher
Joseph Offenburg
Herbert Oliver
Hans Siegfried Oppenheim
Rolf Albert Oppenheim Werner Oppenheim
Carl Oppenheimer
Hans Max Oppenheimer
Kurt Oppenheimer
Kurt Albert Oppenheimer
Leo Oppenheimer
Lincoln Menny Oppenheimer
Paul Erwin Ludwig Oppenheimer
Friedrich Heinz Oschinsky
Kurt Ostberg
Herbert Ostersetzer
Willy Otto
Wilhelm Overhoff

P

Berthold Pais
Eduard Ludwig Otto Moritz Pape
Boris Paretzkin
Hans Pasch
Arthur Henry Paul
Adolf Pauson

Werner Pelz
Siegfried Pereles
Gustav Rudolf Imre Julius Perger
Werner Peritz
Israel Perlberger
Wolfgang Walter Perle
Stefan Peto
Leo Petruschka
Leo Gustav Peysack
Fritz Pfeffer
Heinz Phiebig
Werner Philipp
Franz Adolf Phillipp
Erich Pick
Klaus Hermann E. Pick
Jakob Jankel Pickarz
Mayer Pietruschka
Hans Pinner
Hans Hananja Pinner
Paul Israel Piski
Joann Alex Theodor Erwin Pistori
Erich Plaut
Fritz Plaut
Cornel Polatschek
Felix Wilhelm Pollak
Karl Alexander Pollak
Rafael Felix Pollak
Walter Paul Pollak
Bernhard Moritz Israel
  Poppelauer
Ernst Porges
Jonas Poritzky
Paul Posener
Leonhard Posner
Ludwig Pototzky
Georg Joseph Prager
Wilhelm Prager
Leo Preis
Franz Ludwig Preminger
Klaus Presser
Albin Preuss
John Prey
Louis Primo

Ernst Prinz
Willibald Puchalla
Edmund Pudelko
Fritz Siegfried Putter

R

Gerhard Raasch
Paul Raasch
Moses Rabi
Ernst Radt
Chaim Rädl
Bernd Anselm Rahmer
Georg Rapp
Alfred Raschkowan
Ernst Ratheber
Bernhard Ratner
Jacob Rattner
Arthur Rauch
Walter Rauch
Emil Rauchmann
Georg Rechelmann
Wilhelm Rechnitz
Walter Paul Reeth
Friedhelm Reich
Hans Herbert Reich
Heilech Reich
Ernst Robert Reichelt
Hans Reichenberger
Klaus Reichmann
Kurt Reichmann
Alfred Leon Reichwald
Martin Reichwald
Rudolf Reifurth
Wilfred Olaf Reiners
Hans Robert Reinhard
Max Reinharz
Hans Reinmann
Adrian Reiser
Maximilian Reiser
Rudolf Reismann
Franz Wilhelm Reisner
Ernst Reiss
Fritz Otto Reiss

Hans Reiss

Alexander Nicolai Reissner

Erich Reiter

Julius Reiter

Maximilian Reiter

Franz Rennhak

Wilhelm Josef Resch

Lazarus Ressler

Heinz Riefenstahl

Eduard Ries

Rolf Edgar Rieser

Erwin Riggelhaupt

Alfred Israel Rindsberg

Moritz Rindsberg

Arnold Rink

Leon Rintel

Friedrich Michael Rittermann

Hermann Melchior Robinow

Ernst Rodeck

Jakob Rogoschanski

Robert Rokach

Günter Ernst Rom

Siegfried Heinz Rose

Erich Roseck

Victor Rosen

Werner Georg Rosen

Berthold Rosenau

Kurt Siegfried Rosenau

Gerhard Werner Rosenbaum

Günther Heinz Rosenbaum

Ignaz Rosenbaum

Otto Rosenbaum

Eugen Rosenberg

Heinz Hermann Rosenberg

Herbert Rosenberg

Hugo Rosenberg

Kurt Rosenberg

Martin Rosenberg

Gerhard Rosenblum

Eli Rosenblüth

Ernest Emanuel Rosenblüth

Hans Rosenblüth

Berthold Rosenbusch

Manfred Rosenfeld

Abram Szyja Rosental

Albert Rosenthal

Alfred Rosenthal

Arthur Rosenthal

Ernst Max Rosenthal

Fritz Rosenthal

Georg Rosenthal

Hans Rosenthal

Hans Ewald Rosenthal

Helmuth Rosenthal

Herbert Rosenthal

Röder Alexander Rosenthal

Rudolf Rosenthal

Rudolf Ludwig Rosenthal

Hans Rosensteil

Karl Ludwig Rosensteil

Erich Rosenstock

Charles Friedrich Rosieski

Kurt Rosler

Karl Rosner

Alfred Roth

Josef Roth

Leo Roth

Kurt Roth

Hans Rothe

Konrad Rothenburg

Kurt Rothfeld

James Oliver Rothmann

Heinz Rotholz

Siegfried Rotholz

Bernhard Rothschild

Gottfried Walter Rothschild

Julius Rothschild

Georg Walter Ruben

Rudolf Israel Ruben

Heinrich Rubens

Hermann Rubin

Max Rubinsohn

Isaak Rubinstein

Anton Ruh

Kurt Ruhstadt

David Rummelsberg

Gerhard Ruppin
Julius Russ
Wilhelm Russo

S

Friedrich Sabatzky
Hans Egon Sabor
Heinrich Sachs
Kurt David Sachs
Martin Sachs
Rudolf Sachs
Wolfgang Erich Sachs
Leo Sack
Ernst Sallmayer
Arnold Salomon
Max Salomon
Otto Erich Salomon
Paul Salomon
Walter Salomon
Walter Ernst Salomon
Hans Joachim Salomonis
Carl Salomonowitz
Siegfried Salzer
Abraham Samt
Willi Samter
Konrad Samuel
Wilhelm Samuel
Paul Sanders
Ernst Sandor
Julius Saphirstein
Joseph Saslawski
Leo Sauer
Werner Sauer
Leib Werner Sauerstorm
Walter Saul
Erich Schack
Otto Schächter
Walter Schächter
Kurt Hermann Schädlich
Arthur Schäfer
Johann Schäfer
Kurt Schäfer
Gerhard Franz Schäffer
Siegfried Schaffer

Karl Peter Schafranek
Israel Schapira
Izek Schapiro
Bernhard Scharf
Paul Schatzki
Hans Bernhard Schaye
Julius Schechter
Markus Schechter
Gustav Scheibner
David Schereschewski
Ernst Schick
Walter Schick
George Schidof
Max Schiff
Leo Schifrin
Samuel Schinbach
Adolf Schischa
Martin Schlacheie
Saul Schlam
Erich Schlein
Erich Schlesinger
Kurt Schlesinger
Wilhelm Siegfried Schlesinger
Otto Schlichter
Heinz Hans Schlösser
Hans Schlosser
Kurt Schmahl
Alfred Schmidt
Gerhard Martin Julius Schmidt
Siegfried Schmidt
Alfred Karl Schmitz
Hermann Schmoll
Hermann Schmull
Alexander Schnabel
Moritz Alfred Schnatmann
Peter Schneidemann
Max Erich Schneider
Ulrich Johannes
    Wolfgang Schneider
David Schneier
Friedrich Schönbach
Gerd Albert Schnönemann
Max Schnönemann

Martin Max Schnönlicht
Martin Schnönthal
Heinrich Schor
Salo Schor
Heinrich Schorr
Julius Schott
Rudolf Wilhelm Schreuer
Walter Schreuer
Friedrich August Johannes
    Schröder
Johannes Kurt Schubert
Heinz Hanns Schuftan
Herbert Schuftan
Paul Schulz
Hugo Schuster
Heinz Schwab
Peter Schwab
Wolfgang Walter Schwabe
Dorian Erik Schwadach
Julius Schwarez
Alfred Schwarz
Felix Schwarz
Heinrich Schwarz
Herbert Schwarz
Julius Schwarz
Kurt Schwarz
Max Schwarz
Werner Schwarz
Ludwig Schwarzthal
Kurt Konrad Schweinburg
Heinz Werner Schweriner
Heinz Seekel
Siegfried Seelig
Salomon Seide
Egon Seinfeld
Leo Selig
Martin Selig
Walter Israel Seligmann
Oskar Seltmann
Rudi Sender
Benno Sholna
Edgar Otto Alfred Sögel
Kurt Sibber

Hans Silbermann
Herbert Silbermann
Martin Silbermann
Siegwart Silbermann
Gerhard Silberstein
Leopold Silberstein
Moses Silberstein
Otmar Silberstein
Hans Ludwig Simenauer
Kurt Simenauer
Rudolf Simm
Alfred Simmenauer
Adolf Simon
Bernd Max Leopold Simon
Bruno Simon
Ernst Ludwig Simon
Heinrich Hermann Simon
Hermann Simon
Karl Heinz Simon
Paul Simon
Philipp Simon
Werner Simoni
Arnold Singer
Eric Singer
Ludwig Singer
Peter Senia Sirkin
Fred Skaller
Samuel Sobelmann
Martin Adolf Soberheim
Hans Sohn
Fritz Jakob Sokal
Carl Felix Solmitz
Marcel Maurice Solomon
Kurt Solon
Alfred Sommerfeld
Fritz Louis Ferdinand Sommerfeldt
Günther Sondheim
Arthur Sonnenberg
Wolfgang Heinz Israel Sonnenfeldt
Gerhard Hans Sonnewald
Gerd Salli Sostheim
Erich Spagat
Isaak Spak

Sally Spak
Heinz Günther Spanglet
Ernst Spiegel
Otto Spiegel
Ury Spiegel
Walter Spiegel
Alfred Spier
Julius Spier
Hans Heinz Spira
Arthur Spitz
Karl Spitzner
Erich Stadlen
Peter Stadlen
Günther Werner Peter Stahl
Richard Stahl
Werner Joseph Stahl
Franz Leopold Ferdinand
    Stampel
Walter Steekelmacher
Edward Ernst Stein
Hermann Stein
Lothar Stein
Rolf Stein
Stefan Stein
Hugo Steinberg
Walter Steinberg
Ernst Steindler
Ernst Steiner
Ludwig Steiner
Rudolf Steiner
Gerhard Steinfeld
Kurt Wolfgang Steinfeld
Justin Steinfeld
Walter Steinhardt
Jakob Steinhof
Wolfgang Steinmetz
Albert Steinschneider
Wolfgang Johannes Stekel
Walter Stengel
Adalbert Stern
Alfred Stern
Alfred Jakob Stern
Felix Louis Stern

Fritz Stern
Fritz Friedrich Stern
Hans Stern
Hellmut Stern
Hermann Stern
Isidor Stern
Kurt Stern
Leo Elias Stern
Max Arnim Stern
Max Stern
Oskar Stern
Rolf Alfred Stern
Rudolf Stern
Walter Stern
Werner Stern
Alfred Sternberg
Fritz Sternberg
Jean Sternberg
Kurt Manfred Sternberg
Rolf Theo Sternberg
Walter Adolf Sternberg
Norbert Sternfeld
Fritz Sternhell
Herbert Sternschein
Hans Julius Stocke
Emanuel Straus
Salli Straus
Adolf Fritz Strauss
Alfred Strauss
Erich Israel Strauss
Ernst Strauss
Georg Hermann Strauss
Helmut Strauss
Herbert Strauss
Karl Hans Nathan Strauss
Richard Strauss
Rudolf Siegfried Strauss
Siegfried Strauss
Walter Salomon Strauss
Egon Straussler
Ernst Stroheim
Markus Strohmayer
Sebastian Strohmayer

144

Albert Stübs
Joseph Alter Sturm
Wolfgang Subkis
Zacharias Sucher
Albert Süsskind
Herbert Süsskind
Kurt Süsskind
Alfred Süssmann
Erich Heinz Arnold Max
  Süssmann
Gerson Süssmann
Werner Sultan
Wilhelm Suschitzky
Erich Ludwig Szabo
Erich Heinz Arnold Max
  Szamatolski
Georg Franz Szkolny

T

David Harry Tabak
Walter Tandler
Fritz Rene Tedesco
David Teichman
Georg Anthony Teltscher
Henry Michael Teltscher
Josef Mordko Tetelbaum
Ruben Heinrich Thalheimer
Josef Thiele
Alfred Thierfeld-Barnett
Erich Tichauer
Heinz Tichauer
Willy Werner Tichauer
Peter Tikotin
Leo Tisch
Wilhelm Tisch
Arnold Gustav Friedrich Thoms
Adolf Todtenkoff
Herbert Totschek
Hans Trager
Max Trangott
Eduard Michael Trantner
Walter Trebitsch
Herbert Treidel

Kurt Gert Treitel
Joseph Tremesberger
Rudolph Troll
Werner Türk
Kohos Karl Türkischer
Siegfried Türkl
Franz Alfred Turkheim

U

Michael Ullmann
Richard Karl Ullmann
Wilhelm Ungar
Heinz Unger
Wilhelm Unger
Arthur Isidor Urbach

V

Stefan Vajda
Albert Valentin
Georg Veit
Alexis Johannes Maria Vivenot
Alexander Vogel
Egon Vogel
Kurt Vogel
Marcel Vogel
Alexander Volk
Heinz Vollmer
Heinz Vollweiler
Horst Friedrich von Claer
Baron Martin von Koblitz
Georg Alfred von Kuh
Lorenz Johannes Emanuel
  von Sommatuga
Martin von der Walde
Moritz Vorcheimer
Heinz Vorgang
Herbert Voss

W

Alfred Wachs
Walter Wachsmann
Bruno Wachsner
Otto Wachtel
Naftali Wagschal
Reinhard Waldsax

Hermann Wallach
Georg Wallis
Hans Felix Walther
Bernhard Wand
Julius Wantuch
Friedrich Franz Warschauer
Martin Warschauer
Fritz Warszawski
Ernst Wasser
Albert Wassermann
Jan Weber
John Peter Wehsely
Karl Wehsely
Fritz Weidenbaum
Kurt Weihs
Frank Philipp Weil
Walter Weiler
Leopold Weinbach
Alfred Weinberg
Hans Hermann Weinberg
Hans Robert Weinberg
Harry Hirsch Israel Weinberg
Julius Weinberg
Leo Weinberg
Rudolf Weinberg
Stefan Franz Max Weinberg
Erich Simon Weilburg
Otto Israel Weiner
Julius Weingeist
Joseph Weinsaft
David Weinstick
Maximilian Weinwurm
Isidor Ludwig Weis
Fritz Weiser
Arthur Weisinger
Erich Weiss
Günther Maximilian Weiss
Hugo Weiss
Joachim Günther Weiss
Leopold Weiss
Richard Erich Weiss
Robert Martin Weiss
Mendel Weisser

Hugo Weissmann
Edward Weisz
Hans August Weisz
Heinrich Weisz
Otto Weisz
Peter Ernie Weisz
Aron Wellmer
Artur Wellner
Bruno Weltsch
Erich Willy Wendler
Isak Wenkart
Eliasz Werner
Julius Wertheim
Felix Wertheimer
Max Wertheimer
Edgar Wetzler
Hans Wetzler
Walter Hans Weyl
Alfred Wiener
Saul Wieselberg
Ladislaus Wieselmann
Viktor Wieselmann
Alfred Wiesner
Edgar Wihl
Rudolf Wihl
Manfred Gerhard Wikowski
Hans Klaus Fritz Wilczynski
Hans Wilde
Werner Wilde
Siegfried Wilde
Isidor Wilkenfeld
Georg Max Ludwig Willner
Fabian Windmassinger
Hans Winkler
Ernst Winter
Leopold Winter
Richard Winter
Josef Wiora
Arthur Hermann Wisch
Edgar Witmann
Simon Wittels
Emil Wittenberg
Louis Werner Wittgenstein

Heinrich Wohlfeld
Gotthilf Ludwig Wohlgemuth
Leon Edward Wohlgemuth
Otto Wohlmuth
Erich Wolf
Abraham Selke Wolff
Alfred Wolff
Bruno Wolff
Fritz Israel Wolff
Jean Wolff
Theodor Wolff
Walther Wolff
Walter Wolffs
Heinz Albert Wolffsberg
Otto Theodor Wolfgang
Siegbert Wolfgang
Hans Heinz Wolfsheimer Hugo Ad
olf Wolfsohn
Erich Wolfstein
Christoph Wolkenstein
Oswald Wolkenstein
Manfred Wollstein
Berthold Ludwig Wolpe
Euvin Belmont Woythaler
Georg Wulkan
Harro Wundsch
Alfred Gaston Wurmser
Erwin Wursthorn

Z

Baruch Joel Walter Zacharias
Arthur Zadek
Moritz Zadek
Emil Anton Zaitschek
Abram Zajab
Gustav Wilhelm Zander
Heinz Walter Zantoff
David Josef Zeilinger
Stephen Zeissel
Wolfgang Zeitz
Isidor Zelnanowitz
Hermann Zentner
Charles Ziller
Hersch Jakob Zimmels
Ludwig Zimmer
Siegfried Friedrich Zimmer
Max Zimmering
Siegfried Zimmering
Siegfried Zinn
Heinz Zintan
Günter Benno Zittwitz
Josef Zucker
Stefan Zuckerbäcker
Chiel Schalem Zuckermann
Ernst Rudolf Zutranen
Hermann Alexander Zutranen
Robert Zwicker

CHAPTER SEVENTEEN

In London too, the day on which Erich arrives in Sydney is summery, warm and cloudless. A peaceful inertia is in the air, a distant memory of days when bands played in the royal parks. At 4.15 p.m., the whine of the London air-raid sirens announces the arrival of 375 aircraft of the German Luftwaffe. They fly from the Channel along the Thames towards London and the London docks are the first to go up in flames. As the sun sets, the residents sense that something extraordinary must have happened, as the sun is not setting in the west, as usual, but, incredibly, in the east, where St Paul's and the City of London are. And it does not really set, either, for the sky over the black houses still gleams copper orange.

In Hitler's efforts to subjugate Great Britain, a tactical change has been effected. Over the past two months the Luftwaffe has been attacking the Royal Air Force runways and radar stations: these attacks have been very effective and cost the British many pilots and aircraft. Now it is a matter of destroying London in order to demoralize the population and force the British to surrender. For two hours, bombs hail down on the capital. After a two-hour break, a fresh wave of attacks begins, which lasts until the early morning hours. It is the first day of the Blitz. That night, hundreds are killed. For as long as Erich's stay aboard the *Dunera* – fifty-seven days – London and other cities will be bombed day and night. Great swathes of London fall victim to the flames.

One of the key targets is the district of Battersea and Wandsworth with its extensive network of railway lines and stations, the power station that provides 600,000 people with electricity, factories essential for war production and bridges over the Thames. At night, the river is a shimmering, meandering ribbon, showing German pilots the way.

In Primrose Mansions, sleep is out of the question. But the women stay put in the house. When the bombing gets too heavy, they cower under stairs and tables. The air-raid shelters in the park, hastily built by the government, do not convince them.

Irka has just been given grounds for fresh hope: on 3rd September, a letter arrived from the Home Office, with the message that preparations are being made for the shipment of wives and children of interned foreigners to Australia. However, they must be willing to be voluntarily interned on arrival. Irka is invited to give her agreement to the emigration department in Bloomsbury House, after which they will let her know as soon as there is a sea crossing available. The letter ends with, 'Your faithful servant', and an illegible signature. Irka is willing to do anything just to be near her beloved.

In Battersea Park, anti-aircraft guns and silver barrage balloons are set up to make it difficult for the enemy pilots to fly over the city. From this once green oasis, the popping of the guns can now be heard night after night. But there are too few of them. Churchill orders them to be mounted on trucks and driven from one location to another to afford protection to a greater number of the population. Members of the Aliens' Pioneer Corps dig shallow craters, filling them with a flammable liquid and setting light to them. The German pilots think they have scored a hit, and fly off.

On 18th September, Irka again receives a letter from the Home Office, informing her that her husband travelled under the number 54323 on the ship *Dunera* to Australia and arrived on 6th September in Sydney. 'Arrangements are being made for wives to join their husbands who have already sailed to Australia, out there in voluntary internment. Will you please keep in touch with Bloomsbury House, Bloomsbury St, WC1 who will advise you as to the date of sailing.'

Erich, too, has sent Irka an airmail card, to Mrs Needham's address, as he does not know that she has moved. There is a form with his new address, and the two sentences in English, German and Italian:

> *I am quite well. Letter follows at first opportunity.*
> <u>*If anything else is added the postcard will be destroyed.*</u>

Only Irka's address, the signature, with the internment security number 54323 and the date, 13th September 1940, are in Erich's handwriting. The postcard, stamped by the censor, comes at a time when Irka is already appraised of the situation.

London, 18th September 1940

My darling boy, what a joy it was when I learned that you have arrived. The crossing was very stormy, I read as much in the newspaper. How long will it be before you read this letter? Maybe I will no longer be of this world, as our lives are now hanging by a thread. It's too dreadful to describe. If we ever get together again, I'll tell you. You have a future ahead of you, I'm glad, you'll be able to realise the ideals for which we have struggled, on behalf of both of us. What will happen to me, heaven only knows. In any case, you'll still get this letter. I'm so boundlessly lonely in this world where death rains down from the sky. If I were with you, I'd be less frightened. Do you remember our heartbreaking farewell? Enjoy the time of waiting until the war is over, learn, rest, take pleasure in the sky that only sends rain or sunshine and no bombs. Maybe I'll be with you soon, I hardly dare imagine it, one gets really superstitious. How happy I would be!

Where are our dreams of a happy, peaceful life, my darling? Where is our home? If I am never to see you, I send you all my greatest love and the hottest kisses. The way it's turned out is good, because you're safe. It would be a shame for you, my dearest darling. The hope that I will soon be travelling and able to hold you in my arms might still help me get through this hell. If I had managed to travel then, on 3rd August, you'd have got a nice gift from me: a baby typewriter. Now I don't know what will be left of my things. But I'm talking nonsense, it is all good. If I do get to travel, I'll send you a telegram, so you can count up to the day we meet again. I'm very tired, skinny and ugly, because I've hardly slept for more than two weeks. When I'm with you, I'll recover. I hope you are well in that sunny, peaceful country.

Your Irka

CHAPTER EIGHTEEN

Like moles, the pale, unshaven figures crawl out of the belly of the ship and climb down the wobbly gangway. Dazed, they blink at the sun and breathe in the sea breeze. What a light! One last time the soldiers lining the gangway shove them with their rifle butts.

Disembarkation does not take long, because hardly anyone still has any luggage, so there is not much to check. Partly malicious, partly embarrassed, the guards gaze after the internees. The differences in their social origin, which have rendered the men's coexistence full of interest, but also full of conflict, are no longer recognisable. Tailors, bankers, pianists, university professors and fishmongers are all equally emaciated and ragged. Some are wearing sandals made from car tires, cobbled together during the trip by a clever shoemaker. Like all the others, Erich has trouble enough just keeping himself upright. Accustomed to following the movements of the ship with their bodies, they find the unyielding soil strangely unstable.

Sailors and soldiers stand at the railing and stare silently down at the pitiful cargo that they are releasing into an uncertain future. The military surgeon Dr Brooks, to whom many would have been glad to say a proper goodbye, is nowhere to be seen. But he has thought ahead, issuing the men who stood at his side in the hospital during the journey with a kind of testimony.

On the pier, roped off from the throng, there is a swarm of journalists, photographers and cameramen held at bay by police. The *Daily Telegraph* has announced that 'among the internees were parachutists, other prisoners of war, and hundreds who had been carrying out subversive work in England.' Accordingly, the media are after a nice juicy story. However, what they actually see does not fit into their picture. The emaciated men, Orthodox Jews in traditional black coats with hats, stooped bespectacled men in heavy overcoats and baby-faced youths in light summer clothes on their square shoulders do not look like dangerous spies. What is one to make of this?

The men are escorted by Australian guards, in ill-fitting uniforms and felt hats with broad brims folded up high on the left, across a stretch of port area to the railroad tracks. The internees, used to being pushed along with blows from rifle butts, move with excessive haste, not yet realising that they are no longer actually being driven along. An old-fashioned train with barred windows is ready for them. The wagons look like boxes on wheels, each with just a single continuous compartment and open platforms on front and back. Accompanied by two Australian soldiers, one group after another climbs up the high metal steps into the interior of the compartments. When the first train is full and leaves the port area, another takes its place. There are four altogether.

The *Sydney Morning Herald*, whose reporter cannot be deceived by appearances, reports the day after the loading: 'A number of the older men [...] frowned and scowled through the train windows, looking like cartoons of dangerous conspirators, as they shrugged back into their carriages, out of the sunshine.' Scott is quoted as saying: 'The internees were better fed than any British troops. By the time they reached Australia they had filled out and were dashing round the deck like two-year-olds.'

In the train, the wooden benches are hard, but everyone has their own seat, and that alone is already quite a treat. And no one is hitting them. The Australian guards are older men with sun-browned faces. Legs akimbo, stationed at the doors to the platforms, they weigh up their cargo in silence. Erich is ashamed of his appearance and that of his fellow prisoners. He is curious, alert and excited about everything that might happen.

By the time the last train leaves, it is already five o'clock in the afternoon. At last there is a long drawn-out whistle, a jerk, and with a rattle the locomotive moves off, with a trail of thick black smoke in its wake. Between high brick walls, the railway crosses the harbour area and then reaches Sydney. Stately stone buildings in the centre and long rows of pretty wooden houses with small gardens on the outskirts. After two months on the *Dunera* everything the men see through the closed windows is a true miracle. Trees, gardens, trams, buses, cars, bicycles, children with school bags – and women.

'Parramatta!' exclaims one teenager as they pass through a station of that name. 'I've seen a film about a woman in the nineteenth century who was deported to Australia and imprisoned in Parramatta Prison. So there really is a Parramatta!'

It also arouses amusement that many of the places they pass through are named after English cities: Liverpool, Chester, Canterbury.

Not far from Sydney, in a hilly landscape, the remains of a bush fire can be seen, the trees are still glowing. 'They lit them specially for us,' jokes Erich. One of the Australian guards informs them that in large areas of Australia it has not rained for eighteen months.

'So young and already a Nazi. Can't you think of anything better than that?' the Australian growls, after a while, to the

154

sixteen-year-old Austrian Baron Christian Donnerstein, from whose innocent face he cannot take his eyes.

His English sounds strange. The only word that Christian, who speaks fluent English, can understand, is 'Nazi'. He grasps what the Australian means. 'Hey, I'm not a Nazi!' he exclaims indignantly, and jumps off the seat.

'None of us is a Nazi,' explains Arthur, who is sitting alongside Erich and Otto, forming an Austrian enclave with them and Christian. This is not actually necessary, because there are surprisingly many Austrians, considering how tiny their country is, shrunken after the First World War, and now incorporated into the German Empire.

'We are the greatest enemies of the Nazis. Some of us have been resistance fighters in Austria and Germany. Take him' – he points to Erich. 'Because of his opinions, he's been in prison for almost a year. And besides, most of us are Jews.'

'Jews?' The brawny soldier, who is certainly over sixty, looks puzzled. 'They're being banged up in concentration camps over there. You can even read about it in our newspapers.'

'That's right. We're all refugees who have been interned in England. If we'd stayed in our countries, most of us would perhaps already be dead.'

'I've never seen a Jew.'

'Now you have a unique opportunity to get to know a whole load of them, a real crowd,' laughs Arthur. 'What do you think?'

'Strewth, you're a bit run down.'

'What do you think life was like on board? The fact we've made it to this train halfway healthy is something of a miracle.'

The Australian shakes his head. 'Jews. Well, fancy that. What's happening now?'

'That's what we'd like to know, too.'

'The name's Jack, by the way.'

Otto, Erich, Arthur, Christian, Siegfried, Florian, Heinrich, Hermann, Günther... So many German names, the poor Aussie will never be able to take them all in.

The tension dissolves into relieved laughter. Jack sits down on an empty seat, his gun – a relic from the First World War – between his knees. He is silent. One can almost see the questions circling in his brain.

'But why? I can't get my head round it.'

'You need to ask the government of the mother country about that,' says Erich. 'They've really dropped you in it. Now you've got us hanging round your necks, and we're a real bunch of troublemakers. It's high time you made yourselves independent from England. Where are they taking us, actually?'

'That I'm not allowed to tell you. But it's going to be a long journey. Australia is a big country.'

'A great country,' adds his friend. Love and pride are written all over his face.

'We're used to long journeys. We've all got quite a few big jaunts under our belts.'

Jack takes off his hat, throws it into the luggage net and loosens his leather belt. 'And I was hoping to get my mitts on some real fascists. That's what they'd promised us. If I can't fight any more, I wanted at least to prove myself that way.'

'Too bad, old chum. We'd like to make our contribution, but we're not allowed. But we can be friends. Can we smoke in here?'

'Of course, just light up.'

Of the supply of Waverleys there are only a few sad samples in circulation. Jack pulls a tobacco pouch from his uniform pocket and hands out a small heap of tobacco and a paper to each of the men.

'And you, laddie, you allowed to smoke?' he asks the young baron.

'If I'm old enough to be interned and deported, I'm also old enough to smoke.'

'Too right.'

Jack gets up and busies himself pulling down the improvised bars on the windows with the butt of his rifle. Then he opens the window and shouts to the other guards to do the same. 'These are refugees, not Nazis!' And, turning to the detainees: 'This is strictly prohibited, just so you know.'

'Our lips are sealed.'

'This is getting off to a better start than the last stage,' Erich whispers to Otto in German.

'Give it here,' says Jack, as he sees how clumsy the men are with the tobacco. 'Just keep hold of my gun a minute if you don't mind.'

'You see that?' says Erich in amazement. 'If he isn't giving the newbie his loaded rifle to hold! I'm liking Australia more and more.'

With his own cigarette dangling from the corner of his mouth, Jack spreads a handkerchief out on his knees and turns out an industrial quantity of roll-ups. 'If you're going to survive in Australia, this is something you need to learn.'

Colourless woods alternate with monotonous grey-brown plains. Later in the afternoon, before the onset of darkness that – as Arthur explains – falls suddenly, without any twilight, the train stops at a deserted station with a group of low wooden houses, by Australian standards probably a small town.

'Aha, Goulburn,' says Erich.

In front of the station building with the crooked porch roof there are tables with cloths and, behind them, slim ladies in white aprons. Small cardboard boxes are piled in front of them. The ladies have powdered faces and are wearing lipstick. Their hair is gathered in fixed curls around their heads.

'They look kind of funny,' says one of the youths.

'Still women, though,' interjects one of the older men. 'Can you remember when you last saw a female? Homos are better off. Hasn't any of them hit on you, by the way? A pretty lad like you.'

The boy blushes.

But soon, attention shifts from the ladies to the mysterious cardboard boxes that are being distributed by the guards. They contain ham and cheese sandwiches on white bread, neatly cut into triangles and wrapped in paper napkins. White bread. It's been ages since they ate white bread. Soft white bread, which literally disintegrates in the mouth, with butter and a lettuce leaf between the cheese and the ham. Plus a juicy green apple, a banana and some chocolate.

After this treat, the internees begin to settle down for the night. Some finish the day with a game of chess or cards. It has turned chilly, but no one here has a blanket and few even have a coat. Some lie down on a bench, in pairs, to keep each other warm. However uncomfortable their night lodgings may be, tiredness prevails, and in any case they have finally learned to sleep under far worse conditions.

Early in the morning, a yell rings out through the compartment. Drowsily, they raise their heads.

'Kangaroos!'

They all jump up, galvanized.

The big red-brown animals keep their short front legs comically crossed over their chests, turn their heads inquisitively to look at the train and then jump, with a spring of their muscular tails, at an amazing hopping pace next to the train, as if they were racing it. For a while they can keep up the pace.

'Now we really are in Australia!' the youngsters shout in excitement.

The landscape has become more barren overnight. Flat as a pancake, the Nullarbor Plain stretches out endlessly on both sides of the rails. Reddish earth, sparsely covered by grey-green grass. No bush, no rise in the terrain, only now and then a flock of sheep. Whatever can that solitary wooden house be, with its rusted corrugated tin roof, in the middle of nowhere? A saloon, like in an American Western?

The exotic sight of kangaroos has made even the sleepiest merry. Jack observes them with amusement. Instead of keeping an eye on the internees, he has snored away all night long with his mouth wide open.

More hours pass. The long-legged emus are the only diversion. None of the men has ever seen such a big bird. Sometimes, the train stops at quiet stations, which open to the rear onto a group of gloomy houses. Occasionally a herd of cattle comes into view. There have been no trees for a long time. Gradually, the men start to become aware of just how gigantic Australia is.

Erich sighs. 'It will be ages before we can go to the pictures again.'

'We're in the middle of the outback. How far from Sydney is our destination actually going to be?' Otto asks Jack.

'I can tell you now, we're going to be there soon. I didn't want to make you get stroppy all at once. Over 450 miles.

'Are there really any blacks in Australia?' one man asks.

'Yes, there's still a few Aborigines.' Jack seems to find the subject uncomfortable. 'But not in Hay.'

'Hay?'

'Now I've gone and blabbed. Yes, Hay's where you're getting off.'

'Hay. Sounds promising.'

'Hell is hot, but Hay is a hell of a lot hotter,' says Jack, laughing.

'And summer's almost here,' says Otto.

'Look!' Another shout.

A white cloud is approaching. A giant swarm of birds cuts through the sky. Then the cloud veers off sharply, and when flying in the other direction it shimmers red.

'Galahs,' says Jack without looking up, as if cockatoos in the sky were the commonest thing in the world.

The train finally comes to a screeching halt. 'Terminus,' announces Jack and stretches. They have reached the end of the line: 'Hay.'

'Booligal is even worse,' says Jack.

One of the men who still has a watch glances at it: 'Nineteen hours.'

A pretty, weathered railway station in brickwork painted rust-red and white, with a roof of corrugated iron and a platform with slender cast-iron columns on either side of the main building. At first glance this place under the blazing sky seems completely dead. Somewhere a dog barks. The sun is already high in the sky.

CHAPTER NINETEEN

London is plunged into darkness. People stumble into ponds and fall off the bridges into the river. Everywhere in the city there hang posters warning pedestrians to take care during the blackout: they need to walk against the direction of traffic and wear bright clothing. The roads are divided into two parts by a white line, and even the curbs are marked out in white. Because of the many accidents, the speed limit is lowered for cars and buses in the dark to 20 mph. People wear armbands that absorb light during the daytime and emit it at night. And small flashlights are issued, though the corresponding batteries are hard to get. Those fortunate enough to possess a battery have to wrap tissue paper around the flashlight and direct the light beam downwards. Shopkeepers face the problem of how their customers can leave their shops without allowing a gleam of light to escape. The answer is a double door, as in a photographer's darkroom.

When the war began, the government distributed gas masks and ensured that each household had enough black cotton material for the blackout. It is so cheap that even the poorest families can afford it. But setting it all up is a cumbersome process. To obtain a perfect blackout, two or three layers are required. Getting up in the morning is difficult even when you have not just spent a sleepless night, as no sunlight penetrates the crypt-like bedroom. Some make do with black paper and thumbtacks, but as the paper is often taken down and then re-attached, it is soon torn. In addition, people stick paper strips to the windows to stop broken glass flying around. Everyone lives in semi-darkness. Irka has arranged her strips in imaginative patterns – she has plenty of time.

At first, she finds the complete darkness exciting. How she wishes she could be with Erich, like the couples she senses rather than sees out on the streets at night. A city without any bothersome light at night is a rare opportunity. But like everyone else she prefers not to leave the house in the evening, for fear of air raids. Sometimes she goes with her girl friends to the pictures, to take their minds off things. The film *The Grapes of Wrath*, based on the Great Depression novel, by John Steinbeck, is one they absolutely have to see, bombs or no bombs.

The newsreels are followed with great interest. Mussolini arouses laughter, which liberates the spectators: but they have long since stopped laughing at Hitler, however grotesque this staring, barking puppet might look. How seriously he needs to be taken is something they have all been aware of since his bombs started falling on England. In today's newsreel it is reported that a German U-boat attack has sunk the passenger ship *City of Benares*. Of the 406 people on board, only 159 survived. And Churchill announces in the Commons that the German air raids in the first half of September have caused some 2,000 deaths and 8,000 serious injuries among the British civilian population.

Then comes the film. A family from Oklahoma that has lost everything goes in search of work and heads for California, where it does not fare any better. However, the film ends optimistically, with the mother's words: 'We're the people that live. They can't wipe us out. They can't lick us. And we'll go on forever, Pa... 'cause... we're the people.' At the end of the film, the national anthem, 'God

Save the King'. The crowd rises to its feet and remains motionless until the last note has died away. There is a warm feeling of togetherness.

The women tread slowly and carefully, step by step, as they make their way home from the bus stop.

'The book ends less optimistically,' says Käthe. 'In the novel, the family just falls completely apart at the end. Twentieth Century Fox has turned the film into a message of hope for the future. That's probably what they need for the American market. The main thing is that Steinbeck's socialist views get blurred.'

'But it's exactly this optimistic ending that's socialist. Don't give up, keep fighting, it's going to work out, we're the people,' counters Irka. 'But the way things are, I can't believe in such optimistic messages. I find it amazing that this film was ever made.'

'I like the last words. "They can't lick us." When do we need that message, if not now?' says Lizzie. 'And it's true. Isn't it amazing how the entire audience remained sitting, though the sirens started howling? The English are great. I love them.'

'That says something about the quality of the film, too,' says Dora. 'It was more important than anything else at that moment. More important than their own lives. Only great art can produce an effect like that.'

'Read this, Käthe. Isn't it incredible?'

Irka and Käthe are sitting behind darkened windows in front of the fireplace, reading. The crackling of the flames conjures up an atmosphere of homeliness, which temporarily helps them forget the quite different flames that are licking outside. Dr Pollak has withdrawn to her room. Irka hands Käthe Shaw's *The Intelligent Woman's Guide to Socialism and Capitalism* in which she has underlined one paragraph. She is now reading a lot of the books that are important to Erich, as this helps her feel closer to him. What Shaw has to say about women in the labour market is something she really has to share with Käthe. 'In this way the labour market is infested with subsidized wives and daughters willing to work for pocket money on which no independent solitary woman or widow can possibly subsist. The effect is to make marriage compulsory as a woman's profession: she has to take anything she can get in the way of a husband rather than face penury as a single woman. Some women get married easily; but others, less attractive or amiable, are driven to every possible trick and stratagem to entrap some man into marriage; and that sort of trickery is not good for a woman's self-respect, and does not lead to happy marriages when the men realise that they have been "made a convenience of".'

'Yes, Bebel and Engels say the same thing,' says Käthe. 'Bebel describes prostitution as a necessary social institution of bourgeois society – just like the police, army, church and business community. Either the woman uses her "tricks" to land a husband, or she boosts her income with prostitution. So the liberation of women is an integral part of the struggle for the abolition of capitalism and the construction of socialism. In capitalism, woman is exploited twice over: by the capitalists and by her husband, whose housework she does for free. So woman must also be freed from the bonds of marriage. Under socialism, marriage has lost its reason for existence. If her work brings in a decent wage, the woman does not need to marry. Shaw was right: marriage that is based on a relation of dependency can only destroy love. I'm never going to marry, on principle.'

'I hope Erich doesn't see himself as "entrapped in marriage". When he wants to annoy me, he always quotes Shaw and his attitude to marriage. I wonder why it is precisely this aspect of Shaw's theories that's so important to him. But I myself never wanted to marry. I can see how unequal my parents are. My mother's the educated one, but it's my father who brings the money home. And then allows himself the appropriate freedoms, a little '*gspusi*' now and again. And he was always messing around with my sister Ludka. My mother keeps quiet because she wants to, has to preserve the marriage. But Erich and I were married for other reasons – how else could we have stayed together?'

'Nobody's criticising you, Irka. Of course you had to get married. Imagine if you were in Poland now. You should just make sure you don't end up being economically dependent. Bebel wrote his book about women and socialism at the end of the last century. We've come a long way since then. We've even got the right to vote! And you're educated, you've graduated from high school – unlike Erich, as far as I know – and got good professional training, so what can go wrong?'

'Jewellery? Who wants jewellery nowadays? That's for peacetime.'

'During the Great Depression, jewellery was the only safe investment.'

'Yes, but not mine! In my jewellery, it's not the value in gold that counts, but the artistic quality. You may be right, perhaps my training as a goldsmith will be our salvation one day. I originally wanted to be a great artist, a painter, but I wasn't talented enough. So I became a craftswoman. But what the heck, who knows if it'll be any use. I also learned fashion design and textile design.'

'So hold on a minute! Right now, we're all unemployed. An artistic or artisanal profession has the advantage of being not tied down to any one language. You could also work in Brazil or Colombia. The hardest thing today is to be a lawyer. Who needs a Viennese lawyer in Palestine? The place is teeming with them.'

'Stop talking about Palestine and the Zionists! Oh, Käthe, what dreams we had. Socialism. A free society. A free world. Justice. Equality. Equal access to education and culture. The end of colonialism. The end of anti-Semitism and racism. Free love without the constraints of church and state. It all seemed within reach. We were just dreamers! Me more than anyone! How proud I was when I became an Austrian. Proud in spite of all the negative experiences, proud to be a part of Erich's homeland that I wanted to help shape. And then we even convinced ourselves that the majority of the population stood behind Schuschnigg and Hitler would never dare. And how happy I was when I heard the cleaning women talking on the Belgian border. French! I hugged them and kissed them. And then England. Security. Hitler would never dare. Now we cower under his bombs. And Erich is in Australia. Ten thousand miles away. And I'm here waiting. Waiting. Waiting for a ship that might never leave.'

'We're all living on the edge. It's a terrible time, but things are going to get better. We're going to win. Yesterday, the RAF shot down more than fifty German aircraft. And after the war we're going to build a new world. Perhaps it first needs to be destroyed before it can be rebuilt. Perhaps that's just what the world is waiting for. Be glad that Erich is in Australia. He's safe there. He doesn't have to go into either the Wehrmacht or a Gestapo prison. How many men would be happy to be in his position. And their wives too. You always know where he is, not all wives can say the same about their husbands.'

'You're right. I'm selfish. I'm ashamed of that, too. I'm glad he's safe and has survived that endless dangerous journey. But I miss him so!'

The siren wails. The conversation stops. They remain motionless, and wait. As the droning noise starts over their heads, they crouch down, hunch their shoulders in a senseless attempt to protect themselves and look up. The guns start popping in the park nearby and make their stomachs quiver. Sometimes it sounds as if they were directly in front of the window, then they seem to be far away. Somewhere nearby, a bomb lands. Firefighters call out to each other. Then the siren howls again. Above their heads the crushing sound of the aircraft and shortly thereafter the screech of bombs. So it goes on all night. There is a cellar where the residents have cooped themselves up, but Irka and Käthe have decided to stay upstairs, they want to avoid the hostile eyes of their English neighbours. As if it were their fault that, since the beginning of July, even tea has been rationed.

So they sit and smoke and talk. When the light is turned off in the room, they peep out into the black night and gaze at the flares released by the Luftwaffe. Dr Pollak knits, Dora solves crossword puzzles. The whole of London is waiting for the all-clear siren, which releases people early in the morning. If you can, you go to bed and doze for a few hours in the daytime. Many go outside the house to see what the bombs have done in the night. They sweep up the pieces of shattered windows and nail boards up at the glassless windows. They stand together in groups and talk about the previous night. Children carry homemade guns and play on the rubble of air raid shelters. The air pressure has scattered the contents of shops out onto the streets, and even the shelves on which the goods were piled up. A golden opportunity for looters.

When the sirens sound during the day when they are away from home, the women seek refuge in a public air raid shelter, which can accommodate sixty to seventy people. There, they take care not to speak German, but their German accent gives them away. So they remainsilent.

Even before the outbreak of war, the government recommended the use of private and decentralized air raid facilities and distributed building materials for the construction of Anderson shelters in the gardens. People are not advised to seek shelter in the Underground stations as they do not have enough toilets and people are in danger of falling onto the tracks. People make jokes about this absurd reasoning in the face of the constant danger of death from the sky. The Ministry of Home Security and Transport has published an 'urgent appeal' to Londoners to refrain from using Underground stations as air raid shelters except in absolute emergencies.

On the night of 19th to 20th September, thousands of Londoners take matters into their own hands. By afternoon they are already beginning to settle into Underground stations with bedding and food for the night. During the evening peak travel time, many have already staked out their territory on the platforms. The police do not intervene. The government recognises the fierce determination of the people, and decides to close the short section of track between Holborn and Aldwych and turn it into an air-raid shelter. The tracks are filled with concrete and reinforced flood valves installed that can be closed if bomb damage causes the river banks to be broken. Ninety-seven stations are provided with sleeping bunks for 22,000 people, including standby first aid services, canteens and chemical toilets. Bunker guards are appointed to maintain order, provide first aid and assist people in case the tunnels flood. But if there is a direct hit, not even the stations of the London Underground provide complete protection. On 16th September, twenty people are killed in Marble Arch station. Even so, a few days later, there is a rush to Holborn station.

Irka often goes into town to see what the bombs have done to her beloved London during the night. Another reason is that she cannot stand staying at home doing nothing. Then she always carries a bag with her documentation and the bare necessities for a night in the air raid shelter. Plus her fountain pen and a few sheets of notepaper.

London, 29 September 1940

My dearest Erich, here I am again writing to you and trying to forget that the letter will take months to reach you. It's autumn here, and today is Sunday. In my thoughts I'm flying around the world that lies between, and still waiting. My luggage is ready for departure, they've assured me that I'll be travelling. So I keep on waiting. Frau Baswitz told me you had telegraphed. I know your trip was very stormy, and I'm so glad that you're already there, in safety under a friendly sky.

At first I was fine staying at Dr Pollak's, but since life in London has become unbearable because of the air raids, we've had our differences. Our nerves are tense, and at such times it isn't easy to get along with strangers. Käthe is a nice girl, and so is Dora, but you know they've always made us edgy. Mrs Pollak has been really kind to me, but she's still a somewhat unpleasant person. Probably it would be better if I disappeared.

The life we've been leading here in London over the past few weeks is indescribable. If you haven't experienced it yourself, you can't imagine it. All values have become irrelevant, all that counts is naked survival.

If only my yearning were not so intense! Should I write to tell you how much I love you and miss you? Should I describe the empty days and nights filled with fear that I spend without you? It isn't necessary, you already know it. Once again, white paper and pen must give a definite shape to my love for you.

I am trying to remain steadfast and courageous. Perhaps I'll soon be travelling to join you. They'll keep their promise, don't you think? I have met some women who also want to go. Everyone is waiting. Fingers crossed, my darling, maybe I'll already have set off by the time you get this letter, maybe I'll already be near you. I'll send you some money, but I'm afraid I can't spare much. The support I get isn't enough to live on. I can't take on any work, they tell me, because I'll be leaving soon. It's a real quandary.

Can you imagine holding me in your arms? I get a warm feeling around my heart when I think of your blue eyes. Eri, Eri, who'd have thought it? I can see you in front of me. If you were with me, I wouldn't be scared of anything. But soon we'll be together, that's definite.

Your Irka

CHAPTER TWENTY

In early September in Australia, the spring should only just have begun. But in the morning the sun is already burning mercilessly down from the sky. With stiff limbs, the men clamber out of the train, which immediately rolls, slowly, out of the station. Soldiers on horses prance along the tracks, not letting the prisoners out of their sight. Erich has experienced mounted police in Vienna, he recalls how in 1933 the Left flocked in their thousands to take part in a so-called 'mass stroll', to the ring road, where the government ordered the military to march in and set up machine guns. The police officers on horseback rose above the demonstrators, spreading panic as they drew their swords and slashed the flags and banners to pieces. These here are harmless, that much is obvious, and the whole scene strikes Erich like something from a Western.

The internees laboriously line up in rows of four before marching off. Led and flanked by soldiers, they set off on a broad, sandy road – to where? No one asks. The desolation of the landscape into which they have been unloaded leaves most of them silent. A monotonous, colourless, formless plain: only here and there do the branches of dead eucalyptus trees stretch out into the blue sky. Apart from the clopping of the horses and the muttering of individual conversations, an eerie silence weighs down on the exiles. That is what it feels like: exile to an Australian Siberia.

After a while, some people approach, children with shaggy, sun-bleached hair and parched adults in plain clothes who want to take a look at the foreigners. Uprooted figures who are being brought to their uneventful town, from far away across the sea, for safekeeping. Dangerous men from Europe, where there is war, and whose armies are raining down bombs on England, the mother country. So the natives have only suspicious stares, and no welcoming remarks for the new arrivals. But the children gaze inquisitively, they have never seen such a large gathering of people before. The mounted soldiers circle the internees like shepherds herding their sheep.

In the distance, a familiar sight: barbed wire fences and watchtowers. The men stare in perplexity at the sun-exposed enclosure as, with every step, it comes closer. So here is their final destination. Escape is futile. Any hope they will be freed in Australia evaporates.

Trucks rumble by, leaving a dust cloud in their wake.

'Our suitcases!'

'What a surprise! There are still some suitcases.'

'I'm very keen to see what Scott has left us.'

Then the camp gate. Everything brand new. The barbed wire, about six foot high, in three layers, flashes in the sun, and the wood from which the watchtowers and huts are built gleams and smells fresh. Behind the fence there are recently dug trenches. The corrugated iron roofs shine. No tree. No shrub. Not a blade of grass. Only the earth and sand thrown up by the construction work. And floodlights on tall masts.

'Oy vey!' sighs one of the Orthodox Jews. 'Like Sachsenhausen.'

'They're going to keep us here like serious criminals,' whispers Erich. 'It can't be true.'

'We'll be longing for the dim vaults of the *Dunera*,' says Otto and wipes the sweat from his brow.

Earthen huts are lined up next to each other. Behind the barbed wire there is an empty stretch with scattered dry bushes.

'This is the end,' whispers one man in a choked voice.

Through a wide-open gate the queue of men moves to the blast of a horn, into a fenced area dividing two self-contained departments of the camp. 'Compounds', the Australians call the separate parts of the camp, about a hundred yards apart, into which the men are led, in the groups they were sorted into on disembarkation. About a thousand men to the left, and a thousand men to the right. Behind them, the gates close with a metallic clatter.

Erich and Otto find themselves in Compound 8. This one, they learn later, is for members of different religions and political prisoners, while in Compound 7 only Jews are housed. Perplexed, the men wait for instructions. But no one gives them any commands. After a while the more astute among them realise that it is the same as with the hammocks in the *Dunera*: now is the time to secure a favourable place in one of the huts. Erich drags Otto along with him, Arthur follows. Their new sleeping quarters are in Hut 18 on the left side of the camp. There are a total of thirty-six. They are arranged in a semicircle, standing on wooden stakes that ensure circulation of air beneath the floorboards, they are roofed with corrugated sheet metal, and a short flight of wooden steps leads from the sandy ground up to the door. After the bright sunlight outdoors, it is at first pitch dark inside.

The two rows of bunks are placed close together and provide sleeping accommodation for twenty-eight people. On each bed there is a thin straw mattress and two coarse blankets. No pillows or sheets.

Some of the men in Hut 18 already know each other from the ship: their names are Morduch Brainin, Isak Morgenstern, Wolfgang Steinmetz, Bernhard Goldmann, Heinz and Herbert Baswitz, Richard Kallman, Rolf Stein,

Alfred Landauer, Hans Brühl and Georg Fröhlich. Erich cannot remember any more names just now. Landauer is a painter, someone with whom Otto will be able to talk about art.

The allocation of beds is a civilized process, some would rather sleep up top in any case, while others prefer below. After everything they have experienced, this is a minor issue. There is hardly anything to tidy away as the men have only what they are wearing.

'I feel an exhilarating sense of freedom,' says Erich, spreading his arms wide. 'Isn't it just great to have no possessions? We should try to remember this feeling. It'll never come back.'

'I miss books,' says Brühl, and Erich has to nod at this.

'I miss paper and pencils,' says Otto, and Landauer nods.

'I miss my violin,' says Kallman. 'I haven't practised for two months.'

'All right,' laughs Erich. 'You lot just aren't cut out for freedom.'

'Have you heard?' asks Erich as, with Otto, he explores their future universe. They have no intention of popping their heads into one or other of the huts to see if they can spot familiar faces. 'The Communists aren't staying together like the queers in Hut 24 or the religious Jews. They've spread out through all the huts so they can recruit people – from their beds, so to speak. They're targeting the boys in particular, I saw that already on the ship. The boys are malleable and can be enthusiastic. They get pulled into the web, you'll soon see. Once they've been given a sense of belonging, they're caught.'

'You know, these streamlining organisational structures

174

never did it for me. I can't understand artists who submit of their own free will. I always left that to Else. But what about you? You were in the Communist Party yourself!'

'To begin with, I was with the Social Democrats. There, I also supported the streamlining of structures designed to protect the group. It was clear that a general strike and a civil war would require centralized leadership. But then, it was just this centralization that proved fatal. In February '34 in Linz, the Home Guard fired on the workers, we were all waiting for a signal from the party leadership. So it was agreed: when they start firing at the workers, that's the start of the Civil War. But only one underground leader and a few other comrades knew where the weapons were stored. Since most of the district and county leaders had been arrested two days previously, hardly anyone had the slightest idea of how to get to the weapons. The Dollfuss government wasn't stupid, they knew exactly how to paralyze us. And even when guns were available, we were held back by the command only to defend ourselves against attacks and not go on the offensive. Thus, the initiative was left to the enemy. There was no master plan in the event of armed conflict, nor a central command post. Either these didn't exist, or the relevant comrades were no longer able to act. Also, the general strike on 12th February was patchy at best. But you know that yourself: by afternoon, it was perfectly possible to get a tram into the city centre. That's not a general strike! Telephone and telegraph services were never interrupted. Well, it came to a predictable end, with a fierce clampdown. The Communists' *Red Flag* had already criticised the Social Democrats for taking the path to capitulation on 10th February. Things had been going that way for quite a while. The Dollfuss government systematically

plundered our arsenal without our party leadership reacting. This steady retreat demoralised us. We lost a third of
our protection group, in the best of times it amounted to
some eight thousand men. Who betrayed us? The Socialist
Democrats! Irka and I then joined the banned Austrian
Communist Party in protest, like many of our comrades.
We defectors first made the Communist Party strong.'

'And what later made you change your mind?'

'I'll give you three guesses. The Hitler-Stalin Pact, of
course. Thank God I was already in England. The pact
itself I might have understood – as the desire of the Soviet
Union to gain a breathing space from a possible German
attack and prevent it making an anti-Soviet alliance with
the western powers. But when the Soviets invaded everywhere and chummed up with Nazi Germany to grab half
of Poland, then it was all over. And then the unbearable
pro-German propaganda the Soviet Union churned out to
defend Germany's interests as a great power, declaring the
western Allies to be imperialist aggressors – too much of
a bad joke. I feel sorry for the Communists who are still in
the party, because they want to carry on the fight against
capitalism and against the Nazis and have no choice but
to bear the burden of the unconditional alliance between
the party leadership and the Soviet Union. Count me out!
And I don't even want to discuss it with the comrades
here in Hay. I'm not going to bite: after all, they're decent
people. But what the party says still goes.'

'It's awful. This party loyalty is something that drives
a wedge between Else and me, too. On the one hand I
admire her courage in continuing along the path she's set
out on, but on the other hand she can't allow herself any
real freedom of thought. She has to wear blinkers. Of her
own free will.'

'Irka also tends to be a bit inflexible, but she's generally less political. She reacts very emotionally to injustice, and the Soviet Union's attack on eastern Poland was of course a heavy blow for her. I'd like to learn more about syndicalism, I like that idea. Maybe I'll find someone here that knows about it.'

'Certainly. Here you can find everything. Incidentally, I've just remembered: I recommend you read Arthur Koestler's novel *Darkness at Noon*. For Koestler, it was obvious by 1938 that he needed to resign from the Communist Party, after the Moscow show trials. But right up until the Hitler-Stalin Pact, he'd seen the Soviet Union as a reliable ally in the fight against the fascists – like all of us. But then it was over. They interned Koestler in France in Le Vernet. He called Pentonville Prison, where he was detained after fleeing to England, a three-star prison. Just so we can realise how privileged we are, when you look at it. Even here in "Heu".'

'And how am I going to get hold of *Darkness at Noon* here in Heu?'

'Mmm, good question.'

'Can you smell something?'

'Food!'

'Right. I could eat a horse.'

But then there echoes from the loudspeakers the order that the men present themselves for roll call on the parade ground.

It takes ages for the colourful bunch of undisciplined civilians to manage to line up in neat rows. After the third attempt, the counting is done, and the burly sergeant with the parade baton tucked under his left arm can report to the Camp Sergeant Major Sealdwell. Then the men are told that they can enjoy complete freedom within the barbed wire: this makes the internees giggle. Sealdwell is a thoughtful middle-aged man with a clipped military voice, but his bright eyes observe the men from Europe with keen interest.

After the order has been given to fall out, plates, knives, forks and spoons are distributed. A sigh of relief goes through the ranks. Food! Some cooks, mostly from Vienna, immediately on arrival looked round the two kitchens to the right and left side of the sandy parade ground, discovered some useful implements, and are now setting to work with a will. In one of the kitchens the orthodox Jews, also mainly from Vienna, have created a separate area for themselves. Here, the cooking is kosher and the unclean must not touch their pots and pans. Initially they eat only vegetarian food, but soon a knowledgeable rabbi is allowed, under supervision, to find a slaughterhouse in Hay where he can monitor the slaughter of sheep in accordance with religious rules.

In the dining area, the men sit on benches at long wooden tables and greedily devour a veal goulash, their first decent food for months, apart from the ham and cheese sandwiches on the train. It is very hot. The vents between the roof and the side walls, covered over with mosquito nets, provide little air. And the screen door is completely useless, the fat black flies fall in swarms onto the plates and sweaty bodies. Trying to wave them away is useless, the flies just crawl into your nose and ears.

A military truck has brought clothes into the camp. Old burgundy-coloured uniform jackets, trousers, field coats and also several pairs of boots are piled up under the tarp. Everyone who needs a garment gets one, if not always in the right size. After they've tried an item on, they swap, until everyone is dressed halfway appropriately. There are plenty of tailors and cobblers, though it is not yet clear how they are going to get their hands on working tools, out here in the middle of nowhere.

From the speakers there sounds the Last Post. His lonely lament spreads out across the endless plain behind the barbed wire. Beyond the glaring floodlights the men can see a black, star-sprinkled night, like at Erich's grandparents' home in Windischgarsten. The crescent moon is hanging upside down, and the stars form strange figures; the amateur astronomer is thrilled. The night is very cold. Both blankets are indispensable.

Erich tries to sleep – after all, he is sharing the night with only twenty-seven other men. Otto is near, the two Baswitz brothers he knows from Vienna, so he is not alone, and the ground under his mattress has stopped swaying. He has arrived in Australia. He is going to be here for a long time. This does not worry him, rather he feels an inner peace, a sense of satisfaction. If only Irka can follow him soon. He does not even know if he should allow himself this desire. The crossing is dangerous. But in London, things are dangerous too. The danger comes either from below or from above. Poor little Irka. The men snore, each differently. A sigh. A whistle. One gasps, it's difficult for him to breathe. A fart. A whimper. That must be the one who was in Dachau. Or the one who has been sentenced to death by the Nazis in absentia. Outside, there is complete silence. Not even a dog barks, the town is far away. Before going to sleep, Erich summons up to his memory the image of Irka in the photo he had taken of her on the beach in Varna, wearing white shorts, with a red coral necklace around her neck. Her tanned legs gleam, her smile is happy.

Erich slips into sleep. In his dream, he hears a rustling. Behind the barbed wire something moves. A kangaroo as big as a man is propping itself on its powerful tail and holding its front legs crossed on its chest. Out of the pouch on its belly a baby kangaroo is peeping, tiny, and still without fur. The mother kangaroo remains motionless, staring at Erich seriously, as if to say something to him. Then she turns around and hops away in great strides into the dark night. Erich would like to follow her across the huge plain behind the barbed wire, run like there's no tomorrow, and fall over on the edge. Turn up in the blazing inferno of London. Deafening noise. Then Irka in his arms. Are you afraid, little Irka? Look, I've brought you a fluffy koala bear, a consolation for the lost peace and quiet. I come from a place where it is eerily quiet. Are you up and about now, little Irka? Do you still have a roof over your head? Have the windows remained intact in the night? How is it possible to hear a deafening noise and a deafening silence at the same time? Come on, little Irka, the kangaroo still has room in his pouch. He will carry you into the quiet. Quick, slip inside.

The next morning the baggage is unloaded in the area between Compounds 7 and 8. Everyone rushes over: at last, a chance to have something of their own! Everyone hopes that his suitcase alone has been spared from the vandalism of the Pommies. Great is their disappointment. Hardly a single case is intact. Locks and labels have been torn off, covers ripped open, scraps of dirty clothes are hanging out. In many suitcases there is nothing at all, in others there are clothes that do not belong to the owner. Smelly rotten food purchased in Huyton for the trip. Perhaps ten per cent of the baggage is still unopened and indeed still locked.

'Well, he's got a nerve!' shouts one of the men, and they all turn to look at the area between the two camps that has in the meantime been cleared of luggage. What they see at first takes their breath away with amazement, and then a great chorus of howls of rage bursts out. 'Bloody well go to hell!', 'Fuck off!', 'Thieves!' roar the men in both compounds.

Lieutenant Colonel Scott, Lieutenant O'Neill and the Lion Hunter have come to see how their human cargo is housed in their new prison. What do they expect? Do they actually think the internees will still take a polite farewell of them? Thank them for their safe delivery to Australia? Have they no decency at all?

Faced with this concentration of wrath the alarmed Sergeant Major has to order the 16th Garrison Battalion of the Australian Army in the camp to fall in, in order to protect the three Englishmen. The original intention of Scott and O'Neill to celebrate the culmination of their mission by strutting through the two camps is recognised as unfeasible. Their faces frozen into masks, they beat a retreat. Back behind their bars the internees have found it a relief finally to give free rein to their anger and show Sealdwell that he is not supervising mere numbers here, but human beings, who will just not put up with certain things. This is a fitting end to a humiliating phase of their lives. The men are instructed to make a list of damaged luggage, a tedious job for which an individual working group is formed.

Sealdwell needs reliable partners. Each hut should choose its own speaker, a so-called 'hut father' and his deputy on whom the Sergeant Major can call when there is something to query, and who can convey the wishes of the men in their hut to him. The thirty-six hut fathers and their deputies form the camp parliament that chooses from among its ranks the camp supervisor who will assist the guards in the maintenance of order and discipline. Anyone who tries to escape will, it is clearly stated, be first warned and then shot at.

Erich is elected father of Hut 18.

CHAPTER TWENTY-ONE

When the men take a second look at the camp, after a good night's sleep, they see it in a kindlier light. Between the huts there is enough space for athletic activities as well as for relaxation, the place is just unused and anonymous, like when you move into a new apartment and there are not yet any pictures hanging on the walls. They are still working on the hospital barracks, carpenters in shorts with wide-brimmed hats on their heads, banging and sawing. Behind the barbed wire, in the distance, a green line can be made out. A river?

Swarms of screaming parakeets and colourful parrots fly over the camp. Later in the morning the reddish sand loses its sun-drenched colour and turns pale. For lack of sensory impressions, the men learn to perceive the subtle colour gradations that structure the day. Hardly anyone misses the spectacle of the sunset when the bristly plain glows black and red, and the dying sun colours the clouds first gold, violet, green and orange, until it finally sinks into a sea of flames and makes everyone's skin glow dark brown. Suddenly, night falls and the moon appears in the sky as a blood-red disc. After dinner there is time for reading, writing letters, talking to your friends, and thinking about the inferno in Europe.

For the first few days the men can still enjoy their leisure, allow their skin that has grown pale and flabby in the belly of the ship to get tanned in the hot spring sun, and taste the delicious food cooked up by the Austrian chefs. The Australian chefs take their leave.

All the men are lined up by the crew and vaccinated against typhoid, a process that should later be repeated twice. Like Jack on the train, the guards are mainly amiable older men, veterans from the First World War, who soon realise that with these military internees, a curt military tone would sound out of place. Far from the war events in Europe, they seem to have no prejudices, either against Germans who are not Nazis, or against Jews. The biggest obstacle to fraternization between guards and prisoners is language. Only gradually do the internees learn to recognise the Australian of their guards as the English that they learned in school.

In Camp 7, some lawyers immediately carry out a survey, from which a few days later a memorandum is composed addressed to the High Commissioner of the United Kingdom in Australia, describing the treatment of detainees on their embarkation on board the *Dunera* and during the journey.

But the idleness soon starts to become boring. Under the guidance of the political prisoners, the camp gets organised. After fierce controversies between the various political factions (there are in the camp Communists and anti-Communists, Social Democrats, Trotskyists, Zionists and anti-Zionists, Catholics, Talmudists and secularists, atheists, non-political characters of all stripes, and of course also rich and poor), it is finally the forty-year-old lawyer Paul Auerbach who is elected as camp supervisor.

The daily schedule is structured: 6.30 a.m. wake up, 7 a.m. make beds, 7.30 a.m. breakfast, 10 a.m. morning roll call, 10.45 a.m. camp inspection, 12.30 p.m. midday meal, 1 p.m. to 4 p.m. period of rest, followed by evening roll call, 6.30 p.m. dinner, 10.15 p.m. last call and lights-out. It is not long before the internees do not have to go to roll call on the square. They are now counted in the huts, with every man standing by his bed. After a while, even this is handled more laxly. Where would they manage to get to if they made a run for it? Every escape attempt would mean, as in the days of penal colonies, the almost certain death of the person concerned.

The harsh tone of Sergeant Major Sealdwell cannot conceal his benevolence towards the internees. He observes with astonishment as camp life unfolds before his eyes. In the Hut Parliament, the *Dunera* constitution is soon taken as the basis for the self-administration of the internees. For now, that means primarily cooking, cleaning the houses, washing clothes and cleaning and emptying the latrines. But this in itself does not keep them mentally active. Most of them soon realise that they must either work or study in order not to lose their minds. They make a start with soccer balls, books and writing materials, which Sealdwell willingly provides, but over time the needs of the internees rise skywards.

The centre of attention of many of the men is still the kitchen. The food delivered to the warehouse is in accordance with the rations given to Australian Army members – only the best of everything. What emerges from these abundant supplies depends on the skills of the chefs, and these are self-evident. Thanks to the ever-varied menus, the kitchen boss is a respected figure. Every day there is plenty of meat – one pound per head per day – and vegetables, and there is always bread, butter, cheese and for breakfast porridge, jam and honey. The cooks are soon joined by the pastry chefs, all of them from Vienna.

In the kitchen there is a great need for helpers. Young men turn up to volunteer – after their experiences in the *Dunera*, they still have the tacit idea that they will pick up the daintiest treats in the kitchen. Water for tea, potatoes, stews, casseroles and vegetables are cooked outside the cook houses in round-bellied field boilers. The fire is fuelled with rock-hard eucalyptus wood that the strong young men split into oven-sized logs. The boilers, looking like goulash cannon without wheels, have a fire hole at the front, where many of the men roast their toast for breakfast. The opening needs to be fed, punted and freed of ash. From the rear of the boiler a black vent pipe sticks up into the sky.

One unpopular task is cleaning the latrines, but those who volunteer enjoy the privilege of being allowed to leave the camp in the truck, with the full buckets, in the evening.

The locksmiths too, as well as the carpenters, doctors, nurses, dentists, school teachers, university professors, actors, composers, shoemakers, merchants, clockmakers, lawyers, bankers, singers, musicians, painters, directors and designers gradually start to look for an appropriate activity. For the conflicts that inevitably flare up in these crowded living conditions, a special jurisdiction is created, which also supplies the judges with work.

Soon, the crafty kitchen manager allows cooking skills apart from his own to be recognised. He instructs his cooks to divide up the butter, sugar, flour, fruit preserves, coffee and tea, and opens a privately operated cafe where, in the afternoon, you can buy a small black coffee and some fruit cake.

And at this point, social inequality starts to make its presence felt. Those who have money abroad transfer it to the Commonwealth Savings Bank of Australia in Hay, where they open an account. Via the paymaster of the camp they can withdraw money that is given to them in the camp currency. Australian money is not allowed in the camp. Simple potato-printed banknotes are created and a working group is formed to issue them – the Money Issuing Department. The money is numbered and mostly stamped with the names of two members of the department. As paper is a scarce commodity, they start by printing toilet paper in different colours. For ten shillings you can buy a booklet, in which there are several perforated currency units: twopence, threepence, sixpence, one shilling, two shillings, five shillings.

Erich reckons himself lucky to receive a few pounds from Irka and her sister Ludka now and again. Anyone with money can, in the canteen set up by the camp government, buy not just a small black coffee, but other things too – cigarettes, chocolate, fruit, razor blades, postcards, stamps, a toothbrush. Those who do not have money are dependent on barter or have to sell their own labour, washing laundry for others, cutting their hair, cleaning their shoes – a system that already proved itself in Huyton.

Ten thousand pounds sterling, which an owner of some copper mines, supposedly a millionaire, has transferred to the Commonwealth Savings Bank of Australia, form the starting capital for the cash economy in Hay, organised by a former director of the Bavarian mortgage and exchange bank. With the money, the canteen is stocked with goods, while everybody who is working for the public good can get paid and can buy things with the money earned. The profit is invested in new merchandise.

The special issue of the remuneration of labour for the public good is discussed at a several-hour-long meeting of the camp Parliament, summoned with a horn solo: everyone earns the same, at first little more than a shilling per week of work, whether for cleaning latrines or repairing teeth. Anyone who owns more than five pounds is considered wealthy, and unlike the have-nots, who are dressed in army surplus clothes, he has to pay for his own clothes.

This in itself is a remarkably egalitarian system, but it does not remove inequality, because only those without money have to work. So, in the Camp Parliament, the Austrian political prisoners demand the introduction of a luxury tax familiar from Vienna, the Breitner tax. Its inventor, Hugo Breitner, was a former bank director who after the victory of the Vienna Social Democrats in 1919 took over the financial department of the city. The tax is based on a simple principle: the rich should pay! Those who can afford luxury items (in Vienna at that time, this had meant visiting nightclubs, brothels, cabarets, horse races and boxing matches or owning a car, a racehorse or a luxury villa), has to pay a tax for the destitute. In the camp at Hay, things considered luxury items can be just an ice cream or a pineapple at sixpence a piece.

The debate on the Breitner tax in the Hut Parliament becomes turbulent. The better off, who spend their afternoons with coffee and cake or hanging around at the bar of the canteen waiting for a new delivery of goods, while the other poor wretches clean latrines and chop wood, are denounced as capitalists on the make. 'Class struggle!' shout the bourgeoisie, outraged. 'Of course it's class struggle, what do you expect?' roar the left-wingers in return. It is like a remake of the Weimar Republic, or the Parliament on the Vienna Ring Road before the First World War, which convinced the young Adolf Hitler that democracy was not viable.

Erich gives his first ever public speech. He does not belong to the Communist camp, and the others are readier to give him a hearing. When called by the Chairman, he is inwardly trembling, but outwardly the completely charming tour guide, as he explains the huge success of this tax, which enabled the Social Democrat-led community of Vienna in the ten best years of their history between 1923 and 1933 to put up tens of thousands of public apartments, to create new parks and to electrify the tram system. 'Vienna's appearance today – minus the swastikas – is due to the Breitner tax,' Erich shouts, to the applause of the Left. 'Vienna has become a model of a socially just communal policy. A delegation even came from the Soviet Union so they could be shown the benefits of the communal buildings with their bright, modern apartments for the workers, and their kindergartens, paddling pools and laundry rooms.'

'Exactly!' shout the bourgeoisie. 'No wonder the Communists like it!'

'Bravo!' whispers Otto into Erich's ear when he sits down again, and squeezes his arm. 'The Breitner tax will get through, you'll see.'

And so it does.

The Communists view Erich with mistrust. He argues the same way as they do, but keeps them at arm's length, as they have already noticed on the ship. But they now see him as a potential ally. Erich is also unreliable for another reason: as a trained accountant, he has found a job in the canteen run by Erwin Kallir and with fourteen other internees, including two housemates from Hut 18, is now in charge of ordering and selling goods. So he is sitting right at the source of capitalism, even though nobody can accuse him of being involved in shady business.

The Parliament, which meets in one of the barracks after dinner, enjoys great popularity. In the absence of other evening entertainment, a large number of men in the camp stream to the evening sessions, as if to the circus. The sittings often extend deep into the night, far beyond the last post. Up for discussion: coexistence in the camp, the petitions to the British government formulated by the lawyers, and eventually the planned artistic activities. However, there are questions about the canteen that are always causing trouble, because where money is involved, the class question rears its head. And this interests one bunch of left-wingers even more – it is the main theme of all the debates about a future Europe after the defeat of fascism. The class question also arises in the way work is evaluated. Soon, they are no longer satisfied with the flat rate of payment. Should not heavy work be paid better than light work? Is peeling potatoes heavy work or light work?

The young people cannot take these debates seriously. They find it funny how grown men can argue deep into the night over trifles. Especially when one of them loses his temper and turns abusive – that is the source of much mirth, and the person gets teased the following day. The young men are here without their parents, and many do not know if they are even still alive. They are more independent than their peers in more sheltered circumstances and are not taken in by the adults. The older fellow internees who are trying to keep up the appearances of their rudely interrupted lives, right down to their bow ties, strike them as ridiculous. While most of the boys are excited about the future that lies before them, many of the older ones are in their view irritatingly backwards-looking, lachrymose and pessimistic.

As Erich has already observed, the Communists know how to get on with young people. They know that young men want fun, sport and romance, and offer it to them. If someone stands out for his special abilities, either because he can write or plays table tennis well, he is personally spoken to and entrusted with a task. On the front wall of the barracks, a wall newspaper is attached, and soon, engraved with the contributions of gifted young men, the paper *Youth in the Camp* comes into being, typed on the camp administration typewriter. A Don Cossack choir is founded, to bellow out Cossack ditties and songs of the Red Army. The first concert, for which the singers put on black shirts and borrow Wellington boots from the latrine cleaners, is a great success. In addition, the Communists organise lots of sports activities: football, handball, volleyball, tennis and table tennis.

In the camp you can also become a party member. Your admission is solemnly celebrated in the hut of the party chairman, with a quotation from Stalin. The young men are given the feeling that, despite their current imprisonment, they are a conspiratorial elite, and thus part of a world-embracing plan for the future.

In Hut 18 lives a quiet, withdrawn young man from Düsseldorf. Otto, who has experience as a teacher in dealing with young people, is a little worried about him, as he can see the sadness in him. Max was eleven when his family left Germany. After two years in the Netherlands they emigrated to England in 1936. When the war broke out, he was seventeen, and when he was interned, he had just started his degree in architecture at a polytechnic. His father, a lawyer, of whom his only son was very fond, was detained several weeks before him, but Max does not know where. In Huyton, like Erich and Otto, he volunteered for the *Dunera* even though he had heard about the disaster of the *Arandora Star*, as he had thought that lightning would not strike twice in the same place. A trip to Canada seemed like a good idea, as his parents had good friends in the USA who would help him to emigrate to the

United States. Only in Hay does Max learn that his father was on the *Arandora Star* and drowned when the ship went down. He now has to cope with this news. For days on end he wanders alone through the camp and joins none of the youth groups, and has no interest even in sport.

Max has an unusual hobby: calligraphy. He has taught himself a beautiful handwriting style and set his mind to finding a job outside the camp. The many people around him get on his nerves. Bravely, he shows the commander a sample of his skills, and soon he is actually given a job. Every letter that is written in the camp must be approved by the military censor. Day by day, senders and receivers of letters are noted in a list. It is Max's job to dictate names and addresses to an older internee, who types them out. This all takes place in the commandant's office outside the barbed wire fence, under the supervision of an Australian soldier. This keeps him busy for several hours a day and he has little to do with daily life inside the camp. Only in the evenings, when the Hut Parliament is in session, does he stir his stumps enough to go round with other people and enjoy himself a bit.

After some time, people start talking about the young calligrapher's skills. Since only a very few can afford an airmail letter, they write postcards, and since you cannot fit much writing onto a postcard, and Max has this beautiful fine handwriting, they dictate their messages to him. Max laughs to himself when he thinks of the effort the censor will need to make to decipher his tiny letters. Those who can, pay him for this service with an ice cream or a chocolate bar.

Erich does not need to avail himself of Max's services, as he himself has elegant tiny handwriting, with which he can squeeze a lot of text onto a postcard that will take up to three months to reach its destination by land – which is all he can afford. Internees are now allowed to write two letters a week, of two pages each. Because of censorship, Erich can say only general things about his life in the camp.

Camp 8, Hut 18, Hay, 5th October 1940

My dearest Irka, thanks for your airmail postcard. I hope this card does not reach you because your plans will have been realised in the meantime. Uncertainty about your stay is driving me crazy, and I am waiting and waiting for any small positive piece of news. You now have the task of facing this test, as without you, life would have no meaning for me!

We arrived on 6th September after an arduous crossing. Now we are in a camp where we are well treated and fed, but we are expecting a rather hot Christmas. Life is monotonous, the nights are cold, the days are hot. But my only complaint is that you're so far away from me. Many here get airmail letters and telegrams, but I cannot ask you for that because I'm worried about your financial situation. Amid all these people I feel very lonely and think a hundred times a day of our life together in the past. I am living in a hut with the Baswitz brothers.

Your Erich

At the same time, Irka writes from Welwyn Garden City, where she has recently moved.

7th October 1940

My dearest boy, I am writing again regularly to you, once a week, so that you will receive at least some of my letters. I long so much for a letter from you, so you will not be like a shadow for me, nothing but a memory. This separation is difficult, without letters to give any relief, without the hope of seeing you again soon. For two months I have been waiting for this famous Australian transport, so I did not seek work and am currently in a very uncomfortable position. They are still keeping us in the dark.

Now I am looking for a job, but it's hard, because I don't want to go back to London. No one wants to go there anymore. For the time being I'm living in a small, very pretty place (in peacetime) not far from London, with a lady who has taken me in. Here it's lonely and sad, but a little less exciting than in London, at least during the day. The nights are quieter too, but long and tiring, with not much sleep. It's also dangerous, because there is no shelter here. If I can't sleep at night, I picture our reunion, but this makes reality even more pathetic the next morning. Life is now like roulette, if the odds are against me it'll all be over. If you were with me, I would not be so afraid, I could bury my head in your arms and forget that death is whizzing across the sky. Forgive me for writing such sad things, it's not easy for you, either.

I'm typing on the typewriter that is meant for you. What a joy it was for me to choose it. It's not my fault if you don't get it. Of course I wouldn't have bought it if I'd known I wasn't leaving, I could really use the money now.

If only I knew what life is like for you there, if you are well, what it looks like over there. My boy, my love, if we survive this experience, then there is no power on earth that will separate us, is there? At any event, I am glad that you at least will come through, to achieve something in a different world.

I've lost contact with most of our friends, people aren't in the mood to visit. Times have changed.

Your Irka

Camp 8, Hut 18, Hay, 23rd October 1940

My dear Irene, I received your airmail postcard of 7th August about fourteen days ago. This letter should reach you by Christmas. It is hopeless to write a letter which will take almost a quarter of a year to get there, it is hopeless to be so far away from you and cut off from you. I have now been here for six weeks. At first, I already imagined you on the high seas, and even after receiving your card, I did not give up that hope. I lived in cloud cuckoo land, but my illusions soon collapsed like a house of cards. Since I know you're still in England, and there will probably be no way for you to get here in the foreseeable future, I'm constantly worried. As long as you're not with me, I won't have an hour's peace. But I know that you are strong and will find a way to get through this terrible time.

Ludka has sent me one package, three letters and one pound. With this I bought a few necessities and had my one pair of shoes repaired. She also sent me a photo of herself and the baby. They are fine. I have asked for a photo of you. I don't even have a picture of you!

As for my life here, there's not much to report. Given what you have to put up with over there, I'm not going to complain about the monotony of camp life. I am waiting and I will always wait for you and try to help you whenever I have the chance. For the time being I can only hope that you are not forgetting me.

Your Erich

Welwyn Garden City, 29th October 1940

My dearest Erich, for two weeks I have not written to you because I had a lot of worries and didn't want to whine. My hostess has given up her house, and I had to look for new accommodation. Now, fortunately, I have found some nice people who will take me in for a while, so I can look for work in peace. It is not as easy as it used to be, people don't want to take on foreigners, and everyone is rushing to get out of London. Many of the agencies to which I have written have not even answered. But through the small ads I've now found a place that might be okay. The landlady still needs to get a reference. It would be a post as parlour maid in a large country house in Hertfordshire, far away from the city, which nowadays is an advantage. It will be sad without you, being the outsider in a strange house again. I'll have to serve, brush silver and let them boss me around. But it's necessary, I have to work so that I won't brood so much. And I will indeed send you some money. On Sunday it was your birthday, I thought of you all day. How strange are the ways of life, who knows when and where we'll see each other again? Here it's already cold, and I can imagine how hot it must be where you are. As a replacement for my husband I take the hot water bottle to bed. It's a shame we're missing out on our youth, but perhaps we'll be allowed to be together as old folks – a rather bleak prospect, but better late than never. I'm being silly, aren't I? There are many internees who have been released, either for health reasons or because they are prominent persons. I envy the women who have their husbands back. But it's better that you're there, life is really not very nice over here. Do you know a young fellow named Preminger? I got to know his parents through Dr Pollak. Is Baswitz a nice chap? His wife is in London and has written to me. I also know a Frau Mrak, whose husband is with you, and several others whose names have slipped my mind.

So, soon I'll be in a uniform serving at a table and saying, 'Yes, ma'am.' Brrr. How much I'd prefer to be interned, but they won't intern me. Oh God, if only I could get over to join you! My boy, my boy, do you think about me a lot? Will we even recognise each other when we meet again? No, we'll never be strangers to each other, even if it should take years. There is an idea that unites us, the struggle for freedom. And our love and friendship are much more than mere habit.

196

I'll tell you as soon as I start work. Maybe it will all turn out all right.

Your Irka

Because the letter is written in German, the censor adds at the end: *If not in English, language of letter must be written on envelope. Censor.* From then on, they write to each other only in English.

Camp 8, Hut 18, Hay, 4th November 1940

Dearest Irene, your last two letters were forwarded to me from Camp Huyton. When you wrote it, I had already been at sea for over a week. Since your postcard dated 7th August, I have not received a single letter from you and am very worried. Could you please send me a single telegram, so I know how you are? This letter should reach you at Christmas, I wish you all the best for the day. My birthday wishes for you are too late, but they are no different from what I always wish, from the moment I get up in the morning until bedtime. I myself am in good health, but the whole of life isn't worth much in these times. To keep ourselves fit for a better future is the only thing we can do for the time being.

Your Erich

CHAPTER TWENTY-TWO

In the camp, football fever is going around and those who don't like football play handball, volleyball or table tennis. But most of them do like football, either actively as players or as spectators. It soon becomes the centre of the lives of most of the younger men, apart from the Hasidim, who never take off their black clothes and prefer to stay in the hut, because the Australian sun burns their eyes that are accustomed to reading in dim light. With the energetic collaboration of 'Little Moscow', whose members for conspiratorial reasons call themselves 'friends', clubs are founded with resonant names: Admira Vienna, Hertha BSC, Juventus, Real. On birthdays, each respective club wishes its members a happy birthday with a hand-painted greeting card. The goals are built out of timber, and the goal area and centre line are marked out with light gravel or flour. The teams take their job seriously.

The international match between Germany and Austria, which they have been strenuously training for, is scheduled for a Saturday afternoon. The atmosphere is heated from the start, and deep-seated resentments are running high. The young men fight tooth and nail for the victory of their countries – from which they were expelled not so long ago. There is a hail of insults: 'Filthy Krauts!' or 'Prooshian pigs!' the one lot roar, 'Waltzing wallies!', 'Wiener Schnitzels!' and 'Dirndl dawdlers!' howl the others. Hooting with glee, the victorious Austrians swagger through the camp, while the Germans creep into their huts, downhearted.

Otto shakes his head. 'Will there ever be a time when nationalism plays no role?'

'The need to distinguish oneself from others is mind-boggling,' agrees Erich. 'That's why I've always rejected football. The only purpose of international matches is to fuel nationalism. Why should I just play for "my country"? Especially these days.'

'The only positive thing is that there is still an Austria, at least here in the camp.'

The cultural differences between Austrians and Germans cannot be explained away by cut-and-dried anti-nationalistic attitude. The punctuality and correctness of the Germans, the Austrians' addiction to titles (the camp is full of men with doctorates, who insist on being addressed as 'Dr') and the love of the Viennese for meandering conversation often constitute a source of merriment and sometimes of irritation.

Otherwise, the internees are getting used to the heat of the day and the cold at night. They learn to observe the upside-down starry sky, and the various small creatures that inhabit the camp – scorpions, giant spiders, ants, grasshoppers and flies upon flies upon flies – become part of their everyday lives. One of the men, to whom flies are particularly drawn, has long since given up trying to drive them away. When he sits out in the open and carves spoons, coat hangers, letter openers and cigarette holders from the bits and pieces of wood lying around, so he can later sell them, his naked upper body is covered with flies. He looks as if he were wearing chain mail. Elsewhere a zoologist has put together a display case in which he impales every insect that crosses his path.

In the camp there is plenty of time for spinning fantasies. For those who, unlike Erich and Otto, have no wives back in Europe to worry about, life in camp could be a paradise. You do not have to pay rent, you are clothed and fed, and you work only if you feel like it or need money to buy razor blades or to get your hair cut.

The various religious groups organise themselves, and Australian organisations of the various denominations send donations to the camp. Anyone who identifies as a Catholic, Protestant or Jew is sent a tube of toothpaste, a new pair of trousers, a football or a book, each donated by one of the charitable organisations.

'Amazing how quickly people change religion every time a new delivery of donations comes along,' says Erich with amusement.

'And now the YMCA has also donated Christmas cards. Have you seen them?' asks Otto. 'Specially designed for us. A camp with huts, barbed wire and eucalyptus trees. Each of us receives two cards.'

'The Hasidim will be really grateful!'

There are not any eucalyptus trees in the Hay Camp, and the lack of greenery makes many of the internees depressed. However, it is striking that at the edge of the kitchen barracks, where dirty water is regularly poured away, wild melons are starting to grow. So the only thing missing is water. And soon a garden group springs into being. Camp commander Sealdwell procures some seeds, and shortly a luxuriant small park has grown up around the kitchen barracks, with grass, flowers and all sorts of Australian greenery, which is enthusiastically picked. And soon they are keeping a pet there. One of the men, who was on voluntary work outside the camp, brought back one day a baby kangaroo whose mother had been shot by a sheep farmer. At night the kangaroo sleeps with the Communists in Hut 28, in a cloth pouch hanging from a bed post, and in the morning he is fed with milk from a narrow-necked bottle and hops around happily in the garden all day long. It makes them all sad to think that, one day, they will have to release the animal into the wild.

In the *Camp News*, everyday life is described and commented on with texts, poems, and cartoons. It is composed in the evenings, when the typewriter in the camp office is free, and the following morning four copies are hanging on the walls of the kitchen barracks. It is the same in the neighbouring compound, whose camp newspaper is called *The Boomerang*. Although there is initially no link between the two parts of the camp, almost identical structures develop. An Australian worker who brings the meat into the camp every day sometimes smuggles a newspaper into Camp 8, so that there is sometimes political information in the *Camp News*, and the men fight over who gets to read it.

Especially frustrating are reports from fellow internees who learn by letter of the release of their friends from British camps. They are now serving in the army and contributing to the fight against the Nazis, while the internees in Hay are seen as 'enemy aliens' and condemned to inactivity behind barbed wire while, outside, the killing goes on.

Soon Sealdwell manages to make some Australian newspapers available and Erich, as a canteen employee, has privileged access to them. By the end of October he has a good picture of the situation in London.

Camp 8, Hut 18, Hay, 31st October 1940

My dear Irene, I have just received three letters from you that you wrote in about the middle of July. Since your postcard of 7th August

I have had no news. My love, I cannot tell you how anxious I am about you. All we can do here is ask repeatedly to be reunited with our wives, but we are at the other end of the world, and it seems that they have forgotten us. I myself am well, I am getting letters and reassurance from Ludka, and we all hope you will be able to come. I'd never have agreed to travel if they hadn't promised me that you would soon follow me. Dear Irka, I'm so sorry that you have to go through all of that terror, while I am in relative safety. Maybe the day will come that I can help you. It comforts me to know that you are with friends, please say hello to them on my behalf.

Every morning I read the reports about the bombings in the newspaper and wonder where and how you spent the previous night, poor little Irka. When it gets dark here, it's a relief for me to know that in Europe the day is now dawning and the risk is somewhat less. Always remember that there is someone who loves you and whose life would be meaningless without you!

Your Erich

For the 1st to 4th November, there is great excitement in Hay. As an emissary of the British government, the Jewish banker and stock exchange speculator Major Julian Layton visits the camps and writes a report.

Hay lies in one of the most inhospitable areas of the state, the environment consists of hundreds of miles of desert practically all year round. Apparently, the unappealing region was selected so that if internees do manage to break out, they will only get as far as the river. There is a music society that organises drama performances and literary evenings (including Shakespeare and Chaucer readings), musical comedies, vaudeville, etc. I received a special invitation to a vaudeville show on Saturday evening, the 2nd of the month. One should mention that the invitation bore the monogram of the music society and the show was entitled 'Hay

Days are Happy Days'. Monogram and title were produced with a stamp elaborately carved from a potato, but the only paper available was torn from a perforated roll!

The performance was put together by mainly Jewish artists who had appeared in better times in revues and operettas and Austria and Germany. The stage is built of boards and tables, the curtains are sewn from army blankets, the footlights from jam tins and kerosene containers. The title song has been composed by Ray Martin from Vienna, the one previously known as Kurt Kohn. For days, a male girls' troupe has been rehearsing behind towels, and Sealdwell has had musical instruments, cables, bulbs, cans of paint and material for costume-makers brought into the camp.

The performance turns into a major event. The entire Australian officer corps appears in dress uniform with their spruced-up wives. For Layton and the camp's prominent personages, the first row in the kitchen barracks is reserved. Further back, the off-duty officers and soldiers take their seats. Erich gets a place in the ninth row. As a backdrop, the stage designer has brought together the most important sights of Vienna in a bewitching kitsch panorama: St Stephen's Cathedral, Schönbrunn and the Ferris Wheel, all under a glittering starry sky.

The Viennese in the audience are touched. 'Just look, it's the Steffel,' one of them sighs in the expectant silence. Laughter. On display is everything that will give pleasure to a real Viennese heart: Viennese waltzes, saucy couplets, skits, recitals, cabaret acts. Accompanied by the orchestra, one man sings 'Mei Muata was a Weanerin', which brings tears to the eyes of many of the Viennese. The presentation is in English, simply so that the guards will understand some of it too. At the end the audience stamp their feet in enthusiasm. The Australians are won over. The Commandant comes on stage and thanks them for the wonderful evening. He is all smiles, as if he himself were the director. At the end of the performance, everyone rises to his feet and joins in the British national anthem.

Layton reported that about 120 played a part in the performance, about ten per cent of the residents of Camp 8. He also mentions the 'personal problems' of the internees. They are suffering, he writes, from being labelled as 'dangerous enemy aliens'.

> 700 to 800 interns have visas for other countries, such as North and South America, Palestine, etc., especially for the USA. However, these documents are located in England, and they worry about whether they will ever get them back.

In December, it is the middle of summer in Hay. It gets hotter and hotter by the day. At least now they have all been given hats, but the skin of most of them has long since taken on the colour of rust-brown earth. Every movement requires energy. During the day it is impossible to hang about in the tents. Around midday, strange mirages arise; the nearby Murrumbidgee River bursts its banks, and the rubber trees are lapped around by blue waves. Towards evening the mirage dissolves. Then eerie hurricanes sweep through the camp and disappear in the distance. Water is rationed. After lunch, most doze, wherever they can find shade. At night they roll about sleeplessly on their bunks, tormented by heat, the high-pitched buzz of mosquitoes in their ears and the fear of the itching that lies in wait.

One night heralds a change in the weather. The men cannot sleep, breathing is difficult. In the morning, arms and legs are like lumps of lead. The sun is covered by a thin layer of gauze that gathers to a dark cloud and turns the sky blue-grey. There is an eerie silence, even the parrots are silent. Around noon, the sky turns first orange, then dirty red, and suddenly a storm comes howling up, bathing the sky in deep black. It's like the end of the world. The earth seems to stand up, as if it wanted to fly away. Enormous amounts of fine red sand and black soil are spun through the air. The sand trickles through every crevice of the huts until everything is covered with a thick red layer. It enters ears and noses, glues eyes, crunches between the teeth, pricks the skin as if with thousands of tiny needles. The men are scared they are going to suffocate. Everyone protects himself as best he can. Then, in a single second, the nightmare is over. There is another moment of profound silence, then it starts to rain. The men storm out of the huts, hold up their sweaty, sand-caked faces against the sky, open their dried and sticky mouths and applaud, as if they were at the theatre. The welcome damp rattles down as if from full buckets.

Then a huge cleaning-up session gets underway in the huts.

The next day, the air shimmers as before, and even the flies are back. Those with heart problems, and asthmatics too, have a hard time of it.

At the beginning of December, the British Secretary of Homeland Security announces that the deportation of the internees to Canada and Australia had been a mistake. The men in Australia already know from the newspapers that in London their fate has led to noisy clashes in the House of Commons, that church figures, human rights activists and Democrats are pushing for a revision, and yet they feel abandoned by everyone. They have been shipped to the extreme end of the world and people now hope, so they believe, that they will fall off the edge and disappear into

Hades. Many cannot accept the injustice that has befallen them. Others treat it with a sense of humour. Oswald Volkmann, one of those shipped to Australia on the *Dunera*, writes a poem in which he calls himself and his comrades, 'His Majesty's most loyal internees'.

We have been Hitler's enemies
For years before the war,
We knew his plan of bombing and
Invading Britain's shore.
We warned you of his treachery
When you believed in peace,
And now we are His Majesty's
Most loyal internees.

We left in search of liberty
The country of our birth,
We thought to live in Britain was
The finest thing on earth,
You gave us hospitality
When we gave guarantees,
And now we are His Majesty's
Most loyal internees.

When war broke out, we tried to help
The British war effort,
We could not join, but volunteered
For jobs of any sort,
In our registration book
They stamped 'Refugees'
That's why we are His Majesty's
Most loyal internees.

When Hitler's troops in Rotterdam
Came down by parachute,
And everybody panicking
The thing became acute,
We were with wives and families
Arrested by police,
So we became His Majesty's
Most loyal internees.

They told us not to be afraid
We might be back at night,
We were not prisoners at all
And would be soon all right,
But after weeks of promising
They sent us overseas,
Although we were His Majesty's
Most loyal internees.

The Censor hinders me to tell
The story of our trip,
It is sufficient when I say
Dunera was the ship,
MPs discussed in Parliament
How ere had sailed the seas,
Yet we remain His Majesty's
Most loyal internees.

And here we are, without the means
Of proving our case,
Behind a strongly guarded fence
In a forgotten place,
We wait while the authorities
Consider the release,

Because we are His Majesty's
Most loyal internees.

The lawyers in the camp draw up petitions for the release or return of the wrongfully imprisoned men, and these petitions are discussed in Parliament, right down to the last comma. A letter to Earl Lytton, the Chair of the Advisory Board for the examination of the situation of the interned refugees, points out the paradox that in England they count as German citizens, even though they have all been persecuted by the Nazi regime and ninety per cent of them are Jews, to whom German citizenship has long been denied. The document complains that the men are not regarded as refugees, but as prisoners of war, with all the attendant restrictions, and concludes with a number of suggestions on how the internees' life can be made easier.

Anyone who has friends or family in England bombards them with requests to write to the government, the Jewish community, the churches, and the political parties. They feel that only the camp commandant understands them. He now supports all artistic and academic initiatives that will help to drag the men out of their enforced idleness, he helps to establish connections to Australian universities, and he purchases teaching materials and examination papers. Anyone who is ambitious enough to overcome the inertia caused by the heat goes to the camp school to cram for his future matriculation examination, while others attend the camp university to work towards their exam in economics, philosophy, law or science. In the evenings, after his working day, Erich takes a French course in the canteen.

Camp 8, Hut 18, Hay, 17th December 1940

My dear Irene, Thank you for your letter of 29th September. How relieved I am that things are going relatively well for you in the country, and how glad to finally have a photo of you. Many people here know Welwyn Garden City and tell me that, in times of peace, it was a very pretty place. My love, my heart is full of sorrow, and I must tell you that I will never get used to life without you. The hardship in this terrible time is easy to bear, if you have a true friend and comrade at your side. Now we have to shoulder our worries alone, and I will not stop thinking of you until we are together again. The days, weeks and months are wasted time. It's a meaningless life that is lived only in terms of the future. The only people I share my worries with are your relatives in Sydney. In their frequent letters, they describe the peaceful life of their small family. The boy is growing rapidly, already starting to speak, and needs to be supervised all day long, because he is constantly climbing on chairs and trees. It's difficult for a prisoner to imagine that, somewhere in the outside world, something like a normal life exists, with children and things that gave us pleasure too, in times gone by.

I often imagine where you are and what you're doing. Then I tell myself that you're already close to me, and so nurse an illusion that keeps me going for hours, sometimes even days. This way, I can stand up straight, and I do not want to think that this letter will reach you in Welwyn. They will keep their promise, certainly. I picture the moment when we will have each other again, the days and weeks in which we will tell each other about our experiences. That time will come, until now we have simply mastered every difficulty in life. From your sister I hear that things are fine with your parents, your brother and his wife in Warsaw. They have enough money, she writes, and suffer no hardship, even though life is pretty hard.

My dearest Irka, I beg you once again not to lose heart and to take good care of yourself for my sake. Your photo is now hanging over my 'bed', and I look at it often. It is a comfort to me and helps me

209

to endure the gruesome 10,000 miles that separate us. A job as an accountant at our camp store, that we call the canteen, helps me pass the time that is not pleasant behind barbed wire, even if we are well treated and fed.

Your Erich

CHAPTER TWENTY-THREE

Christmas. Behind the barbed wire, the air shimmers purple along the dead straight line of the horizon. A few crows have found their way into the camp. Just before Christmas, the internees are for the third time vaccinated against typhoid. They apathetically wait for the evening. There is no question of physical activities. Even reading is difficult. The camp university and school are on holiday, as nobody can concentrate any more. Nevertheless, in the evening there is a Christmas concert with a choral work by Orlando di Lasso, arias from Mendelssohn's oratorio *St Paul*, and excerpts from a mass in C major attributed to Mozart. The watercolour picture on the programme shows, together with a Christ figure, a choir loft with audience. Christians and Jews listen intently, Christmas and Hanukkah go well together for the secularists, but the Hasidim stay away. Many huts are decorated to celebrate the day with silver paper, candles and eucalyptus branches. They have even managed to produce a camp wine from raisins, to wash the food down. Late in the evening, they strike up Communist marching songs.

The Catholic hut celebrates a midnight mass, whose sounds waft over to Camp 7, where only Jews are housed.

Camp 8, Hut 18, 24th December 1940

My dear Irene, how sad Christmas is this year, but your letter dated 29th October cheered me up a bit. If there is no way for you to come here, I prefer to make the return journey. People talk a lot about our

being freed, and an official from the Home Office is coming to explore
our situation. Thanks for the three pounds. You shouldn't send me
any money, you need it more than I do. I write almost every week and
wonder if the letters are even reaching you.

Here it is very hot, but I can stand the 43-degree temperature we
had recently. Darling, I'm sure our separation will not harm our love
and friendship. Please do not worry too much and stay cheerful until
we meet again and begin a new life. I think of that all day long.

Your Erich

Because of the heat, the Sergeant Major allows his internees out for an excursion to the Murrumbidgee River, a
tributary of the mighty Murray River, which crosses the
entire south of the continent. For most of them, it is a first
opportunity to experience the world outside the barbed
wire fence. They are greeted by a flock of white cockatoos
with yellow crests that fly away screaming over their heads.
While the other young men enjoy themselves noisily in
the water making noise and squirting water at each other,
Max lies dreamily on his back. Through the silvery leaves
of the rubber trees, the sun glistens. Lying under a tree,
sunlight filtered through leaves, the interplay of light and
shadow – how long it has been since he has seen the like.
Otto gives him a worried look. The boy is too quiet. Often
he has observed him in the evenings, walking back and
forth along the fence like a caged wild beast, over and over
again around the camp. Otto sits next to him.

'Do you know that these red gum trees are called
"widow-makers"? Their branches have the peculiarity
that they snap off without warning. One of the guards
told me. So take heed.'

Max does not respond.

'Max, tell me what's wrong.'

'Nothing. Everything's fine. I just don't want to swim.'

'There's something else, I can tell just by looking at you. Come on, out with it.'

Max smiles sadly, blinking into the leaves.

'You must be missing a girl. We're all missing girls. Just being with men is no joke. I haven't heard any news of my wife for a long time. I don't even know if she's still alive.'

'No, no, it's really not that.' Max is silent. Then violently: 'Did you hear how the Communists in Hut 28 beat up the grey-haired homo?'

'No. Why? What had he done to them?'

'Apparently he came on to one of them. Maybe, but I rather think they just don't like him because he's not like them. Because he's not interested in women.'

'Being interested in women – well, there's not much use in that here. I envy anyone who has another option.'

Max blushes. 'I don't do anything.'

'Congratulations!'

'But it's hard.'

'What's hard?'

'Do you know Simon?'

'The guy with the green eyes? A pretty lad.'

'He reads poetry.'

'Yes, and?'

'Nothing else. He reads poetry. I've noticed. And he doesn't play football.'

'That's to his credit.'

'I like him.'

'Wonderful! Have you told him?'

'No. I don't trust myself.'

'But you're outside the camp all day. Have you got talking to each other?'

'No, I always run away when I see it.'

'Hmm.'

'I...'

'Yes?'

'I didn't know I was like that.'

'Like what?'

'That I like boys. It messes my head.'

'Max, it's normal. Just try it.'

For the rest of the afternoon it is impossible to get anything else out of Max. But on the same evening, Otto sees the two sitting next to each other at dinner, Max and the boy with the green eyes, their tanned arms almost touching. They do not look at each other, but the tension, the tacit understanding, is almost palpable. Otto envies them.

A strange curiosity keeps driving him back to the area near Hut 24. The residents sequester themselves away, like the Hasidim. What is going on inside? So far, Otto has never had anything to do with homosexuality, although some of his friends and students are probably from the other side, as they say. It did not interest him. But now, exposed in this universe of men, and excited by the sight of Max, who looks more relaxed and happier day by day, he cannot keep his eyes and ears off the hut. The camp, with its thousands of men, has become his world, the only one there still is. Else is far away, lost in the mists of memory. What is she up to over in Vienna? Maybe she has fallen into the clutches of the torturers on the Morzinplatz. Perhaps she is no longer alive. What is life like in the underground? She has no address. Even if he knew where she was, he could not write to her. How many years will go by before he hears anything from her?

Otto stares out at the desert and cannot imagine life in Vienna. He cannot even imagine freedom. Freedom spreads out behind the barbed wire. The desert promises everything if you dream of always heading for the horizon, and nothing if you consider it realistically. Out there in the emptiness you are nothing, for the creatures of the desert you are not even interesting as prey, for there are no predators in Australia. Without water, you are dead within a few days. You are safe only behind the fence, with the thousand men who share the fate of unfreedom and yet are so different from each other. They stake everything on being different. Each of them wants to be unique. Everyone does something to prove to himself and to the others that he is. They teach and give lectures and carve figures and rehearse with their choirs and cobble together shoes from car tyres and write poems and puff themselves up with their knowledge and their past lives, just to stay afloat in the monotony of the desert and the faceless huts. Out in the world, millions are being tortured and murdered, while they sit around in the sand and think up activities that will stave off boredom. They play cards and chess, play music, draw, declaim, talk about sex and women, fondle their starved bodies and plan a socialist world.

To kill time, Otto learns from some internees to make woodcuts, a technique for which one only needs a block of wood, a few simple tools and black shoe polish. Sometimes Jakob comes and joins them. But mostly he has other things to do. The cabinetmaker has come up with the bright idea of building a violin out of eucalyptus wood. His first experiences with foreign wood were when he made a bookcase. It is hard and dry and is easily cracked, like chestnut.

'Certainly not the ideal wood for a violin, but here you have to make do', he confides his plans to Otto. 'With a little good will and luck I can use my eucalyptus wood to build the base, sides, neck and scroll.'

What he still needs is the wood for the cover, something that needs to be more flexible than eucalyptus as it must be able to vibrate. One day he comes up to Otto's wood-cutting group, beaming all over; in his arms is a piece of wood that he has found in the vicinity of the hospital.

'What's that wood?' asks Otto.

'I don't know, maybe some Australian carpenter will enlighten me one day. But I think it might do the trick.'

From then on, not another word is to be got out of Jakob.

'Isn't it fantastic?' says Erich, as he walks past Jakob on his evening rounds with Otto. Jakob is working feverishly against the waning of the last daylight. 'I envy him. Apart from reading I don't have any hobbies. While you draw and Ray Martin composes and Jakob carves and the boys belt out their songs, I'm sitting in the canteen and writing orders in block letters. The books that I order from Angus & Robertson, in Sydney, are still the most interesting. The lists are getting longer. If everyone doesn't privatize their books, we'll soon have got together a considerable library. David Low's comic books *Europe since Versailles* are becoming especially popular, recently I ordered eighteen numbers. Otherwise, I calligraphy our latest cheap deals: flannel pyjamas ten shillings and sixpence, dressing gowns seventeen shillings, vests one shilling and seven pence, sweaters fifteen shillings, socks two shillings and twopence. What a creative activity! I also write to Irka in the most beautiful handwriting I can, because it makes her happy. Three months later.'

'You should be a politician,' says Otto. 'You have a gift for it.'

'I would rather be a journalist, a political commentator.'

Otto wonders briefly whether he should talk to Erich about Max, and decides against it. Erich pulls a letter from his pocket. 'Here, read this, Irka's written. Imagine, this letter took less than two months! What speed! She's got a new job. Or had. Today is 3rd January, things might have changed. There is no simultaneity, no point at which we can meet. We jump back and forth as if in a time machine.'

Otto takes the letter and reads.

14 Hillside Road, St Albans, Herts., 7th November 1940

My dear boy, since Monday I've been working as a domestic housemaid, after seven months of freedom I'm back on the treadmill, this time in much more unpleasant circumstances because it's without you. I have quite a lot of work, but otherwise it's not bad here, upstairs I have a nice room to sleep and downstairs another one for sitting and reading, between 2 and 4 p.m. it's perfectly peaceful, and I have every Wednesday and Sunday off. In the mornings I have to clean, and in the afternoon I cook the evening meal. There's a beautiful big mansion with five people who aren't prickly and also lend a hand. Every morning a cleaning woman comes, so I don't even have to do a lot of the rooms. But the loneliness is awful, I have no one to speak to and a longing for you which keeps me awake half the night crying. The wail of sirens reaches us because St Albans is just twenty miles away from London. At night I hear the guns and the horrible sound of the German pilots. But it's better than London anyway. There I had a bad time.

I love you, never forget that.

Your Irka

'Be happy,' said Otto, 'you hear from Irka at least now and again. I can't even imagine Else these days. Maybe she's in jail, maybe she's dead, maybe she's already fled. No, that can't be the case or they'd have written to me. Maybe she wants nothing more to do with me, in such extreme conditions, people change. Who knows.'

'I admire your calm,' says Erich.

CHAPTER TWENTY-FOUR

As promised, Irka writes a letter every week, and Erich does the same.

14 Hillside Road, St Albans, Herts., 12th November 1940

Dear Erich, I'm still waiting for a letter from you. I'm fine, for the first time in my career as a domestic I don't feel like a servant, I even have my own radio they've given me. If I were with you, it would be a really nice place to work. Without you, I often don't know what to do with my evenings, it's so dark by six, and when there's an air-raid warning, you don't want to go out.

Sunday was my birthday, a lonely occasion. No one wished me happy, and anyway maybe it's my last. No, no, that's silly talk! But do ask over there why they won't let me come, I can't figure it out here. Now I speak quite good English. Arthur, who I met a few weeks after your departure, was impressed. I'm really proud, since Arthur knows what he's talking about.

Your Irka

14 Hillside Road, St Albans, Herts., 25th November 1940

My dearest Erich, after months of waiting, finally a card from you. I was so happy that I did not know whether to laugh or cry. But why didn't you write before 5th October? It is so wonderful to get a letter, to know that somewhere far away is a husband who is longing for me as much as I am longing for him. I'm so glad that you miss me. Unfortunately, we'll be writing a lot more letters, as I definitely won't be coming to join you so soon. Meanwhile, too much has happened, and promises are not kept today. Promise me that you will not lose your good temper. You have company, and your life is not in danger – what could be more important? How happy I'd be to have people around me. In my spare time I read books and newspapers, I knit and I paint Christmas cards. Do you remember earlier Christmases? At that time everything seemed so sad to us, but it was wonderful because we were together. Don't worry about my financial situation. I still have about twenty pounds, and I've been working for three weeks and as ever I get 1 pound a week. For your birthday, I sent you a telegram and I'll send you another one, because I know how important it is in this terrible time. When we're together again, I'll tell you lots of stories about the fantastic attitude of the British.

How nice my sister is writing to you. Yes, Ludka leads a peaceful life. Enviable. You can't imagine how tired I am of my adventurous life, my love. I was born in the war, and after that things didn't get much better: revolution, racial and political persecution, loss of my home, forced emigration. And now there's another war with all its horrors. How happy we will be when we've survived it all! It's ridiculous to ask questions when you have to wait six months for an answer. You wait so long, so terribly long for a letter, and then it contains so little. I want to learn so much about your life or at least imagine it between the lines. Please answer: did you receive my package that I sent you to Huyton? Do my letters that I write almost every week arrive? Did you get the money? Let me know what your life is like there. Can you wash properly? Do you have to wear a uniform? Do you have newspapers, books or any work? Please tell me the truth, we have to do that in this country. You can imagine that I'm interested in everything. Are you well? Have you lost weight? Yesterday I discovered my first grey hair and plucked it out, with great anxiety. I do not want to be old. Hopefully I won't have changed too much when we meet again. That depends on how long this war lasts. It's a tremendous opportunity for growing grey hairs. Dearest, I have to stop now, because I have to write

220

to Puppi and Dora Mütz. My free time is always too short. I send you all my love and many kisses across the ocean. Cheer up, my boy, we're having a worse time of it than you here, and we still manage to laugh about it sometimes. But I don't think that human nature is able to adapt to such gruesome circumstances. We read about all that during the Spanish Civil War. Now we understand. But don't worry, Hitler didn't catch me in Vienna, and he won't catch me here. Maybe I can come over to you if the crossings are easier in the spring.

Your Irka

St Albans, 9th December 1940

My dearest Eri, on Sunday I went for a walk, it was a sunny winter afternoon. St Albans is a lovely town, founded by the Romans. The biggest attraction is the ancient abbey, it is said to be the world's longest cathedral. It is surrounded by beautiful old streets, and through Gothic arches you can look out at a dreamy, pale English landscape. It was nice, but you weren't with me, I was alone on this Sunday when everyone has company. Here, many internees are now being released from the camps if they can prove that they have fought for freedom and against Hitler. Already many of our friends have gone home.

Your picture is next to my bed, in it you're sitting, laughing and happy, in front of the steep Raxwand. Will we ever again go hiking in the mountains? If I go out on Wednesday, I'll send you a Christmas telegram, that is probably the best gift these days. Next time you'll get money too. Buy yourself some cigarettes. You mustn't look poor next to the others who have more. I hear that you're all allowed to write. I could actually get a lot more letters from you. Please write, I'm so looking forward to it.

Your Irka

221

Where Erich is, at the turn of the year a vaudeville show is performed, providing for lots of laughter, good cheer and optimism. The mood improves with the amount of camp wine consumed. For midnight, the organising committee has planned a bonfire on the parade square, but this is banned at the last minute because of the risk of a bush fire. The first day of the New Year is a holiday, without roll call or camp inspection.

At the other end of the world Irka receives a shattering piece of news from the office of the High Commissioner for Australia in London:

Regarding your question, I have to tell you that the Australian Government has decided not to allow the wives and children of internees who were not interned in this country into Australia. The Home Minister continues to be committed to these women, but the Australian government has so far not changed its original decision.

St Albans, 2nd January 1941

Eri, Eri, so now we know. Too bad that we didn't know a few months ago. Maybe we'll spend the whole war apart. But don't worry, if I survive everything here, we still have a few years of happiness before we get old. I'm not doing too badly. At the beginning of the Blitz I had a bad time, like everyone, they were the most terrifying nights of my life, but my nerves are obviously weaker than those of the English. The people in this country have demonstrated real heroism. Even I have got used to the sound of enemy aircraft over my head, the crack of the guns and the wailing of the sirens, and even to the bombs. I lie in bed, and these noises go past me all night long, but I don't feel any danger. However, I live in the countryside. We hear the

222

sirens, but mostly we are spared the bombs. There is so much misery in this war that I almost feel ashamed to think of my own grief.

But sometimes I think I just can't bear the loneliness any longer. I think of you, dream of you, my whole life belongs to you. They are playing 'My Whole Heart Is Yours' on the radio, they shouldn't do that, they really shouldn't, it brings back too many memories. That time in Vienna with Zippa, at the beginning of our love. Here I have no friends, on my day off I go to the pictures or for a walk, in the afternoon, because in the evening you can't leave the house because of the darkness and the air raids. Yesterday I was in Welwyn Garden City at the home of a Belgian family I've made friends with. They have two children, and it's all noisy and cheerful there. The woman is a French woman from Alsace and speaks perfect German. But I do not need German, as I'm now fluent in English. Why don't you write about your life? I have no idea what you get up to all day long. Do you have any friends? Are the Baswitzes nice? Are you learning English or any other languages? Do you have books, games, good company? Darling, don't worry about my nights. I spend them in a very comfortable bed in a room on the ground floor (which is supposedly safer), with a hot water bottle. The only inconvenience is that you're not with me. In London, I spent a night in the tube. It was very dirty, noisy and quite funny. One woman said to me, 'If I give you a push with my foot, and you don't budge, I'll take my shoes off.' First I saw no reason to move. But when she did what she'd said she would, I was knocked backwards, and so were a lot of other people. 'This is worse than a bomb!' people shouted. 'A secret weapon!' The Cockneys have an amazing sense of humour. In Kensington, Gusti told me, there's a poster hanging on a half-destroyed door, promising 'business as usual… but please use the door.' Isn't that sweet? You start to really love these people for their composure, their solidarity and humour.

Today I have a lot of free time since nobody's home for lunch, that's why I can write you such a long letter. I type very slowly. You'll

223

certainly enjoy using this little typewriter, once you get the chance. It's yours. You probably won't have any time for me, because you'll only be interested in the typewriter. I don't use it often, so it will be new and in good shape for you.

Your Irka who loves you

Camp 8, Hut 18, 4th January 1941

My dearest Irka, I have just received your letter from St Albans, it took seven weeks to get here even though you sent it by airmail. In addition to the three letters to Huyton that were forwarded to me, I have received one airmail postcard, one telegram, six letters and three pounds. From your telegram of 11th December I gather, to my surprise, that my numerous letters have not arrived. You should have received five airmail postcards and five normal letters, as well as several official communications. It depresses me that not even my words reach you during this difficult time. Twice I've written to Bloomsbury House and asked them to forward my letters to you, because at the time I had no address from you. I'm very glad that your letters get here, and wait for them week after week. It's good that you've found a job that will shorten the waiting time for you. I'm confident they'll keep their promise and send out our wives. This intention was also recently confirmed by the representative of the Home Office in the House of Commons.

I spent the end of the year feeling reflective. In my thoughts I was with you, and I reviewed our previous life. Once again, you are the one who has to make the biggest sacrifices, and I'm ashamed I can't help you. As for my life, there's not much to report, it's empty, as life can only be for a man cut off from his loved ones and worried about them. What will the future bring, how long will this existence last? We can only try to make the best of it. We eat plenty and well, and every fortnight we're allowed to bathe in the nearby river. It's very hot, but then there are pleasant times when the temperature falls. I can't tell you anything about the country that we so longed for, because I don't get to see any of it. A large part of our problems would be solved if we could be together, even in these circumstances. But all hopes seem to dissolve into thin air, and now I think of returning if there is any possibility, because it is unbearable for me to stay separated from you, perhaps for years to come. Write and tell me what you think about this.

Your Erich

St Albans, 12th February 1941

Dearest, I'm surprised that you still think I will be able to join you. The Home Office has written to me that the Australians don't want this. So you have to do something, I can do nothing here but wait and hope.

Your Irka

Camp 8, Hut 18, 14th February 1941

Dearest Irka, this week I had the opportunity to do a bit of gardening outside the camp, and I was be impressed by the beauty of the vegetation – these splendid flowers and the palm trees! We're having a very cool summer. I've been wearing a sweater for a week, and at night I'm glad of the winter coat that I carefully tuck myself in with. But the weather can change suddenly, and tomorrow it might already be 43 degrees in the shade. Again, there is much talk of a return to England, a civil servant is supposed to be travelling from London, but no one knows anything for sure.

Dearest little Irka, I'm writing this letter in the only nice, quiet place in the canteen. It smells of coffee, soap and fruit, but it's rather cosy, compared to our hut that I have to share with twenty-seven men. It's late, and I wish you a good night, or rather good morning! I miss you, Irka, and I love you very much, I just wanted to tell you that before I go.

Your Erich

The next day, Erich orders in the canteen 150 copies of the Penguin paperback *The Internment of Aliens* by François Lafitte, in which the young author sharply criticises the British government's treatment of refugees from Nazi Germany. There is a great press of people at the public readings in the camp. Since the book came out in September 1940, the UK government has revised its policy and now sees the internees in a kinder light. In British and Australian government circles, the matter is discussed, and the refugees in Category C are no longer described as 'enemy aliens' but as 'friendly enemy aliens'. This nourishes the hope of married internees that the Australians will state they are willing to allow in their wives.

St Albans, 19th February 1941

Erich, I long so for you and will never forget you! You are everything in my life, my dream, my ideal, the best, sweetest husband who has ever existed in the world.

Your Irka

Camp 8, Hut 18, 20th February 1941

My love, I think of you so often, that I lose sight of the sober reality from view. I see the pretty little room where we lived in London, I think of our walks and talks in Hyde Park, and all the events of recent months seem so unreal that it's sometimes difficult for me to sort them out myself. I'm in Australia, you're in Europe, how on earth could this happen? Sometimes I expect to wake up from a bad dream and find myself in a better reality, with you and a job and a proper life.

Now it is certain that, in the next few weeks, we are going to be visited by an official from the Home Office in order to assess the different cases again and probably to decide on the question of release. Maybe that will bring us closer to a solution of our problems, but I do not know whether the decision will mean a return to England or something else. In any case, I expect an offer for those who are married, since they are worse off than the others. I hope that the American consulate in Sydney can transfer our application from Vienna to Sydney. I'm also trying to get an affidavit, but I'm not too optimistic about that. Can you please write to your friends in the USA and ask them? Send me a copy of our application to be considered for immigration to the United States in November 1938: the date is especially important. You will find it among my papers and letters. Please write soon and tell me what you think about emigrating to the United States in the event that I manage to get an affidavit. It's terribly difficult to come to a decision, but I beg you to entrust me with all further steps. Please answer me by airmail via South Africa.

Your Erich

Camp 8, Hut 18, 28th February 1941

Irka, little one, will we be together again this year? Even if it were possible, I do not know if I should advise you to come here, because it is very dangerous. I would prefer the risk of travelling back there myself, but now everything depends on Mr Layton from London. We are waiting impatiently for him. In the meantime, we are getting used to the changed conditions of life. Actually, life here is not dead. We have built up many things that were once important to us when we were free. There is a school, a library, a social institution and an entertainment department directed by the film producer Kurt Sternberg, with a theatre that put on a pretty good revue only a week ago – 'Snow White and the Seven Hay Days', with music and lyrics by Ray Martin and Eddy Kassner. All of these activities are attempts to 'replace' the freedom denied us. The beauty of the English country-side, which you describe in your last letter, is something I really miss. We don't have a single tree and hardly any greenery. Outside in the distance groups of trees are visible, and meadows with sheep and farmhouses. But the most beautiful thing is the tropical sunsets that deploy a splendid range of colours. I gaze at it every night until the silhouettes of the eucalyptus trees disappear into the darkness and the stars of the Southern Cross and the Milky Way light up the night sky. In the morning, parrots with bright wings fly over from the Murrumbidgee and come squawking over our huts. That's all I can see of the beauty of the country. I'm familiar with it from books that I read with great interest, I know the main streets in Sydney from photos in the newspaper. I'll probably never get to see any of it.

Your Erich

'Have you seen this?' Otto has come running up, clutching a banknote. 'Erich, have a look at this! It's incredible.'

'Ah. A banknote.'

'A banknote, a banknote… But what a banknote! Take a closer look!'

'A note worth two shillings. And look at all the things on it! A kangaroo, an emu, a sheep. And around it – barbed wire. Is this our new money? I'd better go and change all mine in the canteen.'

'Unfortunately, we have to go on using our humble potato to print them. These notes are only for Camp 7, it's written on them. Georg Teltscher designed them, he's quite a well-known Bauhaus artist. An Austrian, too. Look really closely: in the barbed wire border are some hidden words: "We are here because we are here because we are here." And the serial numbers match the registration numbers of the internees. I'd never have spotted them of course, if Teltscher hadn't written to me. One of the guards brought me the note with a short letter in an envelope. Look at the back! The twenty-five sheep stand for the twenty-five cabins in Camp 7, and in their wool you can read the names of the hut fathers.'

'Clever! It seems amazingly authentic. Who printed them?'

'The printing press of the *Riverine Gazette* in Hay. Whether they had to pay for it, or whether it's a generous donation, I can't say. There are also notes in denominations of sixpence and a shilling, each in a different colour. Apparently, several thousand have been printed. The quality is truly exceptional. You could take it for real money, couldn't you?'

All three notes bear the date of 1st March 1941. Because they are easily mistaken for genuine banknotes and also include the indication that they can be exchanged for real Australian money, they are soon withdrawn, destroyed or invalidated by a red stamp. Later on, all Australian internment camps are given as currency five different chips with holes in the middle.

Camp 8, Hut 18, 11th March 1941

My love, the days are here already chilly and the nights are getting really cold. I am really grateful that you persuaded me to bring my winter coat with me. The climate goes from one extreme to the next, but overall it is not too bad. Ludka wrote to say she recommended you take steps to regain your Polish citizenship, which could make it easier in certain circumstances for you to get a permit. I can't take all this too seriously, but who knows. We are waiting for Mr Layton.

Erich

Under the direction of Hamburg Kapellmeister Kurt Behrens, in March a Beethoven evening is organised. The Prisoners' Chorus from Fidelio leaves a strong impression. 'Oh what joy, to breathe easily in the fresh air! Only here, here alone is life, the dungeon is a tomb.' In the *Camp News* appears an emotional review, in German. 'Twice over did we hear the cry of the imprisoned, arising from the powerless stagnation of an unjust incarceration to a plea for freedom. A ray of light shone on their faces – the light of Beethoven. Its lonely glimmer outshines the darkness of the time that is growing ever deeper and denser, the more it is illuminated by the glow of the blazing cities in Europe.'

Camp 8, Hut 18, 19th March 1941

Dearest Irka, yesterday I received your Christmas letter! Given the fact that this letter took almost a quarter of a year to reach me, I can understand your complaints about missing mail from me. In the first two months I was penniless and could not send you an airmail letter. Now I write at least once a week and always send my letters airmail via South Africa.

Now for a few lines on our situation. This country is not ready to take us in unless we are behind barbed wire. The Pioneer Corps, to which we can report for now, cannot guarantee our return to England. Emigration to the U.S. has proven to be difficult, because even under normal conditions, it is extremely complicated to get all the necessary papers paper. But there is a vague possibility that married people might be able to return to England. I'm asking you to ask your girlfriend Janka for an affidavit for the U.S., if you haven't already done so. I'm also doing my best, but as you can imagine, my options are limited. I've asked for the transfer of our registration forms for the U.S., but still received no response. Can you please write a short personal statement in which you acknowledge that you agree with my eventual emigration to the U.S.? These are all first steps that need to be taken in the event that we are allowed to emigrate. I would then go first, and you would follow. Because of the affidavit, I have written to an American Committee and I am asking you again to turn to Janka and Arnold. We shouldn't expect too much, but we should leave no stone unturned.

Your Erich

In March, *The Boomerang*, the weekly paper in the neighbouring camp, publishes a major article entitled 'Our Future', which against all misgivings preaches unlimited loyalty to England, of course, in English, 'To overcome the gigantic difficulties, we must shake off our German mentality, leave behind everything that is too obviously "continental", and adopt the English or American lifestyle. We must not be defeated, we need to beat Hitler, we need it to survive and help build a new world.'

CHAPTER TWENTY-FIVE

Julian David Layton arrives in Sydney on 24th March 1941. As commissioner for Jewish refugee organisations in England, he has been to Germany several times to prepare for the emigration of Jews. After the annexation of Austria by Nazi Germany, Layton travelled to Vienna and in early November 1938, in the crowded premises of the Jewish community, arranged with the head of the Nazi immigration authority, Adolf Eichmann, for the emigration of 3,500 Jews. His arrival in Australia is eagerly awaited, and not only by Erich.

Promptly, the Australian Defence Minister Spender hastens to assure his countrymen that Layton will not be allowed to open the door to a horde of aliens. 'If the British government wants to release these foreigners, this should be done only under the condition that they will be sent back to Europe. They will not allowed to move freely around in Australia.'

In Hay, Layton is first greeted by a hurricane and then by an uncooperative Australian army officer. As he had done a few months earlier, he judges the camps in Hay to be completely unsuitable for Europeans, and takes measures to move the detainees to Tatura in Victoria, where more pleasant climatic conditions prevail. He also offers to repatriate those who agree to join the Pioneer Corps. In the camp, recruitment lists are hung up for men between eighteen and fifty who are physically fit, though 'minor disabilities' and short-sightedness are not an obstacle. They will be sent back for non-military service in the UK or elsewhere, at government expense. About 400 internees report immediately. Another 200 other men whose wives had been supposed to follow them are assured they will be able to return, provided a suitable sea passage can be found.

Camp 8, Hut 18, 3rd April 1941

Irka, the official I wrote to you about arrived here about a week ago, and we just had to fill out a few forms, which were then sent to Sydney. I have knocked on the door of our emigration to the United States, with little hope.

Erich

Camp 8, Hut 18, 17th April 1941

Mr Layton's visit has ensured that married men are given the promise they will be able to travel back to England as soon as a suitable ship's passage is available. This may take a long time, and Layton has asked us to keep our hopes on a low flame. The return trip is voluntary and is on condition of another period of internment in an English camp until every case has been investigated individually. I would like to know what you think about it. Please confirm you've got my letters because I never know which letter you've received, and so I repeat myself more often than necessary. I'm still trying to emigrate to the U.S., but I have little hope, actually I have no hope at all. Also, the traffic to England is uncertain, given the circumstances. I'm still in hospital with my tonsillitis, but I'll soon be allowed to get up and about, and hope to be out in a few days. I've enjoyed the luxury of a proper bed, a reminder of earlier times. The whole life here is getting on my

nerves. But there is no reason for despairing, separation can last only
so long.

Your Eric

On the day when Erich writes this letter, the inmates are asked to fill in triplicate forms in the presence of a justice of the peace for compensation for items 'lost' on the *Dunera*. Erich notes his Waterman fountain pen, his Doxa watch and the leather briefcase from Vienna. The men have the impression that things are finally starting to move and the internees are being taken more seriously.

Camp 8, Hut 18, 2nd May 1941

Emigration to the U.S. seems to be out of the question, and anyway it would be meaningless if you weren't with me. So I've registered on the list of those who want to travel back to England. Otto has decided to do the same. Now that's done, I've been much calmer. This terrible distance between you and me needs to be made shorter. Even so, it may be a long time until we meet again, but if I hadn't done this, I'd definitely have blamed myself later for missing out on the opportunity.

Your Erich

St Albans, 5th May 1941

Erich, please consider your decision carefully. I'm glad if you're safe and sound over there. The crossing must have been horrible, I recently read about it in the newspaper again. And now you'd have to do the whole thing all over? Life here is not particularly pleasant. If only I could be with you! It's a shame I don't have a baby, then I would have something of yours. If I'm not already too old, I could still have one. I'm crazy, aren't I?

Your Irka

At the instigation of Major Layton, the first group is taken to the Tatura camp before sunrise on 5th May. A large crowd gathers at the camp gate to watch as the luggage is loaded onto trucks and its owners jump on after it. Followed by many shouts of 'hallo!' and wishes for a better future, the men disappear gradually on the horizon while, in Hay, a new day dawns.

Erich still cherishes a faint hope of emigration to the United States and is glad to stay in Hay for the time being. Some of the men who had their papers with them have already left, most to the U.S., others to Palestine or even to Cuba. Gradually the camp empties. It is autumn.

Camp 8, Hut 18, 8th May 1941

Irka, dearest, here it is now getting quite cold, especially in the evening, at night and in the early morning. I wear flannel underwear, two sweaters, my jacket and sometimes the winter coat. In the daytime it sometimes gets really hot again, so you have to change several times a day. Compared with the continental climate in Europe, it's not really cold, but you feel it more because the temperature difference between day and night is so great. Today the weather changed, the first rain in many weeks, it's pouring with tropical violence. When it rains, it feels like home, because we mainly have blue skies and sunshine. I long for snow and mountains. The rain has turned the camp into a lake, it looks really romantic.

Liebste, you shouldn't complain about getting older, we all do from the day we're born. And you're thirty-one so you have no reason — I'm already turning forty. I envy you your youth. I'm not joking!

Your husband who loves you

CHAPTER TWENTY-SIX

Towards the end of April 1941, Londoners can breathe a sigh of relief, as Hitler seems to have lost interest in operation 'Sea Lion'. The pilots of the Spits and Hawkers have done a great job, the invasion of Britain has failed. The priority for the Germans is now 'Barbarossa', the attack on the Soviet Union. The culmination of eight months of devastation in Britain is a week of violence launched against Liverpool, Glasgow, Sheffield and Hull. After that, only a symbolic proportion of the Luftwaffe is to remain in France as a base. But on 8th May the Royal Air Force retaliates. Nearly 400 bombers attack Bremen and Hamburg. The casualty figures are low compared with what was inflicted on British cities in recent months, but Hitler is foaming at the mouth.

On 10th May, the sun shines golden in the morning high in a clear blue sky, it is just unusually cold for the month of May. Irka has got up early, as usual, she has to prepare breakfast. Her family wants to set off at nine, to spend the weekend with relatives on the coast. As soon as they have left the house, Irka also gets ready to travel. She stuffs her documents, make-up and a clean pair of knickers into her purse and decides to spend the weekend in London. Since Käthe has moved away, there's a free room in Primrose Mansions that she can use any time. She could go to the pictures with her girl friends, as a few days ago the double summer time was introduced, so it is light until ten o'clock in the evening. This Saturday, the blackout does not begin until 10.21 p.m. The Londoners catch up on their lost sleep and begin to look towards the future with confidence. For three weeks there have been no more air raids. The newspapers fuel the optimism of the population and celebrate the losses inflicted on the Germans by British air raids.

Irka is in a good mood as she goes to the station. She is wearing her grey suit, the jacket of which clings to her slender body by, as usual she has her high-heeled shoes and a hat set at an angle on her head. Her lipstick is dark red. This is how Erich likes her to look. As soon as she has left the brick house, her maid's existence falls away from her. To the chirping of birds her heels clatter along the pavement. An appreciative whistle from the other side of the street enables her to hold her head a little higher.

Irka is lucky, a train is ready waiting at the platform, by eleven o'clock she has reached Victoria Station. She's going into the West End to buy something warm for Erich, as winter is just starting in Australia. She does not have much time before the battered department stores close. On Oxford Street, road builders are hard at work, the devastation of April has not yet been fully repaired, but by Monday two lanes should again be open to traffic. After a sandwich and a cup of tea in the Lyons Teashop, Irka spends a lazy Saturday afternoon in Hyde Park. Almost a year has passed since she was sitting here with Erich. That their separation would be long was something she had suspected at the time, but the invasion of Britain has failed – one more reason to rejoice in life. As it gets chillier, Irka crosses the Thames on a bus, Battersea station has been closed since it was struck by an incendiary bomb on 20th October.

At eleven o'clock at night, the first sirens wail. At half past twelve the storm breaks. After the smoke of the incendiary bombs has lifted, the Londoners can lift their eyes to a clear sky, studded with Luftwaffe bombers. Acoustically, they can be identified by their irregular drone. By desynchronizing their aircraft engines, the Germans manage to disrupt British air defence, whose guns are equipped with sonic monitors and fire only when there is a continuous roar. The whole of London goes up in flames, neither rich nor poor neighbourhoods are spared, although the inhabitants of the proletarian East End are more affected because they have neither cellars, nor Anderson shelters in their gardens.

With an ear-splitting whistle, an incendiary bomb hits two houses in the front garden and bathes the whole area in a gleaming saffron-coloured light.

'I can't take this anymore!'

'Do not be hysterical!' Dr Pollak orders Irka. 'While you retreated to your rural idyll, we've put up with this for a full two months, day and night. We've survived, as you can see. And we will also survive tonight.'

'And what's wrong with the shelter in the park?'

'You really can't trust them. We haven't been in it a single time. In October a bomb caused a massacre in Kennington Park. The shelter collapsed and the people were buried. The exact number of deaths has never been made public. Do you want to be buried alive?'

But Irka will not be stopped. When there is a break at a quarter past one, she rushes out with a blanket under her arm, crosses the road and runs over to the air raid shelter which the government had erected in Battersea Park even before war broke out.

She climbs down a wooden ladder. Halfway down, she is already greeted with the stale smell of the densely packed crowd in the unventilated underground space. Several wooden, interconnected trenches are furnished with benches, where women, children and old men sit, their gas masks in their laps. The construction is not very deep under the earth, it's easy to predict that in a bomb attack, hardly anyone will survive.

The people shift closer together to make room for Irka. In her panic, she does not notice who she sits next to. It's cold and damp underground, Irka wraps herself in her blanket. Conversations buzz around her. Despite the uproar over their heads, women knit and share recipes. Nutrition is an ongoing issue. There is little fruit, hardly any sugar, eggs only now and again. Meat, butter, flour and almost all other foods are rationed. With the slogan 'Dig for Victory!', posters instruct Londoners to create vegetable gardens in their front yards and parks.

People also tell jokes. 'Hitler's dog has no nose. – Really? How does he smell? – Terrible!'

'Two Jewish murderers lie in wait for Hitler who comes to this particular spot every day at twelve noon on the dot.' The man telling this joke is sitting next to Irka. He has a German accent. 'They've got everything they need: pistols, grenades, bazookas. It's 11.55 a.m. and the one says to the other: "Get ready." Twelve o'clock comes, but no sign of Hitler. They wonder what's happened, and meanwhile it's 12.10 and then 12.20. Then the one Jew says to the other: "He's late, I hope nothing's happened to him."'

Some of the listeners laugh. Irka turns to him and smiles. He has dark eyes and hair, but she cannot make out anything else.

Just before 2 o'clock, it gets louder again. The anti-aircraft guns, whose popping sounds like music to the ears of the British, are firing nearby. The conversations fall silent, all eyes gaze anxiously upward. Irka is gripped by an uncontrollable trembling, she presses her hands together, but this does not help. She trembles, and her entire body is immediately as if paralyzed, if anyone asked her to get up and run away, she would not be able to stir. From outside, the shouts of the firefighters and the ringing of the fire engines penetrate inside. Irka feels her heart racing. She closes her eyes.If only the shaking would stop.

'Shh, it'll be all right, calm down.' A warm hand is laid on her shoulder. Even this little contact helps to diminish her trembling. The hand grips her shoulder firmly, and the trembling stops. Irka breathes in deeply. 'I'm so sorry,' she says, 'I'm not used to it these days, I live in St Albans.'

'It's all right,' says her neighbour. 'We'll get through. We won't be licked by Hitler. No way.'

'No, we won't let him win,' says Irka, pushing a strand of hair from her face and smiling bravely.

'Let's talk,' says the man, 'that helps. My name is Leo Singer and I'm a refugee like you.'

'How do you know that I'm a refugee?'

'You can see it.'

'You can see it?'

'Yes, your eyes are different from English people's. And you can hear it too. You're from – let me guess: Hungary.'

Irk has to laugh. 'Why just from Hungary?'

'Because you're so elegant. I've never been to Hungary, but I have a good idea of the way those smart women from Budapest look.'

'And what would you say to Warsaw? After all, they say Warsaw is the Paris of the East.'

'Oh, Warsaw. They've bombed it flat. London will probably look much the same when we get out of this hole. So you're from Warsaw? Then you can be glad you're here.'

'I am indeed. I'm Irena or Irene, whichever you prefer.'

'I like Irena better. Very pleased to meet you. I'd have happily met you in different circumstances, but this is fine too. Look, those women are praying. Shall we say a prayer too? I doubt if anyone will object if we say a Shema Yisroel.'

'Pray! Are you crazy?'

'Okay, okay, it was just a thought. You probably don't have much time for religion?'

'No, none at all. I believe in the ability of people to fight for a better life in this world.'

'Right now, that's a pious wish, whether you're religious or not.'

Irka sighs. 'That's true, unfortunately.'

'Do you have family in Warsaw?'

'Yes, my parents are there, my brother and my sister-in-law.'

'You must be really worried. You never know exactly what's going on there.'

'They've sent me a telegram via the Red Cross saying they're all right.'

'Let's hope it's true.'

'Do you work in London?'

'Yes, I found a job in a print shop and so I'm working in the profession I learned. In Cologne I was a graphic artist.'

'You're very lucky. I work as a maid.'

'Don't you like that?'

'What a lot of questions! I hate it. I find it extremely difficult to accept commands, but they won't let me do anything else. I entered the country as a domestic from Vienna in '38, and a domestic worker I must remain. I had a dream job at a school, but the Labour Department didn't allow me to keep it.'

'Vienna! Ah! Another city I long to see!'

'Yes, and full of anti-Semites! I have the worst memories of Vienna. Long before Hitler it was already swarming with Nazis. I was turfed out back to my native land of Poland in 1936 for illegal political activity. A policeman took me to the border. As soon as we were sitting in the train, he pulled out a copy of the *Völkischer Beobachter*! It was still banned in Austria. A policeman! And just imagine: he left it up to me whether I got off the train or not, he couldn't care less. That was how loyal to the Austrian state he was. But I didn't want to get off, I'd had Austria up to here.'

'Interesting. So it's true that the Austrians welcomed Hitler?'

'Oh yes, and how!'

Irka is amazed that she is being so chatty. And she has found someone who understands her, with whom she does not have to pretend. In England she has met with so much ignorance and disinterest about her fate. There are crashes and bangs over their heads, but somehow they cannot hear them. She resists the temptation to lean her head on Leo's chest. And as if he has sensed her impulse, he puts his arm round her shoulder and hugs her.

'Think of all the things that could happen in a night of bombing like this! I don't live very far away. When they've finished dropping their bombs up there, I could treat you to breakfast.'

Irka does not answer, but she likes the sound of the invitation. She feels at home with the stranger even after this short time. A shared breakfast, the warmth of a hug, a test of whether she is attractive even in her old age. She dares not think about it in any more detail.

There is again a terrible thundering noise. The wooden walls shake. Sand trickles down their necks. Irka buries her face in Leo's shoulder, and he embraces her in both arms. It does her good.

'Come with me,' he whispers.

At half past four, silence falls. The people in the shelter stare quizzically at one another, unsure whether to wait or go home. They are afraid of what they will find up there.

At some point, Leo takes Irka's hand and pulls her away. She unresistingly follows.

The dawn cannot break through the thick curtain of smoke that hangs over the whole of London. Irka holds a handkerchief to her mouth. From the railroad tracks, pitch-black clouds of smoke rise to the sky and plunge this end-of-the-world scene even deeper into darkness. Over Westminster, the sky is red from the glow of the fires. In Battersea Park Road, fire hoses lie on the wet road, a house has been completely burned out. Isolated people wonder in a daze through the deserted streets.

'Come on! We'll be there soon. But if my house is no longer standing, I don't reckon much to our chances of breakfast.'

Edna Street is a cul-de-sac. It has been spared. Leo heaves a sigh of relief. 'Up there, that's my place.'

The gas is turned off, and out of the tap comes not a single drop, but there are buckets filled with water and an electric kettle. Tea and toast are soon on their way.

Irka drops into one of the two armchairs covered with flowery patterns like at Dr Pollak's, and warms her hands on a mug with the inscription, 'Mary'. The bed is right next to them, covered with newspapers. The rooms of refugees are all so alike.

Leo sits on a stool next to her. 'We're both admittedly a little worse for wear, but you're a real treat for the eyes.'

'Don't joke. I'm dead tired, I could fall asleep on the spot.'

'I'll clear some space for you on the bed.'

Fully dressed, they lie down on the bed. Leo covers Irka gently and leans her head on his shoulder. The first rays of the sun come streaming in through the window.

'So we'll get a bit of sleep and then we'll see. Okay?'

'Okay,' mutters Irka and cuddles up to him. 'I wonder if the trains are still running? How will I get back to St Albans? I've got to get back to work tomorrow.'

'But we can think about that later.'

'How quiet it is.'

'Yes. Now I'll just quote you a line from Goethe, then I'll let you go to sleep. "If to the moment I should say, 'Tarry awhile, you are so lovely!'" Nicely put, isn't it?'

'You saw my wedding ring?'

'Yes.'

CHAPTER TWENTY-SEVEN

Camp 8, Hut 18, 15th May 1941

Irka, my love, I've been so worried ever since I read in the newspaper about the terrible bombing of London. I just hope that you didn't come up with the idea of spending this Saturday of all days in London. Won't I find out for three months? An unbearable thought.

Mr Layton's visit has led to us being moved to another camp, where supposedly better conditions prevail. So everyone's storming our canteen, and I have a lot to do. I've become a real individual sales-man – another job that doesn't bring in much money – and I can sell everything that a provincial store can offer, plus ice cream, which you don't usually get there. My sweetheart, we mustn't give up our hope of seeing one another again, a small possibility of my getting back has opened up, at least I'm on the list of those who want to return. So long as nothing has happened to you in London.

Perhaps it's ridiculous to think of it at such times, but I am firmly convinced that a better future lies ahead of us, in which peace will form the basis of a shared human life, and here I am daring to utter a bold idea – a baby. It would be the greatest happiness on earth for me. What do you think?

Your Eric

Five days later, Erich and Otto are taken with the other remaining men in the Hay Camp to Tatura near Melbourne. As a farewell present, Erich as hut father receives one of Alfred Landauer's customized water-colours, signed on the back by the residents of Hut 18.

Depicted are a parrot with pink wings, an emu and two galloping kangaroos. In the background, the camp is suggested with a few strokes of the pen, like a mirage gradually fading away.

Sealdwell says goodbye with tears in his eyes. Compounds 7 and 8 will now accommodate just Italian prisoners of war.

Hut 6, Internment Camp Victoria, 22nd May 1941

Dearest Irene, your last post was dated 5th March, a sweet postcard. As you can tell from the address, I have been moved to another camp. It is much greener outside the camp, and inside there are a few trees and flowers. But it is very cold, and I'm once again glad to have the warm overcoat that you talked me into. Camp life still gets on my nerves, but my health is fine, and I'm keeping myself fit for our shared future. Oh, how I long for you and a normal life!

Your Eric

Erich and Otto soon have to leave Tatura, too. They wish they had been taken there sooner. In the less extreme climate that prevails here, the internment would be more easily endurable. But none of this is relevant now, since something incredible has happened: their return journey to Europe is imminent. Many of their travelling companions want to stay in Australia, especially the younger ones. For them, there is little reason to return, and adventure lures them. Erich and Otto take their leave of Max. He has grown in recent months, wiry, sun-tanned and confident.

They spend eight days in a filthy transit camp in Liverpool near Sydney. On 2nd June the forty members of the group are given new clothes. The men have to hand over their blue overalls and military coats. Erich gets a new pair of shoes, a brown jacket and grey trousers.

'You look quite the dandy,' says Otto.

Erich cannot help but giggle. No hand-me-down trousers in the world are long enough for Otto. When he pulls on the coat they have given him, he looks even funnier.

The next day they are all issued with felt hats. Though Layton has asked the men not to go on board as a group, their identical hats suggest the suspicion that they belong together somehow. In the evening, the paymaster comes and distributes money: two pounds for anyone who has nothing, while the 'rich' are allowed to take five pounds out of their account. They will be travelling as free passengers on parole for the duration of the voyage. The officers are already addressing them as 'Gentlemen'.

Early on the morning of 4th June, they have made great progress: bags are packed, blankets handed out, luggage given in. For a few more hours they hang around waiting. They betray a certain nervousness. Finally, it's back to war for them, they know only too well that anything can happen on their journey. And yet they are relieved that the endless waiting, the torpid paralysis, is now coming to an end.

After a short train ride they transfer to a bus that takes them to the port. Two ships are at anchor there. Erich's group is for the smaller of them, the *Largs Bay* from the Aberdeen & Commonwealth Shipping Line, a medium-sized passenger steamer. On board they are assigned to double cabins with real beds and white linen. Erich is passenger number 368.

Shortly after half past twelve, the ship weighs anchor. Erich and Otto, now provisionally free men, stand at the railing and look and look. In the anticipation of reunion with Irka, there is a feeling of sadness mixed. Erich would have liked to stay in Australia. Will he ever see this splendour again, ever feel the scorching sun on his skin, admire the long evening sunsets? He needs to fix the sight before his eyes in his memory. The Port of Sydney, the bold arch of the Harbour Bridge, the skyscrapers of the Inner City, the bustling traffic of small steam boats, palm-fringed islands and bays. And in the port lies the world's largest ship, the *Queen Mary*.

British, Australians, New Zealanders, French, and the German and Austrian returnees, soldiers and civilians, all stand on the highest points of the ship, the crew on rope ladders and masts, to enjoy the show one last time. The sailors of the 'Forces Navales Françaises Libres' sing the Resistance song 'Sous les plus beaux drapeaux'. In the distance the smoke plume of *Themistocles*, on which the second group of returnees is travelling. Gulls circle the mast.

'Farewell, Australia!' says Otto.

Both are stirred. The misery of captivity is almost forgotten.

'Again I'm setting out on a journey across the oceans, without being able to give Irka due notice.'

'And no one is waiting for me at all. I could just as well have stayed put.'

It's a journey without barbed wire, without out-of-bounds decks, without armed guards, without orders, beatings, humiliations. Erich knows that his future life, wherever it may lead him, will be full of privations, and he is determined to enjoy this luxury to the full. The *Largs Bay* has only one class, and the internees on parole can, like any other passengers, make use of all the ship's amenities. They can use the leisure areas, buy food in the canteen and eat in the common dining room. In addition to the 'Free French', there

249

is on board a group of British sailors who, it is rumoured, got into a fight with a man on the *Queen Mary* and threw him overboard, so they are going to stand trial in England. The passengers travelling in private capacities are primarily English and Scots, who happened to be in Australia when the war broke out, and are returning home to their families in London, Manchester, Glasgow and Birmingham. The trip costs 150 pounds, a sum for which an English worker would have to work up to three quarters of a year.

In the following two months, Erich develops a routine from which he deviates only in the event of a torpedoing completed. He goes for a swim in the pool each morning, then goes for a walk, has a really high-quality breakfast, plays a game of deck tennis, rests up before lunch reading a book in a deckchair, wearing a pith helmet when it is hot, and in rainy weather he is in the salon, has lunch, coffee in the smoking room, an hour's nap in the cabin, in the evening after dinner a game of chess, concert and singing in the bar. In ports with no blackout there is dancing on deck. Erich remains an interested observer, although so many ladies would have gladly been asked for the pleasure. He cannot dance, to Irka's chagrin: she was a competition standard dancer in Warsaw.

In their party, there are some musicians and actors who in the Pacific Ocean put on a Non-Stop Variety Show, with great zest – comic dialogues, Viennese songs, Hawaii melodies, Santa Lucia. It is a huge success, and further performances on behalf of the Red Cross follow, under the auspices of the Captain.

On 9th June, they reach the Cook Strait and, accompanied by a group of dolphins, approach the coast of New Zealand. They sail through a bay fringed by rocks and cliffs into the port of Wellington. There the *Themistocles* soon sails in, too, and the internees crowd along the rails to wave to each other. Erich is still happy. The sea air, the glistening water, the princely food – what a contrast to his journey on the *Dunera*.

After the piece of Austrian Alpine landscape with pine trees on the mountains and palm trees on the coast, two days later, in the endless expanse of the Pacific Ocean, they pass the International Date Line and change the calendar from Thursday to Wednesday. The Antipodes mean they have the same day, the 11th June, twice over.

On 22nd June they listen in breathless anticipation to the crackling and humming ship's radio in the smoking room, where they hear the news of Hitler's invasion of the Soviet Union. Erich suspects that this date of historic importance will be the beginning of the end of the war, and notes the sequence of courses at dinner that the evening: Consommé au Riz, Poached Kingfish with hollandaise sauce, Leeks au gratin, Cumberland pudding with custard, then coffee in the smoking room.

From now on it is always crowded in the living room when the news is broadcast on the radio, and the Communists suddenly enjoy a high reputation as a source of information about 'Russia' and the question of whether Hitler has bitten off more than he can chew by facing the Red Army. Many Communists consider the war to be won already. Although the Wehrmacht is advancing, that means nothing: the attacked party is always at a disadvantage initially. It will take a huge country like the Soviet Union a while to get moving. But then it will strike.

Despite this grim news, boxing matches and concerts with pieces by Beethoven, Schumann and Grieg take place on board.

A few days later they reach the equator, then Balboa, the entrance to the Panama Canal linking the Pacific to the Atlantic Ocean. Newspapers are brought on board. They report the capture of Minsk and Riga. Erich and Otto, like the Communists, are depressed. 'When I think that the Fascists are bulldozing everything the people in the Soviet Union have laboriously built up, I could go mad with anger,' says one of the men. But he also remains confident. The only question is: How long will it take Stalin to get into gear?

The journey through the Panama Canal, a system of dams, artificial lakes and gigantic locks, takes a full day to complete. Six electric gear engines pull the boat into the locks, three locks raise it 400 feet to the height of the dammed Gatún lake in the middle of the Canal. Not only the technology, but nature too arouses considerable enthusiasm here: dense jungle with wild bananas and exotic trees in full bloom, tropical islands that it is best not to land on because of their poisonous snakes and alligators, hundreds of steep, cone-shaped hills. Butterflies and parrots fly out of the jungle onto the ship. A parrot is captured and taken to Europe. Three locks bring the ship to the mirror-calm Atlantic. Only the moist heat gets to the passengers.

'Tens of thousands of lives this marvel of technology cost,' says Erich.

'Yes, like the pyramids. Previously, ships had to go around all of South America, what a gain in time and money this is! The path of technological progress is paved with corpses.'

Through the Caribbean they sail on to Willemstad, a Dutch town on the island of Curaçao, where the *Largs Bay* puts in for the night. Many only know this name from the blue liqueur. Everywhere in the harbour lie British tankers. A Dutch newspaper is brought on board. It reports on Stalin's appeal to the workers of the occupied countries and the acts of sabotage in the Škoda Works in Czechoslovakia.

From Curaçao, every morning a practice drill is held for emergencies. Each passenger has a card pressed into his hand, with the number of his lifeboat on it. Erich and Otto are given number 5A, located on the starboard side of A Deck. At a signal, all passengers have to gather with their lifebelts to receive instructions for the real thing. It is reassuring to know that this time, at least they will not be left to fend for themselves. On 6th July, a Sunday, the lifeboats are lowered in order to be ready for use in an emergency.

The *Largs Bay* sails along the coast of North America and on 11th July reaches Halifax in Canada, where the ship is moored for a few days. A merchant approaches in his motor launch and offers treats and items of daily use. With a fire bucket tied to a rope the items are brought onto the ship.

The peaceful tropics lie far behind them. Also, it has become cold, jackets and coats are fetched from the cabins. A convoy of seventy ships takes shape, freighters and tankers of all sizes, with the *Largs Bay* as the sole passenger ship and some frigates that circle the periphery of the convoy at high speeds, keeping watch for U-boats and indicating when the ships need to change their position in the formation.

In the notorious fog banks of Newfoundland, the passengers cannot see their own hands in front of their eyes. This lasts a full three days. The ships are brightly lit and maintain contact through foghorns that emit blasts every minute, day and night.

They give a tempestuous reception to the first British destroyer. Soon, British fighter planes can be seen circling over the convoy until the end of the journey. They are back at war.

Erich writes in feverish anticipation to Irka:

Liebste Irka, I'm back! I'm writing this on board ship at the very last moment before we land. Can you imagine how I feel at the prospect of seeing you again after so long? As I assume that you have moved in the meantime, I have no address for you, so I'll ask Bloomsbury House again to forward the letter to you. And since I don't know what they plan to do with us once we've arrived, I can't give you any address either.

I long to see you,

Eric

On 29th July, they reach the Hebrides. The passengers begin their preparations for landing. The convoy splits into two groups. The sea is smooth, the sun is shining. Erich and Otto enjoy their last hours aboard in their deck chairs. Accompanied by screeching seagulls, the *Largs Bay* sails through the North Channel and the Firth of Clyde to Glasgow, where they arrive on 1st August.

'We've had a trip round the world for free, isn't that great?' says Erich.

'I'm just curious to see what happens to us now,' retorts Otto grumpily.

When all the others have disembarked and only the interned are to be kept for one more day on board, they suspect that their time as free men is at an end.

CHAPTER TWENTY-EIGHT

Hutchinson Internment Camp, Douglas, Isle of Man, is Erich's next address.

'*Welcome back to Great Britain!*' says a special edition of the Camp P newspaper as it greets the new arrivals. That they have managed to land safely in Great Britain is the most important thing, writes chief editor Carlo Pietzner.

> *For the first days or weeks (let us pray it won't be months) you will be in this tiny domain, overlooking the sea with the English coast appearing only on days of rare light and purity of air. – It is Britain all the same. Some time more: and you will all move freely on the greater island across the sea, an island of men and women, where you'll find the barbed wire put up against the real enemy, all along the coast, against the invader whom you are going to going to fight, too, by your work and help.*

In the meantime, the cultural delegate informs them, the internees can make use of a language school and a technical school that might help them make the best use of their time in camp. And although he also wishes the newcomers as short a stay at Camp P as possible, the old 'inmates' are glad of the cultural and intellectual contribution, with which the newcomers will enrich the life in the camp. On the back of the four-page mimeographed leaflet follows information on the rights and duties of the camp residents. Twice a week, letters on official headed paper may be written, up to twenty-four lines in length. In urgent cases, additional letters are allowed, that like telegrams require the authorization of the intelligence officer. As in the Hay camp, the internees organise themselves, with a camp supervisor, two organisers and an advisory board of three persons.

The camp consists of some street districts in the island's capital Douglas that are separated off and surrounded by barbed wire. In the centre is a splendid large park with flowering bushes. Erich and Otto are assigned to house number 20.

To sweeten this new internment, on the very next day, to honour the returnees from Australia, the group from Camp P puts on *Thunder Rock*, a play by the Hollywood screenwriter Robert Ardrey. A few days later there is a performance of *The Silver Box* by John Galsworthy, a comedy with the Austrian actor Otto Tausig, later to have a very successful career in the role of Mrs Barthwick. Women's roles inevitably have to be taken by men, which only enhances the comedy.

2nd August 1941

Irka dearest, what a joy to be back in England! Since your last airmail postcard of 5th March, I've had no news from you. We are well accommodated, live in real houses, and have our own kitchen, and culturally there is a lot going on, we can even go to the pictures. You'll also be able to visit me – with the permission of the Home Office. I'm so glad to be closer to you now, so we can stay in touch more easily. Write to tell me what you have done regarding my release, I need to know, before I do anything myself. Write and tell me if you are willing to do heavy work together with me. Maybe I could work in agriculture: that would mean we would live in a hostel in Berkshire.

Your Erich

5th August 1941

Dearest Irka, hopefully you received my card and the letter I wrote immediately after my return. Now I'm waiting impatiently for some sign of life from you. I'd rather you didn't come to visit me here, because I want to face you as a free man. I'm dreaming of it day and night. In the last postcard that you wrote five months ago, you say that you would soon be working in a factory, so I suspect that you've moved. I can't decide on anything until I get a message from you. Many of the returnees have received telegrams from their wives. Please send me a couple of shillings, because I'm completely penniless.

Your Erich

Three days later, Erich receives a letter from the Germany Emergency Committee, in which a Mrs Jane Unwin tells him Irka had appeared in her office because she had heard nothing from her husband for so long.

I was glad to be able to tell her you were on the list of those who had returned from Australia.

In order to help to find a prospective employer for you I should be glad if you would give me a few more details about your experience. I see from your file that you have worked for jewellery firms, and I should like to know in what capacity. If you have actually repaired or made jewellery you would obviously be skilled with your hands. I believe too you have had a short course as a welder and I hope this may be of some help. Have you any experience of bookkeeping and shorthand or typing in your clerical work?

You will know, of course, that there is an employment exchange on the Island where you will be able to register for employment, and your wife is going to ask her present firm if they can offer work. There is a new engineering firm being started which will take all the Germans and Austrians we can provide and as soon as they have got into production with their present staff they will apply for others from the camps for training and I hope this will be before long.

I hope you have by now had news from your wife. It was a great surprise to her to know you were back, and I know how much she is looking forward to seeing you again.

8 Worley Rd, St Albans, 11th August 1941

Darling, I've got news that you will definitely be glad to hear: today I spoke with Mr Williams, my employer. He wants you to write to him. Then he asked me: 'Do you think that he can tolerate heat? It's a job in the department of heat treatment. The tools are heated to 415 degrees, bent and tempered in oil. Some of the other parts are heated to even higher temperatures.'He needs a bit of information about yourself, i.e. education, experience, etc. I told him of your three-month welding course, and he asked me if you have any knowledge of chemistry. Of course you are sufficiently qualified for this work. Please write him a nice letter. It's very hard work, hot and dirty, but other people do it, and it's not forever. You simply have to stay there as it's not allowed to change jobs. Working time is 8 a.m. to 8 p.m., I work until 7, with one hour lunch break. But the factory is not unpleasant, and I like my job. Just imagine working in the same place with me! So you'll acquire a new skill, and St Albans is a lovely town. Liebster, everything now depends on your letter, don't write too much, be modest, intelligent and clear. And please answer his question about the heat. Write straightaway, it doesn't bother me if I have to wait for a letter from you, maybe they'll also give you permission to write an additional letter. I showed him your photo, and he asked me if you're tall or short. Now I'll find out what he needs to do in order to ask you. I told him that you were a civil servant in Vienna and had to leave the country because of the Nazis.

Your Irka

12th August 1941

My dear Irka, I'm worried because I've still heard nothing from you, even though I wrote my first letter on 1st August. My return journey was very pleasant, two months' idleness, but in the end we were happy to be back in England. Some of married men have heard from their wives or from the Committee that an employer has already been found for them. Perhaps the Quakers can help. I can't tell you, little Irka, how much I long for you all the time! When I was on the ship, I imagined our reunion as too radiant, and now – after a fourteen-month separation – there is another camp between us. This is depressing.

Your Erich

14th August 1941

Dearest Irka, how glad I am that you are well and that you like your work. A request from an employer will probably be the fastest way for me to be set free. Perhaps I could also work in the area of your residence in agriculture. We just have to find an employer. I don't want you to change your job on my account, so I'm willing to take any job that will allow me to be near you. I'm also writing to Mrs Unwin to tell her that, and I'm asking you to do everything humanly possible. Just in brief: I don't need any clothes, shoes, or underwear, because I'm pretty well provided for. Also, no cigarettes, I still have some from Australia, only a few shillings, please. There's a cafeteria here where you can buy cigarettes and food. We take a daily walk in the beautiful surroundings, and sometimes go swimming, and once a week to the pictures in town. Next time I'll write more, we're only allowed a limited number of lines.

Your husband Erich

21st August 1941

Dearest Irka, I wrote to Mr Williams straightaway. I very much hope that he will ask for more, otherwise I'll be out of a job for quite a while. If he doesn't want me, I'll apply to the Committee. In the last months in Australia, we couldn't send any more airmail letters, and about six weeks before our departure we weren't allowed to even mention our return. So I could communicate to neither you nor Ludka, which I'm actually glad about, because you certainly would have worried, if you'd known that I was travelling the seven seas of this world. How happy I am to be back again, because it is atrocious to receive letters from my girl that are two or three months old, reports of feelings in the spring that arrive in the autumn, while in the place where they were written, it's already summer. Over there everything is messed up, the moon hangs upside down in the sky, in the spring there are raging sandstorms, the sun blazes all year long, while at the same time, the nights are freezing cold and the flies keep you on your toes so you can't laze around in the heat. We were treated very well, had plenty of food, butter, meat and everything else. It's a delight to be back living in a brick house, although I'd just as much live, as a free man, in a hut with you.

Eric

23rd August 1941

Dearest Irka, thank you for the package that arrived today. Hopefully you also got the chocolate and cigarettes, a poor gift that I brought you from my world trip. And what a trip it was! We saw dream lands with palm trees, high mountains and beautiful cities. But the beauty of this world is nothing to get excited about in times like these, though I often thought how wonderful it would be to experience all this together with you. Here, the cinema is a small window that gives us a glimpse into real life, and it opens once a week. Apart from my longing for you I'm fine. I had no problems with the transition to rationed food and am reading a lot, books and newspapers. Mostly I spend time in the beautiful park with its fantastic views of the sea, and now I'm just off to swim. But what good are all these amenities, if I cannot share them with you? I look forward to a life with you, even if it's harder than the previous one, I look forward to work and the opportunity to finally make myself useful.

With love, Erich

24th August 1941

Liebste, I'm sorry that I irritated you with my letters urging you to write, but I hadn't heard from you for almost half a year. Now that I know that you're fine, I have no more worries. So, Liebste, no excitement, I am prepared for the fact that things won't develop as quickly as we would like, but this is unfortunately inevitable. Don't imagine I hold you responsible when I express the wish to finally leave this camp life behind me. For our wedding anniversary I send you my most tender wishes and my longing for our life filled with love together in the future.

Your Erich

A few days later, Mr Williams writes to Erich, saying that he is asking him to work at his factory as an oxyacetylene welder and toolmaker. For a week's work of forty-seven hours, he offers him a weekly starting wage of three pounds, and if Erich like the other workers does overtime, he could make this up to four pounds a week. 'We expect,' writes Mr Williams, 'that you will put your heart and soul into this new work. After your return to ordinary family life, there should be no reason why you should not be happy in St Albans.'

Even before this letter reaches Erich, Irka has sent him a telegram to tell him of the good news. Now it is up to Erich to apply to the Home Office for his release.

1st September 1941

Dear Irene, I'm very pleased with the way things are developing, and although I am still emerging from a long internment, I can see light at the end of the tunnel. Without Australia I would have already been free for a long time. How happy I am to be back in England! Over there I felt rather lost. There is so much I can look forward to here, not just you and freedom, but also my new typewriter. A few words about my life here: once a week I leave the camp to do heavy digging work, so I earn two shillings. The island is incredibly beautiful, and our job is half an hour away from the camp. The vegetation and the green hills especially make those of us from Hay happy. The rest of the week I spend reading, playing chess, doing the laundry, going for walks or swimming in the sea. The water is terribly cold. I should call it a lazy life, although I have little leisure at the end of the day.

Your Erich

4th September 1941

Today I had an interview at the employment office on the island. All will be well, hopefully we'll be together for my birthday and hopefully for yours, too. Please don't waste any money on sending me packages, I have everything I need. Be a good girl and wait patiently for your husband, who is no longer quite as far away from you.

Eric

8 Worley Rd, St Albans, 5th September 1941

Dearest Eri, I haven't written to you for a long time because I was so busy. Now I'm pinching half an hour of my lunch break. The application from the employer was first sent to the wrong address, a further delay. Please let me know in advance when they release you because I have to look for a larger room, which is not easy in St Albans. Next week I have two weeks of night shift, and from then on every fortnight, each time for two weeks. I'm not thrilled about this, but I can't do anything about it. The weather is fantastic just now, and I hope you'll enjoy it while you have no work. I spend all day in the factory, with only one hour in the fresh air. More on Saturday.

Your Irka

8th September 1941

Dearest, now I have to ask you for something: can you go to a bookshop and order The B.O.C. Handbook for Oxy-Acetylene Welders? *It costs a little over three pounds. Maybe you can also find literature on tool-making. I need these books to learn the technical terms in English. Now we can do nothing but wait for the decision. In the meantime, I would like to use my time well, hence the request for the books.*

Eric

15th September 1941

Dear Irka, I did not get your promised letter from Saturday. So it's again been a fortnight without news from you, I hope you are well. I asked you to send me a book about welding. A few days ago we were informed that we can only receive books when they are shipped directly from the bookstore. So if you've already sent the book, I won't get it. Also, the parcel you mentioned in your letter of 28th August has not arrived. You poor girl, you're working ten or more hours and yet you have to do things for your husband stuck behind barbed wire too! But it won't be long now. From the day the applications is made you can reckon on four to six weeks, but usually it's less. It's pretty cold, and I'm spending more time indoors. It's a pity that we won't have many sunny summer days left when we are together again. Note: I now live in house 2.

Eric
22nd September 1941

Dearest Irka, your letter of 5th September took a long time because there wasn't a stamp on it. Darling, have you got used to working at night? I'm so sorry that I'm sitting idly around here while you have to work so hard. I'm very pleased that the Home Office and the Employment Office have been in touch with the factory. I'll definitely be able to celebrate your birthday with you. I'm not afraid of hard work, the only thing I fear is that you'll be working nights and me during the day, and so we won't see much of each other. Do you actually have time and patience to read? Probably not. Because I'm better placed, reading is the only pleasure I have here. I'm sorry that this letter is so boring, but it's the way I feel.

Love, Erich

25th September 1941

Irka, darling, thank you for the book, which now keeps me busy through-out the day. Several 'Australians' have already been released. I often think about what our reunion will be like, after one and a half years of separation. It will be a great day, my whole life is going to change. I'm already getting ready for it, though it may still take a few weeks, I'm darning socks, a lousy job, and arranging things so that nothing apart from the factory will get in the way of our life together. Unfortunately, I have to wear my only good suit in the camp. If I had an old pair of trousers, I could save it for later. If you find a pair, please send them my way. Now it's too cold for shorts, and it's a shame to wear the good suit to work. Darling, only a few weeks, and then we will stay together forever. Send me the photo that you promised me ages ago!

Cheerio, Eric

29th September

Irka Darling, don't worry about the room, just a room is perfectly fine to start off with.

Eric

2nd October

You ask what I'd like for my birthday. If my dreams come true, then I'll get the most precious gift of my life: you, the freedom to work and – finally – the typewriter that you bought me an eternity ago.

Your Erich

52 Beech Road, St Albans, 5th October 1941

My dearest Erich, I'm sorry but I haven't found any old trousers, there are only two new suits, new flannel trousers and an unworn jacket. But wear shorts at work, children do it here all year round. But not, of course, if you're freezing, perhaps the English children are hardened to it. Last night I moved into a new house, the room is very small, but quite nice. I sleep in a huge double bed in which I feel completely lost. This room will probably not be suitable for both of us, it was stupid of me to take it, I was too polite to refuse the offer. It came as a surprise, because these people have no need to rent out a room. It's a modern house, bright and clean, but the downside is that the owners interfere too much in my affairs. I'm seldom at home, and they always want my company. Unfortunately we will have to live with them for a while. But if we don't want to stay here, it will be easier for you, as a man, to find an excuse. If you would just come soon! Darling, I have no photo of myself, and it would be a waste of money to get one taken now. Just wait until you can take a good look at me, the way I am now, quite old. Tomorrow I'm going to our work dance, one of the women on the staff here bought me a ticket. Darling, come soon, everything is ready for you – I'm taking a day off to enjoy the event fully.

Your Irka

Monday 6th October

Dearest Irka, you've probably already moved, and I hope you're happy. Are you living together as a family? I'm very sociable and I appreciate an occasional chat, I just hope we have enough time for each other. I've also moved again and now live in house 7. Every day, people head off (but most have been waiting a lot longer than me), and then they put the remaining detainees together. But I'm used to raking my belongings together and moving on, as we've been doing since 1934. Apart from this, the house where I live now is really comfortable, but hopefully it will be my last abode in this camp. Can you imagine us seeing each other again? I don't know if I can still move about in traffic, or how I'll take care of you after such a long period of isolation. But you're going to teach me and look after your returnee, aren't you? Once again, paper kisses and imaginary hugs

From your Eri

10th October

Irka, sometimes I wonder if it will ever be granted to us to look to the future with any confidence. Then I answer my own question with a resolute yes. If I'm wrong, I don't want to go on living. Please write soon.

Eric

16th October

Darling, if only the news were better, I'd be full of hope. In our living room there's a nice fire burning, and it's raining buckets outside. I wish I could give you some of the time I spend reading, nobody can read all day long. Darling, I remember the time when we read every book together, sometimes reading out portions to each other aloud. Now I have no one to share good and bad things with, but just wait, soon! Can you write and tell me about the work I'll have to do in the factory?

Your Erich

22nd October

Dearest, thank you for the beautiful picture that you sent me with your last letter. I can see no difference in your appearance from the time when people asked if you'd left school yet, and since then so much time has passed! I still hope to be able to leave the camp in October, because things gradually seem to be stirring for our group from Australia. A few were released yesterday. Once you receive the notification of my release from the Home Office, please send me a message because I won't know it until after you. I can only send you a telegram on the day of my departure, which I will do. Should I maybe send it to the factory so that it reaches you straightaway? From the date the women notify us, it usually takes three or four days.

Your Eric

26th October

On the 24th I had the hearing, which usually precedes release. Then it takes fourteen days to six weeks. So we have to be patient again. Now every week a couple of *'Australians' leave, so there is hope. The nearer the moment approaches, the more excited I get, and I often look at your photo. I know that we cannot really be happy as long as there is so much* misery in the world, but inactivity is almost as depressing as all this evil. I want to immerse myself fully in the work so I have no time to think. My English has probably improved only in writing, because you have very little opportunity to speak English when you're locked up with German people. I read many books and three daily newspapers, which enriches my passive vocabulary. You're the better linguist of us, I've always admired your ability to learn new languages and apply them without delay.

Your Erich

52 Beech Road, St Albans, 27th October 1941

My dearest Eri, today's your birthday, it'll be sad and lonely for you. I'm concerned that you're still in the camp, while many of your fellow internees are already free. I'm beginning to lose hope and I'm depressed because we can't tell when it will all be over. In our factory, it is cold and not exactly pleasant. But I wouldn't care if you were only with me. Isn't there anything you can do to speed things up? It would be much easier to be alone if there were no hope, but since you've been back in the country, I've been gradually cracking up. My brother has the same birthday as you. On this day, I think more than ever about the misery my family must be suffering in this cold winter, in the midst of the murderous Nazis in Warsaw. Will I see him again? And my parents? What has become of your brothers Georg and Heinz? So many questions that won't be answered until the war is over. I am sad.

Your Irka

52 Beech Road, St Albans, 28th October 1941

Eri, my darling, I got your letter of 22nd October and will have to admit that it rather makes me despair. Why are all those people going home but not you? Advise me as to what I should do. The wait has made me terribly nervous, I can't laugh, I can hardly do my work. I can think of nothing else but you, talk of nothing else. It's not much fun for the others. If you're released, don't send the telegram to the factory, but to my house, my landlady will bring it over to me. Please also write to say when and at what station you arrive, so I can pick you up in London. Please write to the Home Office and tell them to get a move on. I've already written twice and I've lost confidence.

Besides that, I'm healthy, just a bit tired. The people where I live are extremely nice, but living this close to them doesn't suit me. I'm waiting for you, and then we can decide how to proceed. Eri, dearest, what can I do to get you back? I would give half my life, if I could have you with me.

Good night, my dear.

Your Irka

29th October

Irka: I love you 365 days a year and can't wait for the moment I can prove it to you!

Eric

52 Beech Road, St Albans, 2nd November

My dearest Erich, I'm desperate at the length of our separation. Why are the others free, and not you? Last week I waited every day for a letter from the Home Office. Again, nothing. Now you tell me it can take weeks. Mr Williams has also enquired because he needs you. It is now bitterly cold, and I have no heat in my room, so I sit with the people downstairs, but I don't always want to. Yesterday I was at the pictures and went home in the moonlight. In my mind I had a long talk with you and gave you the sweetest nicknames in all the languages I've learned. Back home I cried my eyes out.

And now some good news: I'm getting a wage increase of five shillings a week! This is the second rise since I started here. You can be proud of me, because I'm very proficient in an area that was completely foreign to me before. Hopefully it'll turn out the same way for you, even though I'm afraid that your work will be harder and less pleasant than mine.

Darling, for my birthday, you'll definitely not be with me, so I won't celebrate it. Who would I celebrate it with? I'm still hoping we'll have Christmas together. Aren't you cold? Do you have enough to put on? Clothing is rationed now, we can only buy something for you when you've got your food stamps.

Farewell, my sweetheart, and come to me soon.

Your Irka

2nd November 1941

Irka My Darling, it's your birthday soon, and I doubt but that we will spend it together, although what is longed for eagerly can happen every day. I wish you, my brave little wife, all the very best for the

271

future. After all that we've been through, we deserve some happiness and family life. Under normal conditions this would go without saying, and once the madness is over, things will get back to normal again. Then we will have a child. Today, a few people have left the camp who were only informed yesterday. So it can really happen any day. It makes life more exciting here, compared to the long and lazy months in Australia. And even there, one day a friendly breeze wafted us back to Mother Europe. Maybe I will still get there, as the most fully alive birthday gift you've ever received.

Your husband Erich
52 Beech Rd, St Albans, 5th November

Eri, darling, I'm sure you won't be here for my birthday. Probably something went wrong with your request. I know that the request from the employer has already reached the Home Office, and the Labour Department is waiting for a decision from there.

As I knew already, to be honest, it was stupid of me to get accommodation with these people. There is a great shortage of housing in St Albans, and in my earlier pretty room we wouldn't have been able to live together. As I was then offered this room for both of us, I jumped at it, as I'm now paying for both of us just as much as I was there for my single room. It has turned out to be a misunderstanding. Yesterday, the man told me that we must not use our bedroom as a living room, so we'd have to spend all our free time in their living room. He also insists that only English is spoken. I can't accept this. We can't have visitors, either, and our bedroom has no heating. There is a beautiful bathroom, in which for some unfathomable reason I'm not allowed to have a bath. I told him yesterday that I'll find somewhere else as soon as you arrive, but I've already started looking. It takes time, and most rooms are very expensive. If only I knew when you were coming, we'd be able to afford it together, it will cost maybe thirty shillings a week. Shall I wait until you get here?

Dearest, today I went to bed at nine o'clock in order to write you this letter. It is the only place where I feel at home. Will we always have to live with strangers? It's been this way for so many years, I've had enough. When you're with me, everything will be easier.

Irka

7th November 1941

Darling, all we can do is save up our patience for the final sprint. The processing of my case is no slower than for the others, believe me. There are even pioneers who volunteered for Australia and have still not been released. I'm working regularly now, but next week I'll probably stop because the weather is really horrible. Today we had to stop our work in the garden several times and shelter from the rain.

When I come 'home', I always ask first for letters and a telegram. Unfortunately, I won't be able to tell you the time of my arrival, because we can only send a telegram in which the fact we've been released is communicated, nothing else. So you won't be able to meet me at the train station. I can manage. Most of the trains arrive in London in the evening. Just tell me which bus I should take from Euston station and how long they run until. Stay calm, we'll soon be together again.

Eric

St Albans, 9th November

Dear, I got your birthday wishes, but I can't take pleasure in anything, not even your sweet letter. I never would have dreamed that we wouldn't be together on my birthday. I can't understand why we

273

are being treated so badly, I'm desperate, I'm homesick and wish I could run away from myself. A year ago, when the bombs were falling all around, I just wanted peace, now the bombs aren't falling any more, but I feel the same way. This afternoon I went to the pictures, it was a beautiful autumn weekend. I saw a film showing an air attack on Warsaw, and recognised familiar, though bombed-out roads, and heard Chopin. I was so overwhelmed by homesickness that it still hurts. Where is my mother? Where are my people? Why do I have to live among strangers?

My character has changed, I'm always on the defensive, at any moment, I expect to be attacked. In my heart there is no room for love, only hate. Love is solely reserved for you, my love, you, Ludka and my poor family. I've also stopped believing that you'll come, and I ought to stop waiting, it consumes too much energy. I couldn't care less about my birthday this year. I don't feel comfortable in my current 'home'. If I want to be alone, like now, I have to sit in an unheated room, which the people here don't like. I can't stand their smug, self-satisfied faces. I have nothing in common with them. I'm so different from them. I prefer to speak with the shade of my past happiness than with them.

Darling, your letter is so sweet. But don't get your hopes too high: for us exiles, a family life and a baby are not possible. Our battle will be even harder, we must always be on our guard, there is no law and no state which will protect us. And once the madness is over, I won't be able to have any more children, you'll have to look for a younger woman.

Darling, I'm so tired.

Don't be angry with me because of this letter. I only have strangers round me, but to you at least I have to write and say how I feel. Farewell, Eri.

Your Irka

12th November

Dearest Irka, yesterday I was busy, so I'm writing to you on another birthday, the birthday of the Republic of Austria after the end of the monarchy. It doesn't mean anything that it's taking so long, I'm just afraid Mr Williams won't want to wait for me. That would be terrible, because then the whole process would start over again. I congratulate you on your wage increase and your ability, I am very proud of you. You are a brave girl who deserves a husband who is not held behind barbed wire so he can't be with you. My little Irka, hopefully we will soon be marching one 12th November which, as in 1918, is the birthday of a better world. Don't lose heart, we've had so much bad luck, and then the opportunity arose to make a new start. So it will be again.

Eric

14th November

Dearest, Your letter of 9th made me very sad. Your letter of the 5th also came, talking about a room. Yes, it's unbearable not to have a room to ourselves. From what you say, I understand that you've already started looking. However small the room is – it will be big enough to start with. It's essential for the time being that we have a home where we can relax after work. After one receives notification from the Home Office, it usually takes a week, but I don't think you can move in such a short time. If you find something suitable earlier, then please jump at it! Don't worry about the money! After a hard day's work you have to feel comfortable, otherwise you wreck your nerves. Darling, I cannot find words to comfort you, it's just bad luck. I'm waiting for your telegram like I've never waited for anything before. However, we must not despair, that would be the stupidest thing we could do. Your sadness and despair I understand only too well, but Irka Darling – please – pull yourself together! I want you to be in good health when I take you in my arms.

Love, Erich

St Albans, 18th November 1941

My dear, I hope that one day we will witness the rebirth of all oppressed countries. This is the only hope that keeps me going in my lonely, joyless and hardworking life. I've stopped waiting for you and I don't believe you're going to come. Once again I've been taken in, like last year when I was waiting to travel to Australia. They've told me that your waiting time is exceptionally long and that something is wrong. But I don't know what to do, besides, I'm too tired. I'm more unhappy and worried than ever. Mr Williams will definitely not give up on you, there's a general lack of manpower. I'm seeing him tomorrow. He wrote a letter to the Home Office and has still received no response. Thousands of refugees have been free for over a year, only you are still interned. Isn't that strange? It's not long now until Christmas, and I tell myself that you'll be with me then. How sick I am of always feeling miserable, I want so much to laugh and enjoy life like most of the other women who work in the factory. They already call me 'grandma' because I'm always moaning about my age.

Your Irka

52 Beech Rd, St Albans, 23rd November 1941

Darling Eri, maybe I feel so miserable because I don't like my current home, but without you I can't look for anything else. If anyone finds something, they have to decide quickly and pay the same day. And what if you then don't come? So I'll wait, and then we can decide together. If you don't come soon, I'd like to visit you, let me know where I should apply for a visitor's permit. Yesterday night I dreamed of you, a sweet dream, and when I woke up alone in a double bed, everything was so incredibly sad. I love you, Eri, and I will never forget you, even if it still takes years. It's just so tiring, living by oneself with nothing but memories.

Your Irka

Friday 28th November 1941

Darling, I will write in the next few days to the Home Office. Maybe my request was lost. Already more than half the returnees from Australia have been released, and every week more leave. It's a long road, but by Christmas we'll definitely have it sorted. I'm taking a chemistry course to freshen up long-forgotten knowledge, and I read a lot. I've just read Priestley's novel Far Away, *and Hašek's* Svejk, *which is even more delightful in English than in German. Maybe I'll be with you on the 18th to celebrate the anniversary of our first meeting in December. It was all easier then than now.*

Your Erich

Friday 12th December

Dearest Irka, I'm aware of your difficulties, and I'm sorry I can't help you, but I can't give you any advice, as I haven't the least idea of how much longer it will be. It could be over any day, but it could also take weeks. Baswitz left today, and he waited for as long as I have. His brother is still waiting. In Australia, I was less edgy than now, when everything is so

277

close and nothing can be done to shorten the waiting time. A quarter of the returnees are still waiting like me. I would be calmer if I knew that you weren't worrying so much. Actually, we should be glad I'm here and not in Australia, for those who couldn't decide to come then will now have to wait for a long time because of the new war. I hope you will be patient.

Your Erich

17 Alma Road, St Albans, 15th December 1941

My favorite Eri, I'm so tired that I've stopped sleeping and eating. In such a state of mind one does everything wrong. I've rented two rooms, one of which is uninhabitable because water is literally running down the walls. It's supposed to be a bedroom. The other is dark and musty, but at least not humid, that's where I sleep now. For this bargain I pay twenty-five shillings a week, which leaves me little to live on. Fortunately, I eat so little that I hardly spend anything on it. I tried to find something else, and almost managed, a beautiful room in a modern house, but when the woman asked me where you were, and I told her that you were interned, she turned me away. Now I'm too tired for any further change. I just want to know whether you're coming or not, because for myself I just need one room. Mr Williams has finally received an answer, the decision will be made in the next two weeks. That means nothing, two months ago they wrote telling me the same kind of thing. My second letter was not answered. Mr Williams no longer believes you'll come, everyone thinks there must be reasons why you're still interned, and look at me suspiciously. My position is more difficult than yours, which is a paradox, because I'm a Pole and so I have nothing to do with the Germans. I don't care whether I live or not, before me there's just a bleak future in which I will always be alone. There is no one to help me, to advise me, to take the burden of responsibility from me. Darling, try to find out whether you're coming or not. I can't go on like this, I'm working ten hours a day and hardly sleeping or eating. I'm living on my nerves.

Look after yourself and pretend I didn't exist. I like your letters, but I myself would prefer to stop writing because my letters are no fun for you to read. In these eighteen months, I've changed a lot, there was too much cruelty, injustice and loneliness in my life. I'm exhausted like a hunted animal in a foreign country, always on the defensive, although I'm trying to go on the offensive. I have no wishes any more, no hopes. I can't stand anyone. Maybe it will be different again when you get here, I'll cry for hours in your arms and feel better afterwards. But you will never come, our destiny is separation. Maybe they'll let you go, if I fall ill.

Now it's 1 a.m., and I have to work again tomorrow. But I can't sleep. My confused thoughts switch between deepest grief and burning hatred. Do not be alarmed, my dear, this letter is merely an explosion, so that I can carry on, it's better than a nervous breakdown. And don't worry about Christmas. One day I'll be working, and the other I'll get by somehow. Don't think of me, think only of yourself, in this horrible world you have to be selfish. One day you will be happy.

Your Irka

In response to Irka's request of 9th October, on 17th December the Home Office sends her a form in which she is informed that its Department for Foreigners' Affairs will be releasing her husband for the purpose of taking up employment. Irka immediately sends a telegram to Erich bearing the joyful message. But they are not granted to spend Christmas together.

24th December 1941

Dearest Irka, thanks for the long-awaited telegram. Unfortunately, I will only be able to wire you the exact date of my arrival on the

279

day of my departure. You will therefore find out only a few hours in advance. I'm writing to you even though this letter will probably arrive only after my arrival. Christmas will be lonely again, but with a heart full of hope and joy. As I have already told you, it usually takes one week after the official confirmation. So don't trouble the lost property office if I arrive later than you expect. I haven't been lost, just you wait. Wait, wait for the great moment.

Your Eric

31st December 1941

Darling, for a week I've been living in an atmosphere of feverish expectancy and I'm writing you what is hopefully my last letter from here. I was officially notified of my release on Christmas Day, I filled out the papers a few days ago and thought I would leave yesterday. But as has already happened before in individual cases, my de facto release is being held up by a few formalities with the employment office in London (in theory I've been free since Christmas). Therefore, it seems unlikely that I'll be leaving the camp this week. Too bad we can't spend New Year's Eve together. This latest delay has thoroughly shattered my nerves. Now, however, it may really be only a matter of days. Darling, be patient and not depressed, look forward to the happier days that lie before us. Darling, I long so much for you, for a normal life and for meaningful activity. I love you.

Eric

CHAPTER TWENTY-NINE.

Irka smoothes down the tablecloth. The telegram arrived a few hours ago. She has taken a half-day off to prepare the room, and herself, for the great moment. She has managed to rent two more rooms in the house in Alma Road, a living room and a heated bedroom with no damp walls. Literally at the last minute – the landlords took pity.

On the table are items that Erich knows, so he should not feel strange in his new home: a candlestick, an ashtray, a small fruit bowl with apples, all made by her in bronze, when she was in Vienna. On the mantelpiece are the Christmas cards that friends have sent her, and from her sister in Australia, a red-robed Santa Claus on a sleigh pulled by reindeer in deep snow. Irka has to smile, it is typical of Ludka, in Australia it is now high summer, she never had any taste. Irka always had to give her advice when they were choosing clothes in Warsaw, and even then her sister never looked very elegant. What Irka has in her fingers, Ludka has in her head. Irka arranges the holly branches with the red berries in the glass vase, and on the door frame she has attached mistletoe, in accordance with English custom, so that Erich will have to kiss her straightaway.

Evening has fallen. She lights the candle, unfortunately there were only white ones. Irka loves colour. Several times she darts into the bathroom to examine herself in the mirror, her lips are red as Erich likes them. She pulls her hair into shape, straightens her stocking seam. She returns to the living room.

Irka twists her wedding ring, which has become too loose on her. She hopes she is not too skinny for Erich. And she hopes he will not realise that she met Leo. She should not have gone with him. She should have refused him when they woke up late in the morning and the sun was shining into their eyes. Her guilty conscience throws a shadow over their reunion. The women in Primrose Mansions noticed that something had happened when she arrived in the afternoon, grabbed her handbag and silently rushed to the train station. But they will not give her away.

Do not think about it. They have not seen each other again since that terrible night of bombing and the sweet awakening. Although they would both have liked to. So lonely it was then, so great the fear. Leo, a refugee and a Jew like her. It did her good. Erich would certainly forgive her this moment of weakness. But that is all over now. From now on there is only her husband, forever and ever, as they have promised each other. Erich and the new life. A real family, maybe.

Irka walks up and down the room. Will he like it here? She has sewn some curtains, hung up a photo, enlarged it specially: it shows them both as domestic workers in Wiltshire, he with a rumpled suit and trousers rolled up, she in a white Austrian sweater with red pompoms. So happy they look. Actually, it was already daring to wear Austrian clothing. Probably the English did not recognise it as such, in their insular ignorance – how often they have confused Austria with Australia. At that time the war had not yet started.

In the kitchen there is waiting a meatloaf with potatoes and Yorkshire pudding, the landlords have allowed her to cook. Tinned mincemeat can sometimes be obtained, and she has saved up the three eggs to which she is entitled each month for the big day.

Irka presses her hands together as she had done back in the air-raid shelter. Why doesn't he come? The bus must have arrived long ago. Maybe he missed it, and will have to spend the night away from home. Maybe he got lost in St Albans. This waiting is unbearable. She takes up a book, *Three Men in a Boat*, cannot concentrate, the letters become blurred before her eyes. Should she put on water for tea? Erich will be thirsty after the trip. What will they do? Throw themselves immediately into each other's arms, or first gaze at each other for a long time? Perhaps they have become strangers to each other. Maybe he has changed, he will have lost weight too, and grown tanned from the Australian sun. But no, he has been in England for five months. Five months! And now it is already 1942, 2nd January 1942.

In two days it will be Sunday, a day of rest. She will show him St Albans, the city has really grown on her, it is her new home. The Cathedral, the pond, the swans, the ancient pub 'Ye Olde Fighting Cocks' from the eleventh century, perhaps they will be able to treat themselves to dinner there. Erich will enjoy that. He is capable of such enthusiasm, she loves this about him, he is curious and easily roused. Alive. They will have a lot to tell each other. Between them lie a trip round the world and a bombing campaign.

The doorbell rings.

Author's Note

This story is based on real events. However, apart from my parents and well-known historical figures, all the characters have either have been given altered names, or been freely invented. Many of the scenes depicted happened as I relate them, or in a similar way, while others were imagined by me. I have drawn on historical documents, scholarly publications, the correspondence of my parents, published interviews, interviews I conducted myself with witnesses of the events, and novels and memoirs by survivors of the *Dunera*.

Erica Fischer

Translator's Note

The German title of the novel, *Königskinder*, is an allusion to a well-known ballad in which two lovers, the 'children of kings', are separated by water. The first stanza goes:

Es waren zwei Königskinder,
die hatten einander so lieb,
sie konnten beisammen nicht kommen,
das Wasser war viel zu tief.

There were two children of kings,
They were so madly in love,
But could not be together, for
The water was much too deep.

Merely to mention the name of the ballad evokes, for the German reader, a story of a love that survives in spite of the watery miles between the lovers. The ballad and Erica Fischer's story have different endings: the author suggested 'Over the Ocean' as an English equivalent, and the internees (in chapter 8) sing a stoically comic variant of the Scottish ballad 'My bonnie lies over the ocean'.

ACKNOWLEDGEMENTS

Without the wealth of information and suggestions from the following works and websites, the book could not have been written:

Bader Whiteman, Dorit: *The Uprooted. A Hitler Legacy*. 1993

Balestracci, Maria Serena: *'Arandora Star': Dall'oblio alla memoria*. 2008

Bartrop, Paul R. Eisen, Gabrielle: *The Dunera Affair. A Documentary Resource Book*. 1990

Cincotta, Gianfranco *L'eruzione del 1930 ed altri ricordi*: http://www.swisseduc.ch/stromboli/about/visitors/cincottai.html

Clerque, S.C.: *SOS – Rettet unsere Seelen*. 1953

Dümling, Albrecht (ed.): *Zu den Antipoden vertrieben. Das Australien-Exil deutschsprachiger Musiker*. 2000

Dümling, Albrecht: *Die verschwundenen Musiker. Jüdische Flüchtlinge in Australien*. 2011

Everett, Sue: *Not Welcome*. 2010

Gillman, Peter and Leni: *'Collar the Lot!' How Britain interned and expelled its wartime refugees*. 1980

Kaufmann, Walter: *Die Zeit berühren. Mosaik eines Lebens auf drei Kontinenten*. 1992

Kaufmann, Walter: *Unter australischer Sonne*. 1965

Lafitte, François: *The Internment of Aliens*. 1940

Loewen, Fred: *Dunera Boy, Furniture Designer, Artist*. N.d.

Mortimer, Gavin: *The Longest Night. Voices from the London Blitz*. 2005

Patkin, Benzion: *The Dunera internees*. 1979

Pearl, Cyril: *The Dunera Scandal*. 1983

Pelz, Werner: *Distant Strains of Triumph*. 1964

'The London Blitz, 1940.' Eye Witness to History: http://www. eyewitnesstohistory.com. 2001

Wilczynski, Klaus: *Das Gefangenenschiff*. 2001

Wing, Sandra Koa (ed.): *Our Longest Days. A People's History of the Second World War*.

Zimmering, Max: *Die unfreiwillige Weltreise*. 1961

*I'd also like to thank my parents,
Irena and Emmerich Fischer, excerpts of
whose letters I have used, Massimo Cortini,
Alan Morgenroth, the 'Dunera Boys'
Alfred Jason, Kurt Levinsky,
Henry Lippman, Hans Löwe,
Hans Marcus and Oswald Wolkenstein
and my cousin Syd Nade.*

BIOGRAPHICAL NOTE

Erica Fischer was born in January 1943 in St Albans,
Hertfordshire. Her parents had fled to Britain from
Austria in 1938, faced with the annexation of Austria by
Nazi-Germany. In the summer of 1948 Erica's parents
returned to Vienna together with her and her brother.
She went on to study translating and interpreting there,
before becoming a founding member of the Austrian
feminist movement in the early 1970s. Since then she has
worked as a journalist, translator and writer. In 1988, she
left Austria for Germany, where she now lives in Berlin
with her Italian partner. Her bestselling novel, *Aimée &
Jaguar* was published in 1994 and translated into twenty
languages (including English), a film adaptation appeared
in 1999.